Sport in the Global Society

General Editor: J.A. Mangan

SPORTING NATIONALISMS
Identity, Ethnicity, Immigration and Assimilation

CASS SERIES: SPORT IN THE GLOBAL SOCIETY
General Editor: J.A. Mangan

The interest in sports studies around the world is growing and will continue to do so. This unique series combines aspects of the expanding study of *sport in the global society*, providing comprehensivesness and comparison under one editorial umbrella. It is particularly timely, with studies in the political, cultural, social, economic, geographical and aesthetic elements in sport proliferating in institutions of higher education.

Eric Hobsbawm once called sport one of the most significant practices of the late nineteenth century. Its significance is even more marked in the late twentieth century and will continue to grow in importance into the next millennium as the world develops into a 'global village' sharing the English language, technology and sport.

Other titles in the series (ISSN 1368-9789)

Sporting Nationalisms:

Identity, Ethnicity, Immigration and Assimilation

Edited by

MIKE CRONIN and
DAVID MAYALL

FRANK CASS
LONDON • PORTLAND, OR

GV
706.34
.S66
1998

First published in 1998 in Great Britain by
FRANK CASS PUBLISHERS
Newbury House, 900 Eastern Avenue,
London, IG2 7HH, England

and in the United States of America by
FRANK CASS PUBLISHERS
c/o ISBS
5804 N.E. Hassalo Street
Portland, Oregon 97213-3644

Website: http://www.frankcass.com

British Library Cataloguing in Publication Data

Sporting nationalisms: identity, ethnicity, immigration
and assimilation. – (Cass series : sport in the global
society ; 6)
1. Nationalism and sports 2. National characteristics
3. Ethnic groups 4. Minorities in sports
I. Cronin, Mike II. Mayall, David
306.4'83'089

ISBN 0 7146 4896 5 (cloth)
ISBN 0 7146 4449 8 (paper)

Library of Congress Cataloging in Publication Data

Sporting nationalisms: identity, ethnicity, immigration, and
assimilation / edited by Mike Cronin and David Mayall.
    p.   cm. – (Cass series – sport in the global society, ISSN
1368–9789 ; 6)
    Special issue of Immigrants & minorities, vol. 173, no. 1, March
1998.
    Includes bibliographical references (p.) and index.
    ISBN 0-7146-4896-5 (alk. paper). – ISBN 0-7146-4449-8 (pbk. :
alk. paper)
    1. Nationalism and sports. 2. Ethnicity. 3. Sports – Sociological
aspects. I. Cronin, Mike. II. Mayall, David. III. Immigrants &
minorities. Vol. 17, no. 1 (Special issue) IV. Series.
GV706.34.S66   1998
306.4'83–dc21   98-18870
                                                          CIP

This group of studies first appeared in a Special Issue on
'Sporting Nationalisms: Identity, Ethnicity, Immigration and Assimilation'
of Immigrants & Minorities (ISSN 0261-9288) 17/1 (March 1998) published by Frank Cass

Printed in Great Britain by Antony Rowe Ltd, Chippenham, Wilts

Contents

List of Illustrations

List of Tables

Series Editor's Foreword

With malefic purpose, and a far from modern sensitivity towards ethnic minorities, identities and susceptibilities, the Johnson of Dictionary renown not drugs notoriety, considered that it was the duty of the English to civilize the cherokees, orang-utans and the Scots. He would not have understood, far less sympathized with, Tiger Wood's view quoted in the Introductory Remarks to this collection edited by Mike Cronin and David Mayall, that 'ethnic background should not make a difference'. Neither do Cronin and Mayall. In their view, sport is a vehicle, in a variety of ways, for the construction of individual, ethnic and national identities, and in this volume they gather together a set of contributors to make precisely this point.

Their point of view is wholly reasonable. As Eric Hobsbawm has remarked, in the post-1918 era in Europe, in part the gap between private and public worlds was bridged by sport.[1] Initially international sport was established 'with the object of integrating the national components of multi-national skills';[2] later it became an expression of national struggle and sportsman heroes became symbols and expressions of their imagined communities.

The efficacy of sport as 'a medium for inculcating national feelings' resided in the simple fact that sporting heroes represented the dream fulfilment of practically every man – young and old. Nothing has changed except that these roles and dreams are now as commonplace in Africa, for example, as in Europe. Modern sport has played a catalytic role there in fusing together ethnically diverse communities into the synthetic nation-states inherited from the Age of European Imperialism. The extent to which this fusion is complete, of course, remains to be seen. The point was made in the concluding remark to the Introduction to *Tribal Identities* and it is made here again: that 'the potential of sport for unity and disunity should never be underestimated'.[3]

Globally there may be trouble ahead – and for certain, sport will be a focus both for political cohesion and confrontation. In *The Future of Population,* John I. Clarke states:

> The current prevalence of ethnic, religious or linguistic groups increasingly expressing their desire for autonomy or independence is indicative of their uneasy accommodation within the modern system of centralized states, and challenges our accepted notion of a 'population'.[4]

He goes on to observe that the boundaries of many new states, *especially in*

Africa, are unrelated to ethnic distribution and diversity. In addition, 'international migrations have intensified ethnic and cultural diversity within states'.[5] He is far from optimistic about the future, observing that many governments have made strenuous efforts to establish nation-states out of diverse cultures but that it has too often proved to be an arduous and intractable task. One reason lies in collective memory. In the words of Paul Valéry, 'are you not the future of all the memories stored within you? The future of the past.' David Brown suggests another reason for the increasing challenges by ethnic communities to the nation-states. They have been weakened by their failure to deliver social justice; in consequence old imagined nations are under threat from new imagined nations promised by counter-elites.[6] Without a doubt they will make use of sporting myths, rituals and symbols in an era mesmerized by such things, to forge new collective identities.

By way of a prologue to a consideration of nationalism and sport, in their short discussion of nationalism and national identity Cronin and Mayall praise the much thumbed works on nationalism of Breuilly, Hobsbawm, Gellner and Anderson. Reference could also have been made to J. Hutchinson (*Modern Nationalism*, 1994) E. Kedourie (*Nationalism*, 1983) and A.D. Smith (*Nations and Nationalism in a Global Era*, 1994). Cronin and Mayall include Adrian Hastings in their list. Hastings, taking the long view of history, searches for the origins of nationalism in the fourteenth century – a confident and bold ethnocentric perspective, that the Chinese, in particular, would find both amusing (and irritating). There is a world beyond Europe (and America) as the Chinese among others, would be quick to point out! And it should never be overlooked, as Richard Davies has recently noted, that the non-European experience of nationalism has long informed the construction of European nationalisms and identities if only as manifestations of 'a significant other'.[7]

Furthermore, the reminder by Hugh Thomas that the earliest reference, in the Oxford Dictionary no less, to the 'nation state' was 1918 should give pause for thought. Thomas, incidentally, would take issue with Hastings over the timing of the earliest origins of (European) nationalism. A 'Europe of nation states', according to Thomas, replaced the universal empire of the Middle Ages in the sixteenth century![8] Then there is the curious coincidence that the consolidated and emerging nations of late nineteenth century Europe aggressively metamorphosed into empires reducing numerous other nations in the process. Among other things, 'Greater Britain' was born – at least in the mind of Sir Charles Dilke. In passing, incidentally, is it significant that the French refer to 'l'état-nation' not 'la nation état' (as do the Spaniards – 'estado-nacion')?[9]

What all this amounts to, of course, is that the concept of nationalism has a complex, stimulating and provocative as well as a long intellectual provenance. Only selected aspects can be covered in the pages that follow but the coverage, albeit restricted, is itself thought-provoking. Nationalism in sport as in war, politics, economics, culture or religion, on occasion, can be ugly – in the sardonic words of Richard Aldington, 'a silly cock crowing on its own dunghill'.

If the thrust of this volume is essentially and enthusiastically European, Cronin and Mayall, however, do raise the minatory aspect of the impact of globalization on nationalism. Closer to home, of course, and worthy of closer scrutiny there is the impact of the European Union on nationalism and even more interestingly perhaps, the impact of continuing nationalism on the European Union. Happily these are two significant issues raised in the specific context of sport in two recent complementary volumes published by Cass: *Tribal identities: Sport, European Nationalism* (1995) and *European Heroes: Myth, Identity and Sport* (1996).[10]

Even closer to home what about nascent nationalism in the United Kingdom and the associated role of sport? Norman Davies, making up for his analytic shortcomings regarding sport and society in his otherwise brilliant *Europe: A History*, has recently observed: 'The ... United Kingdom ... does not have its own football team in a television age when teams are one of the most effective motors of national identification ... and the moment to raise one has passed.' Why? Davies provides his answer: 'If one looks at the 1966 World Cup, the vast majority of English supporters were waving Union Jacks, oblivious of their mistake. This year, in a sea-change of attitudes, most of them will brandish the English flag.'[11]

Cronin and Mayall point out that individual and collective identities are not exclusively defined by nationalism or the nation-state. Thus ethnicity and ethnic identities are also the appropriate and absorbing concerns of this volume. Defining ethnicity, like defining nationalism, is not easy and to their credit the difficulties are squarely confronted by the editors and contributors in their consideration of ethnicity as constructed or innate, fixed or ascribed, changing, fluid and variable, in their consideration of the ways in which ethnic identity is created, confirmed and reproduced, and in their consideration of the complexities resulting from migration, colonization, assimilation and intermarriage. Additional concerns throughout the collection are the preservation of community identity and assimilation into the wider community.

Across the globe nations and cultures are now bound tightly to sport in its many manifestations. This is the reality of the twentieth century; it will be an even more visible reality in the twenty-first century. And across the globe, sport is now too important to be left in the hands of sportsmen and women. More and more, it is the property of the 'People' in their various manifestations as politicians, entrepreneurs, educationalists, commercialists, publicists and, not least, academics, as this volume and the series 'Sport in the Global Society' bear ample and appropriate witness.

If the academics in this volume provide a European ethnocentric emphasis, as the editors are the first to admit, none the less it will undoubtedly stimulate Asian, African, Australasian and American studies on the themes of nationalism, ethnicity and sport within this Series sooner rather than later. Among other things, to take but merely one cluster of issues of relevance, interest and concern, this will allow an exploration of the subtleties of the relationships on and off the playing field and sports arenas of the imperial proselytizer and proselytized, an investigation of the complexities involved in modifications to, re-interpretations of, resistance to and rejection of some (more infrequently all) of the hegemonic cultural efforts of the European but especially the British '*homo ludens imperiosus*'.[12]

This is a massive subject of massive significance for modern nations and ethnicities. There is still much challenging and stimulating work to be done locating, recording and explaining the tensions, past and present, inherent in the hegemonic actions of the former imperialist particularly in the setting of Africa, Asia and South America. Above all, there should be a keenness to confront the disparities between ideological assertion, intention and realization and an appreciation of the independent, creative capacities of non-European nations and ethnic communities. All this has been said before but *Sporting Nationalisms* could give fresh impetus to old demands.[13]

In confronting these demanding and fascinating intellectual challenges R.H. Tawney's dictum leaps into the mind: the certainties of one age are the problems of the next – to the advantage of the historian. The challenges are certainly worth it. If the cultural history of sport is to grow to maturity, it must be unassumingly mature cultural history or it will remain an intellectual infant, or at least be regarded as such by the pre-eminent who set the standards in the arts and social sciences. Of course, those who rise to the challenges will require a sensitivity to the dangers of stereotyping, reductionism and condescension that Dr Johnson clearly lacked.

> One of the paradoxes of historical writing is that even its ablest practitioners are soon neglected. Indeed, where their ability has been literary they suffer at the hands of posterity even more than their fair share of oblivion ... Yet, even unread, certain historians exert an influence over later ages which ensures them a kind of anonymous immortality. Their immediate successors transmit an interpretation which, in the hands of later exponents, is divorced from its first begetters.[14]

If one swallow does not make a summer, one location most emphatically did not make a discipline. Sports History is polyphyletic. Subtle reality must prevail over simplistic myth; careful inquiry must prevail over casual assertion. Scholastic integrity requires it. The philosopher, politician and essayist Francis Bacon had the answer a long time ago – 'He that questioneth much shall learn much … but especially if he apply his questions to the skill of the persons whom he asketh'!

J.A. MANGAN

NOTES

1. E.J. Hobsbawm, *Nations and Nationalism since 1780: Programme, Myth and Reality* (Cambridge, 1990), p.142.
2. Ibid.
3. J.A. Mangan (ed.), *Tribal Identities: Nationalism, Europe, Sport* (London, 1996), p.9.
4. John I. Clarke, *The Future of Population* (London, 1997), pp.14–15.
5. Ibid., p.15.
6. See David Brown, *Nations and Nationalism*, Vol.4, No.1 (1998), pp.11–15.
7. Richard Davies in his review of Stuart Woolf (ed.), *Nationalism in Europe: From 1815 to the Present* (London, 1995) in *Nations and Nationalisms*, p.131.
8. Hugh Thomas, *Europe* (London, 1997), p.13.
9. Ibid., p.15.
10. J.A. Mangan, *Tribal Identities: Nationalism, Europe, Sport* (London, 1996) and R. Holt, J.A. Mangan and P. Lanfranchi, *European Heroes: Myth, Identity and Sport* (London, 1996).
11. Norman Davies, 'Britain is breaking up faster than you think', *Sunday Times* (Review Section), 31 May 1998, p.5.
12. See J.A. Mangan (ed.), *The Cultural Bond: Sport, Empire, Society* (London, 1992), pp.1–10.
13. Ibid., p.7.
14. Denys Hay, 'Flavio Biondo and the Middle Ages', in *Art and Politics in Renaissance Italy* (London, 1993), p.59.

Sport and Ethnicity:
some introductory remarks

MIKE CRONIN and DAVID MAYALL

In 1997 Tiger Woods, the professional golfer, joined an elite band of modern sports people. He succeeded at the highest level at an early age in taking the US Masters title, he signed sponsorship deals with the major corporations and countless column inches were dedicated to him in the world's media. One issue which featured prominently, almost to the point of obsession, was Woods' ethnic origin. It was deemed noteworthy and newsworthy that a black man was succeeding in what had previously been a predominantly white man's game. In addition, Tiger Woods was not simply black. He was, in his own words, 'Cablinasian': a quarter Thai, a quarter Chinese, a quarter white, an eighth native American and an eighth African American. Yet despite this clear mix of distinct cultures and immigrant groups that had come together to make the man and golfer that is Tiger Woods, he has clearly and publicly stated that he believes his ethnic background should be of no significance:

> This statement is to explain my heritage. It is the final and only comment I will make regarding the issue. My parents have taught me always to be proud of my ethnic background ... The media has portrayed me as African-American, sometimes Asian. In fact I am both ... The critical point is that ethnic background should not make a difference. The bottom line is that I am an American ... and proud of it. Now, with your co-operation, I hope I can just be a golfer and a human being.[1]

Is Woods correct in his assertion that the ethnic background of sports men and women is unimportant and should not impact on the way they are perceived by others, or indeed in the way they construct themselves? The aim of this volume is to explore and challenge the central argument which is put across by those such as Woods who attempt to champion the view that sport plays no role in the creation and recognition of identity. Sport has undoubtedly served many different functions historically and continues to reflect and shape society in the contemporary era.[2] We would suggest, however, that there is a common theme which runs through the history and current practice of sport. Put simply, sport is a vehicle, in many different ways, for the construction of individual, group and national identities.

The issue of identity has become a central concern for academics in many different fields since the 1960s. There has been a plethora of work on the general issue of nationalism and national identity, and this has been further refined as work has emerged which concentrates on concepts of ethnicity and race, much of which has used the specific socio-historical experience of immigrants as a vehicle. In the 1990s academics have begun to use sport as a way of understanding issues surrounding identity, and this volume is partly a product of, and partly a contribution to, those debates. We will now briefly consider the three strands which have informed this collection.

Nationalism and National Identity

The starting point for anyone interested in issues associated with nationalism and national identity must be with the now standard and seminal texts by Eric Hobsbawm,[3] John Breuilly,[4] Ernest Gellner[5] and Benedict Anderson.[6] The work of Anderson is particularly useful for the way it moves beyond a merely political focus and examines the construction of the nation at a variety of political, social and economic levels. It is within this idea of the imagined community, as set out by Anderson, that sport functions. As will be shown later, sport has been used to symbolize the prowess and success of the nation, but it is a symbol of the nation which is benign. Sport cannot win territory or destroy an opposing ideology or religion which the nation seeks to demonise. It can only support the construction of a nation which has been imagined.

The debates around nationalism, ethnicity and identity have now begun to move on to the next stage and, for example, Adrian Hastings' recent study of the construction of nationhood serves as a critique of those key texts identified earlier.[7] He argues that the work of the 'modern theorists of nationalism appear somewhat weak on hard history'.[8] He also suggests that the origins of nationalism should be located in the fourteenth century and not be seen as products of the period of modern history which began with the French Revolution. This critique by Hastings is a welcome and timely contribution to the growing body of literature, from historians, political scientists and others, which sets out to explore the processes by which nationalism acts as the driving force underpinning notions of identity.

Flags, anthems, geographical boundaries, commonality of language, political structures and ideas of shared culture all contribute to a sense of belonging. At times this can lead to an identification with the nation which excludes the 'other', such as in Nazi Germany or in apartheid South Africa.

In its more 'mature' form, a national identity can permit the blurring of differences and serve to unite a multi-ethnic people behind a single national ideal, as is encapsulated in the notion of the American Dream. It is doubtful that there can ever be an academic 'last word' as to the origins, nature and meaning of nationalism and national identity, but the existence and contribution of nationalism to the notion of identity is undeniable. Finally, in this context, we should note the arguments which point to the challenge and threat posed by globalization to the forces of nationalism, especially the presence of a world-wide media, the internet and other electronic forms of information.[9] However, an alternative argument concerning the impact of globalization suggests that the resultant attempt to recapture the past serves to strengthen the ideal of the nation.[10] The concept of nationalism must be seen, therefore, as both an historical reality and as a contemporary continuum which has been, and still is, central to the construction of identity and one which performs a vital function in sport.

Ethnicity and Ethnic Identity

Alongside the historical and political considerations of nationalism and national identity have emerged studies which examine identities not defined by the the nation state. In particular, and common to the articles contained in this volume, there is now considerable interest in those collectivities within the larger societies generally termed 'ethnic groups'. Of course, a nation and so a national identity might directly coincide with an ethnic group and a sense of distinctive identity, thereby forming the majority element of that society. More usually, though, the term is used to refer to minority groups, whether indigenous or immigrant, within the larger whole.

The concepts of ethnicity and ethnic identity have occupied the attention of a wide variety of commentators, from varied disciplinary backgrounds, for many years. Given the volume of material and the multidisciplinary nature of the approaches, it is no surprise that there is little agreement and some considerable confusion over meanings. As John Hutchinson and Anthony Smith note in the introduction to their recent, and excellent, edited collection of essays and extracts on ethnicity: 'A major element in the confusion and conflict surrounding the field of 'ethnic phenomena' has been the failure to find any measure of agreement about what the central concepts of ethnicity signify or how they should be used.'[11] While it is beyond the scope of this book to consider the varied and plentiful literature on ethnicity, some brief comment is necessary. A useful starting point is provided by Cornell and Hartman: 'Ethnicity, then, is identification in ethnic terms ... A population or social collectivity may be simply an ethnic category, assigned an ethnic identity by outsiders. Once that objective becomes subjective – that is, once that population sees itself in ethnic terms, perhaps in response to the identity outsiders assign to it – it becomes an ethnic group.'[12]

Already, then, we can identify some of the problems: is an ethnic group and an ethnic identity something formed and then imposed by outsiders, usually the majority society? Or, is it a self-forming process by the group themselves? What role does opposition or antagonism play in this process? Immediately, this then leads to other questions concerning boundaries, the characteristics which provide the kernel of separate identity, the importance of objective criteria as against the subjective, or the 'sense' of common ethnicity. Also, importantly, we have to ask whether ethnicity and ethnic identity is something constructed (the 'instrumentalist' view) or whether it is natural (the 'primordialist' view). This in turn questions whether ethnic identity is fixed and ascribed or, alternatively, whether it is something more fluid, changing and variable. And, as well as considering ways in which ethnic identity is built, confirmed and reproduced, we must also consider the challenges which result from migration, colonisation, assimilation and intermarriage. In short, a range of extremely problematic controversies surround this seemingly straightforward and commonly-used concept.

The various contributors to this collection each, in separate ways, contribute towards these debates. Sport has been used by the nation state for different purposes since the foundation of 'modern' sport in the nineteenth century, and in a similar fashion it has been used by those wishing to promote (either in a positive or derogatory fashion) the idea of separate ethnicities. The most common practical embodiment of this has been amongst immigrants as they seek either to preserve the cultural separateness of their own ethnic group, or as they strive to assimilate themselves into their host community. These processes, preservation of community or the acceptance of assimilation, are key themes in the treatment of ethnicity in this text.

Sport

All societies have played sport. Some, such as that played in Mayan ball courts or huge folk football games, may be barely recognizable to us but they nevertheless performed vital functions within their respective societies. Since the mid-nineteenth century and the emergence of commonly recognized codified games, sport has played a large role across the world. Events such as the Olympics and the Soccer World Cup are played out in front of ever greater global television audiences, while other sports which have a more limited spectator and participation base, such as basketball, have a huge impact because of the marketing of individual players and their links with multinational corporations.[13]

Sport also has a major place in the everyday life of any nation. Most states now have dedicated sporting channels on television, will have a separate sports press, will make heroes of its sporting champions, and will celebrate any national victory. Sport and leisure is now a major industry in most western nations, and MacClancy has argued that it is now the third biggest in the world behind oil and cars.[14] As the money involved in sport becomes ever greater the nature of its followers has changed. There are few if any major sports which can survive without sponsorship – the names of McDonalds, Coca-Cola, Pepsi, Fuji, Mastercard, to name but a few – are inseparable from sporting events. The sum of money now involved in sport drives the salaries of sports stars ever higher and feeds the media an increasingly heady diet of famous household names who are playing for corporate as well as individual or team glory. Television coverage follows (usually sold to the highest bidder) and the demand for tickets in the stadium and the spiralling admission prices increasingly exclude all but the elites of society. This has been especially true in British soccer where the nature of the crowd at Premier League level has changed from traditional working class to an eclectic list of pop stars, media dignitaries, politicians and the chattering middle classes. An editorial in *The Independent* on 29 July 1997 drew attention to the way in which working class sports have become colonized by politicians, seeking another dimension to their public faces, and the middle classes generally: 'There is scarcely a Whitehall permanent secretary or a deputy governor of the Bank of England who does not append a football club, preferably northern, to their CV to show their continuing closeness to the people through the people's sport.' Sport then is ever changing. It is an industry, a focus for the media, a source of local or community pride, and a means of securing a lucrative livelihood for its best exponents.

Given the previous and growing importance of sport in society it is little wonder that it has occupied the attention of a range of academics to the extent that it is now possible to identify a distinctive area of sports studies and even sports history. Approaches to the topic, especially from an historical perspective, have shown significant changes and developments over the years. The first sports histories were written primarily by amateurs, recording the exploits of certain clubs, organizations or players. These antiquarian-style works, although important in their way and still representing a significant proportion of all studies, were then followed by those written by historians whose backgrounds lay more in the fields of social, economic and educational history and the history of ideas and grew out of an interest in ideological, educational and social class history. Studies by Allen Guttman,[15] Richard Holt,[16] J.A. Mangan,[17] Tony Mason[18] and Wray Vamplew,[19] and the publication possibilities offered by distinguished publishers such as Cass and, in particular, *The International Journal of the History of Sport*, have elevated the academic study of sports history to a new and impressive level and facilitated the emergence of the study of sports history globally at undergraduate and postgraduate levels. Mention should also be made of the seminal works of the educational historicans Peter McIntosh and Sheila Fletcher[20] who, with others, prepared the way for later studies of ideology, sport and society, and of John Lowerson,[21] who demonstrated that in the historical study of sport there was more to social class than simply the working class. In addition, in Britain, the growth of organizations such as the British Society of Sports History is a further indication of the current healthy state of sports history.[22]

The growing academic interest in the subject is mirrored by a much more widespread public fascination with sport, its past and present. This can be seen, for example, in Britain with the BBC television series *Kicking and Screaming*, which traced the history of soccer, the success of Radio 5, and the enormous expansion of 'fanzines'. The general popular interest is further indicated by the appearance of articles in specialist sports magazines, such as *Total Sport, Inside Sport* and *Ninety Minutes*, dealing with historical themes and also the development of new sports' museums such as those at York for Horse Racing, Preston for soccer and Twickenham for Rugby Union.[23]

The Collection

This text emerges out of a broader development which is currently taking place within sports history as it opens itself to a more interdisciplinary approach. Until recently, little attention has been given by the academic community to general questions surrounding identity, ethnicity and immigration in the context of sport.[24] As Jeremy MacClancy stated in his introduction to *Sport, Identity and Ethnicity*, echoing our own observations on the relative absence of work in this field, 'Sport is a central activity in our societies, one embodying social values, and, as such, deserving of systematic investigation as any other. Sport might be fun. That does not mean it should be disregarded by academics.'[25] This text aims to draw together developments in our understanding of the issues surrounding identity in its many different forms and apply them to the increasingly sophisticated and wide ranging understanding of the place of sport within our society. In doing so we believe that this volume will challenge Tiger Woods' assertion that identity is not important.

The creation of identity through sport takes place at many different levels, as evidenced in the chapters collected here: sport can be used by the sports person or team to create and sustain their own identity (as is the case with Croatians in Australia); sport can be used to demonize or champion an athlete as either one of 'them' or one of 'us' (as with the media destruction of Ben Johnson and the starkly contrasting positive construction of Michael Jordan); sport can be used to replace one identity with another as it functions as a vehicle for assimilation (as with nineteenth-century immigrants from Britain arriving in Australia); sport can be used to perpetuate antagonistic notions of identity (as with the sectarian nature of Scottish soccer); and it may be used to create an international and all encompassing identity in place of the national (as was attempted by the Gaelic and Australian football codes).

Daryl Adair provides a wide perspective on the relationship between immigration, ethnicity and race in the long-term evolution of organized sport in Australia. Unlike previous studies into this theme, Adair does not turn his attention to the post-1945 experience of diverse immigration to Australia and the impact of official policies of multi-culturalism. Instead, he extends the study backwards to the initial 130-year period of white settlement, exploring the earlier relationships, immigrant and colonial, between ethnic groups and the development of sports. Inevitably any such discussion brings to the fore crucial questions concerning identity – ethnic, national, majority/minority – and in particular we are shown how an imported sporting culture which celebrated Englishness came to be mediated and transformed through the immigrant experience. In effect Adair is using sport as a vehicle for examining the early history of immigration to Australia, inter- and intra-group relations, and the negotiation of separate and shared identities through sport.

In the second contribution, Roy Hay looks at the role played by soccer in the creation and moulding of a distinct identity for those Croatians, and their descendants, who migrated to Australia in the years after the Second World War. For the newly-arrived immigrants, notwithstanding the Australian government's policy of assimilation, the Croatian football clubs through their various activities, contacts, social networks and ownership provided all that was hoped for: recreation, work, a home and a family. In short, security and identity. But, as Hay illustrates, the role of the clubs went beyond even this, performing important educational, socializing and political functions also. It is perhaps when we move into what Hay describes as the integrating role that we enter more ambiguous territory, addressing an issue central to many immigrant studies. By providing a range of services and opportunities for the newly-arrived immigrant, the clubs were assisting in their integration into the receiving society by reducing opportunities for conflict and confrontation. Equally, however, by strengthening a sense of Croatian identity and heightening the visible separation from the indigenous population, it can also be argued that integration was impeded by the resultant enmity and distrust from other groups.

One theme common to both Adair and Hay, providing some context to both their studies, is the nature of government policy towards immigrants, which in the Australian case witnessed a shift in the post-war years from one of assimilation to multi-culturalism. Such a change in official attitudes was not merely empty political rhetoric, as shown by the considerable funding provided by the government to enable and encourage immigrants to retain their own ethnic identities as well as to develop a new 'Australian' identity. In parallel with the Croatian experience described by Hay is the way in which the Macedonian Rom formed their own Romani football club as one means of establishing their own distinctiveness.[26] Similarly it is possible to see like processes at work with the existence of Jewish soccer clubs and leagues in London. However, perhaps it is worth noting just a brief word of caution concerning this policy. Its critics suggest that the only kind of ethnicity permitted is that based on the harmless display of dress, dance, diet and dialect. It is likely that football would be seen in the same non-threatening light.

In his examination of American basketball, Murry Nelson makes explicit use of the theoretical work on the notion of cultural capital by Pierre Bourdieu.[27] Nelson argues that basketball, a largely working class and ethnically-based sport, became cultural capital for many immigrants, and their children, to New York City in the early 1900s. His focus is primarily on the Original Celtics professional basketball team and the major immigrant groups represented by the players – Irish, German Catholics and Jews. Nelson shows how the involvement of these groups in the early days of professional basketball facilitated the acquisition of the habitus (or disposition) of the dominant cultural faction (or class), thereby permitting the assimilation and acculturation of these groups into American society.

Steven Jackson, David Andrews and Cheryl Cole are broadly concerned with the role of sport in defining national identity and of sports people as symbols of that identity. They look at the contrasting experiences and significance of two of the most famous black sporting personalities in recent years, Michael Jordan and Ben Johnson. By examining the discourses surrounding these two men, they look at how racial and national identities are defined, contested and reproduced. In particular their focus is on media discourses. The chapter critically examines the construction of Jordan as symbolically transcending his skin colour and emerging as the authentic, all-American hero and personification of the 'American dream'. This is located in the context of the American, Reaganite New Right's analysis of urban problems whereby instances of black achievement, such as Jordan's, were used as an example of levels that could be attained with determination and enterprise. Failure to achieve, especially among the urban black population, therefore becomes not the fault of the political system and government policies, or of society's racism, but the absence of will and application among the 'problem' population themselves. By way of contrast, the discourses around Ben Johnson are seen as being as much about black and Canadian identity as they are about the politics of the Olympics and the illegal use of steroids. This is seen against the background of Canada's long-standing preoccupation with its own identity, especially in relation to its southern neighbour, the United States. Issues of identity became embroiled in the fears of Americanization which existed in the late 1980s and were personified in the rivalry betwen the American athlete, Carl Lewis, and Johnson. By employing contemporary cultural analysis with recent studies of identity and imagined communities, the authors offer a distinctive reading of two, recent sporting icons.

In their contribution Joseph Maguire and Jason Tuck examine the dynamic nature of the relationship between sport and national identity in the British Isles, locating their arguments within the current debates concerning 'globalization'. Their piece starts with a consideration of the meaning of national identity, drawing on the work of Elias, Hobsbawm and others, in relation to notions of 'construction' and invented traditions.[28] This is then followed by a detailed study of the role of the media in presenting a particular version of national identity through newspaper (*The Times*) reporting on rugby union since 1945.

Although somewhat tangential to their main argument, this study helps to inform wider concerns relating to the relationship between national and ethnic identities and sport. A common analysis, and one that appears at various points throughout this volume, is that sport provides a major avenue for the expression of local, regional, ethnic, immigrant and national identity. Indeed the evidence to support such an argument is in many respects overwhelming. However, as briefly indicated in the work of Maguire and Tuck, this analysis can also be taken a stage further to incorporate the more paradoxical, ambiguous and multi-layered aspects of identity. It is possible, for example, to have a genuine and real pride in the achievement of a national sports team but otherwise hold to an internationalist worldview. The two are not, by any means, as incompatible as is sometimes implied. Similarly, it is possible for immigrants to express their distinct ethnic identity by participating in or supporting a (native) sport or team, but otherwise and for the most part seeking, consciously and deliberately, to assimilate into the host society and to lose any signs of separateness in a multi-cultural whole.

This though is to head the discussion towards issues relating to group and individual strategies of identity retention and assimilation. While such questions are raised in this contribution they are not central to Maguire and Tuck's main argument and the emphasis is rather on the way in which the media represents sport as an expression of national culture, politics and identity. In terms of the newspaper selected, the ambiguity referred to above is not in evidence.

The main question asked in the essay by Joseph Bradley concerns the role played by Celtic Football Club in forming and maintaining a distinct national identity for Irish Catholic immigrants, and their descendants, in Scotland. Bradley highlights the immigrant origins of the club and the importance of the national question to its officials, players and supporters in the period at least up until the 1920s. More controversially, he suggests that the cause of Irish nationalism remains a strong feature of the club and its supporters up to the present day. In establishing his argument Bradley necessarily locates the processes of identity formation and strengthening in the wider context of anti-Catholicism and anti-Irishness in Scottish society. This is to pick up a common theme in studies of ethnicity and ethnic group relations concerning the role of opposition in the making of group identities. By way of comparison, the importance of anti-Semitism and anti-Gypsyism for Jewish and Gypsy identity is widely acknowledged. The antagonism between Celtic and Rangers is seen as a product of the separate ethnic origins and evolution of the clubs. In this way, they act as the location for distinct ethno-religious identities, echoing how, on a larger scale, sport acts as a conduit for regional and nationalist sentiment and fervour.

However, Bradley's study also hints at some of the problems and difficulties of over-stressing these associations. He indicates how the football club, as well as contributing to the expression and maintenance of separate ethnic identities, can also, and perhaps paradoxically, act as avenues for immigrant interaction and assimilation with the host population. We have already seen a similar argument in the chapter by Roy Hay on Croatian clubs in Australia. Bradley talks of the identities being constantly interrogated, as being fluctuating and indeterminate, and as confused and in dispute. We are left, then, with a sense of the ambiguous nature of Irish identity in Scotland, especially among the Scottish-born descendants of the original migrants, and of immigrant identity as something multi-layered rather than one-dimensional.

The main theme of Tony Collins' contribution is the issue of racial integration and racism in sport. Collins finds that rugby league achieved higher levels of racial integration than other sports. Essentially Collins argues that the bitter split in the sport of rugby, stemming from the Rugby Football Union's insistence on amateurism which forced key northern groups to splinter and form the Northern RFU, led to two different paths of development for the sport. Rugby league developed into a distinctive game with its own rules, culture, ideology and ethos. The professional/amateur debate was echoed in a working class/middle class and north/south divide, and combined, according to Collins, to form among the supporters of rugby league a sense of injustice, exclusion and marginality. This in turn, he argues, led to the development within the game of an ideology of egalitarianism borne out of an almost siege mentality, not to be found in the strictly amateur rugby union, which in turn prepared the way for the entry of black players into the sport. The sport then developed in a way which made it at least marginal to, and arguably counter to, the more mainstream sporting national identity by virtue of its emphasis on commercialism, its working class character and the multi-racial composition of its players. This idea of professionalism and the class character of the sport make an interesting contrast with the school-based amateur games ethic discussed in the contribution by J.A. Mangan, seen by him as an essential component of character building for the Empire. Such notions do not appear to be in evidence in the sporting ideology of rugby league.

However, Collins also, and importantly, points to some of the limitations of this picture. Commercalism may have been as important a factor in opening the door to black players as any ill-defined sense of egalitarianism. The failure of the sport, as he notes, to find any base in the black and Asian communities of the north also at the very least must cast a shadow over any claims to successful integration and the combatting of racism.

Native sports, such as sumo wrestling in Japan and basketball in America, are by their very nature isolated from the international arena of competition. This, argues Mike Cronin in his study on Gaelic games in Ireland, denies the sport, its players, supporters and administrators, the opportunity to participate in and exploit the sporting nationalism associated with international competition. On the one hand, he argues, native sports play a considerable part in creating a sense of national identity, with the distinctiveness of the people being reflected in and confirmed by the distinctiveness of their (national) sports. However, such an expression of separateness also, and paradoxically, prevents the development of national pride and unity which is engendered through competition with other nations.

In an attempt to overcome this dilemma attempts were made in the late 1960s to internationalize Gaelic games and break what had previously been a self-imposed isolation. A number of reasons combined to ensure the failure of this endeavour thereby limiting, according to Cronin, the nationalist potential of the game.

The final essay in the volume, by J.A. Mangan, is concerned with the evolution of a British identity for Scotland. Mangan extends the arguments of Linda Colley on the eighteenth century by looking at the part played in this process by what he describes as a Scottish educational revolution in the second half of the nineteenth century.[29] In particular, his focus is on the development of the games ethic in private and state schools in Scotland. The motives behind the introduction and assimilation of this ethic, due in no small measure to the efforts of certain pioneering headmasters and teachers, are seen as a combination of pragmatism and idealism. Mangan argues that the successful incorporation of the games ethic into the schools system led to a revolution in manners and morals amongst the Scottish middle classes and that it contributed to the building of a distinctly British as opposed to Scottish identity among the middle-class pupils. In the glory days of the Empire this brought with it a much-desired social acceptance as well as rewarding occupational opportunities.

Adair, in his study of immigrants and sport in Australia, points to gaps in his essay – he admits that he does not cover the full range of immigrant and ethnic groups and that the important area of women and sporting identity remains neglected in his work, as indeed it does in others. Adair's self-criticism could also be taken to apply generally to this volume. It would have been an impossible task to consider anything other than a selective sample of sports, groups and identities. Similarly, the geographical focus is restricted and, unfortunately, does not consider sport in areas of continental Europe, Asia, Africa or South America. To say that this volume is merely a reflection of current research into the topic is not to offer a defence or excuse but rather an explanation. We share Adair's view that more detailed analysis and study is required to fill these significant gaps and to test the arguments presented here. It is hoped that this collection, by reflecting on current theoretical debates and approaches and by adopting a range of methodologies and case studies, contributes in some measure to this enterprise.

NOTES

1. *Total Sport*, July 1997, p.89.
2. The historical and contemporary literature on the function of sport is huge, but as examples, see R. Holt, *Sport and the British. A Modern History* (Oxford, 1989) for historical functions and B. Houlihan, *Sport, Policy and Politics: A Comparative Analysis* (London, 1997) for the contemporary.
3. E. Hobsbawm, *Nations and Nationalism since 1780: Programme, Myth and Reality* (Cambridge, 1996).
4. J. Breuilly, *Nationalism and the State* (Manchester, 1993).
5. E. Gellner, *Nations and Nationalism* (Oxford, 1983).
6. B. Anderson, *Imagined Communities, Reflections on the Origin and Spread of Nationalism* (London, 1983).
7. A. Hastings, *The Construction of Nationhood: Ethnicity, Religion and Nationalism* (Cambridge, 1997).
8. Ibid., p.2.

9. Robins has talked of the 'Transnationalisation of Economic and Cultural Life'. See K. Robins, 'Global Times: What in the World's Going On?' in P. du Gay (ed.), *Production of Culture/Cultures of Production* (London, 1997).

10. For example, see S. Daniels, *Fields of Vision: Landscape, Imagery and National Identity in England and the US* (Cambridge, 1993).

11. John Hutchinson and Anthony D. Smith (eds.), *Ethnicity* (Oxford, 1996), p.15. For a good recent discussion see S. Cornell and D. Hartman, *Ethnicity and Race: Making Identities in a Changing World* (London, 1998).

12. Ibid., p.21.

13. The use of basketball players such as Michael Jordan by companies like Nike have taken the game to a far wider audience than would have otherwise been possible. Movies such as *Space Jam*, again featuring Michael Jordan and made by Warner Brothers, combined basketball, Bugs Bunny and a host of other legendary cartoon characters to take the game into the world of international celluloid.

14. J. MacClancy (ed.), *Sport, Identity and Ethnicity* (Oxford, 1996), p.1.

15. For example, Allen Guttman, *A Whole New Ball Game* (London, 1988) and *Games and Empires* (London, 1994).

16. Holt, *Sport and the British.*

17. For example, J.A. Mangan, *Athleticism in the Victorian and Edwardian Public School* (Cambridge, 1981 and Falmer, 1986) and *The Games Ethic and Imperialism* (Harmondsworth, 1986 and London, 1998).

18. T. Mason, *Association Football and English Society, 1863–1915* (London, 1980).

19. W. Vamplew, *The Turf: A Social and Economic History of Horse Racing* (London, 1986).

20. Peter McIntosh, *Physical Education in England since 1800* (London, 1986); Sheila Fletcher, *Women First: The Female Tradition in English Physical Education 1800–1980* (London, 1984).

21. John Lowerson, *Sport and the English Middle Classes, 1870–1914* (Manchester, 1993).

22. The first British Society of Sports History Conference was held at Keele University in the early 1980s. The publisher Frank Cass offered immediate and active support and launched *The British Journal of Sports History*. This growth has parallels in Finland, Sweden, Denmark, Brazil, South Korea and Japan, and with works by Roberta Park, Gerry Redmond, Katherine McCrone, William Baker and Patricia Vertinsky to name but a handful of nations and authors. Such developments bode well for studies of sport, nationalism and ethnicity *beyond* Europe and this volume. See J.A. Mangan and Roberta J. Park (eds.), *From 'Fair Sex' to Feminism: Sport and the Socialization of Women in the Industrial and Post-Industrial Eras* (London, 1987); Gerald Redmond, *The Sporting Scots of Nineteenth-Century Canada* (London and Toronto, 1982); Kathleen E. McCrone, 'Play up! Play up! and Play the Game! Sport at the Late Victorian Girls' Public Schools', in Mangan and Park, *From 'Fair Sex' to Feminism*; William J. Baker, *Jessie Owens: An American Life* (New York and London, 1986); Patricia Vertinsky, *The Eternally Wounded Woman: Women, Doctors and Exercise in the Late Nineteenth Century* (Manchester, 1990).

23. For a more general discussion of these themes see M. Polley, *Moving the Goalposts: A History of Sport and Society since 1945* (London, 1998), pp.166–71.

24. The only major published works which are primarily concerned with an examination of these themes are those edited by Grant Jarvie, *Sport, Racism and Identity* (London, 1991); Jeremy MacClancy, *Sport, Identity and Ethnicity*; and Philip Moseley *et al.*, *Sporting Immigrants* (Crows Nest, NSW, 1997). Other than these, discussion has been restricted to the occasional chapter in a book, such as Martin Polley's 'Sport and Ethnicity' in his recent *Moving the Goalposts* (pp.135–59).

25. MacClancy, *Sport, Identity and Ethnicity*, p.2.

26. See K. Lee, 'Australia – Sanctuary or Cemetery for Romanies', in T. Acton and G. Mundy (eds.), *Romani Culture and Gypsy Identity* (Hertford, 1997), pp.67–81.

27. See P. Bourdieu, 'Sport and Social Class', *Social Science Information*, Vol.17, No.6 (1978), pp.819–40.

28. See N. Elias, *The Germans* (Cambridge, 1996); Hobsbawm, *Nations and Nationalism since 1780*.

29. See L. Colley, *Britons: Forging the Nation 1707–1837* (New Haven, CT, 1992).

Conformity, Diversity, and Difference in Antipodean Physical Culture: The Indelible Influence of Immigration, Ethnicity, and Race during the Formative Years of Organized Sport in Australia, c.1788–1918

DARYL ADAIR

For historians of Australian sport, the post-Second World War era has been of greatest interest with respect to the combined impact of immigration, ethnicity, and race on Australian sport. This focus on the relatively recent past is understandable. Demographically, the overwhelming majority of Australians in the nineteenth and early twentieth centuries were either immigrants from Britain and Ireland or their descendants. Not until the four decades after 1945 did the Commonwealth's ethnic composition become noticeably diverse, during which time around six million immigrants from various parts of the world – many from non-English speaking backgrounds (Nesbs) – made Australia their home.[1] In doing so these people brought with them their traditional sports and pastimes, such as the Italian game of *bocce*, while they also stamped their influence on locally played sports familiar to Europeans, such as soccer, wrestling, and boxing.[2]

There are two further compelling reasons for a focus on immigration, ethnicity, and race during the recent history of Australian sport. First, in 1967 a national referendum was passed authorizing the federal government to count Aborigines in the Commonwealth census, and to assume new legislative powers with respect to the condition of indigenous people. Historically, Aborigines faced both official and *de facto* restrictions to their freedom of movement and rights of association. In terms of the 'white world' of organized sport this had either limited or complicated Aboriginal involvement.[3] Second, in 1972 the new federal Labour government announced that Australia, as a nation of immigrants from diverse (though predominantly European) backgrounds, should embrace multiculturalism. In terms of sport this Commonwealth policy provided credibility to an existing practice of Australian-based soccer clubs representing particular ethnic communities.[4] Just as significantly, the ideal of a multicultural nation also suggested that Australians from NESB's and racial minorities *ought to be* welcome in so-called 'mainstream' sporting pursuits like the English imports cricket and rugby league, and the locally invented Australian Rules football.

Such changing ideas about the status of minority groups reflected a formal end to the Commonwealth's White Australia Policy (1901–73), but they also forecast greater ethnic and racial diversity during the last quarter of the twentieth century. A more 'colourful' Australian society was emerging slowly, with regular intakes of Asian, Arabic, and other NESB migrants from the 1970s onward.[5] Additionally, Aboriginal people, though still small in number at around one per cent of the nation's total population, were becoming more vocal about their sense of collective self-worth, and more visible as residents in white-dominated urban areas. In terms of sport, Asian-Australians became conspicuous in martial arts, table-tennis, and badminton – games that were popular in their respective homelands.[6] Concurrently, Aboriginal men began to figure prominently as professional players in two of the most popular winter spectator sports – Australian Rules football and rugby league; while tennis great Evonne Goolagong and sprinting star Cathy Freeman have been among a handful of Aboriginal women to make it to the sporting 'big time'.[7]

This overview suggests that discussions of immigration, ethnicity, and race in contemporary Australian sport will elicit a bevy of questions, arguments, and discussions. Hence it is no surprise that the first book about Australian sport to examine these topics collectively, by Mosely *et al*, focuses on 'the post-Second World War decades when immigrants from Non-English-speaking backgrounds (NESB) arrived *en masse*'.[8] The editors point out that this is a pioneering study, so it is pleasing to find that their book, despite its explicit focus on sport in recent Australian history, also offers brief insights into physical culture since the beginnings of white settlement.

That said, the following contribution contends that in order to understand the long term evolution of sport in Australian society, historians need to focus *just as much* attention on immigration, ethnicity, and race in the colonial and post-colonial eras before the Second World War. Australia was certainly far less cosmopolitan then, but the cultural baggage of different immigrant groups and their descendants was fundamental to the evolution of local sporting experiences. Just as significantly, colonial sporting events provided a public domain in which wider inter- and intra-ethnic group relationships were displayed – or indeed played out – symbolically. Finally, the involvement or otherwise of NESB ethnic and racial minorities in dominant or so-called 'mainstream' sports may shed light on what type of society WESB's (Australians of white, English-speaking backgrounds) were trying to establish and, subsequently, preserve.

With these twin themes of group inclusion and exclusion in mind, this article focuses on the respective places of majority/ minority ethnic and racial groups in sport during the first 130 years of white settlement in Australia, 1788–1918. Such an exploratory macro-historical inquiry cannot hope to provide steadfast conclusions. But it should serve as a basis upon which new micro-historical studies will spring forth, and from which further wide-ranging discussions, taking in the inter-war period 1918–1945, emerge subsequently. The current study is limited to a discussion of prominent ethnic or racial groupings in colonial Australia: the English; other Britons (Scots, Welsh, and Cornish); the Irish (both Catholic and Protestant); NESB white immigrants (specifically the Germans); and NESB non-whites (Aborigines, Chinese, and Pacific Islanders).

Australia's Sporting Roots

Contrary to common belief, British settlers were not responsible for the genesis of sport in the continent we now know as Australia. Aboriginal tribes had their own games of physical strength, endurance, and dexterity. These localized sports were, however, not simply recreational since they promoted hunting skills and they prepared young men for inter-tribal warfare. Foot races tested speed, wrestling required guile and physical strength, while spear and boomerang throwing contests demanded expert eye-to-hand co-ordination. As a consequence of regular physical activity in food gathering and tribal sports, Aborigines were characteristically fit and athletic.[9]

Habitation of Australia by whites began when convicts from Britain and Ireland were transported to New South Wales in 1788. The later arrival of ship loads of free settlers, particularly from the 1830s onwards, suggested that the Australian colonies were destined to become more than simply dumping grounds for felons.[10] Land grants, leasehold properties, and sale of Crown territory enabled fledgling agricultural and mining industries to begin. Concurrently government or parish-assisted passage was made available to 'respectable and industrious' emigrant labourers from various parts of the British Isles.[11] This transfer of able-bodied settlers also resulted in the transmission of Anglo-Celtic cultural baggage, including Protestant and Catholic forms of religious practice, and traditional recreational customs, such as drinking alcohol and playing sports. The church and the public house were major social institutions in the early settlement period to 1850, particularly as there were few established sporting venues during that time.[12] That helps to explain why publicans were the first sports promoters in the colonies: they offered traditional British games of quoits and skittles to their drinking patrons; they staged single-wicket cricket matches on land adjacent to their hotel; and they sponsored boxing bouts, wrestling contests, and (while they were still legal) cock-fights and dog-fights on their licensed premises.[13]

Formally organized sporting events were usually held spasmodically before the 1850s, and with scant resources. It was difficult for early settlers from the British Isles to replicate the traditional village green in a 'foreign' environment, but colonial improvisations enabled sport to make symbolic cultural connections with emigrants' homelands. Horse races were staged on hard and dry ground rather than lush turf, the steeds were at first hacks rather than thoroughbreds, but bookmakers and punters still traded cash with customary zeal. Socially exclusive hunt clubs set hounds loose on kangaroos and, later, in keeping with English field sports tradition, on foxes or deer imported from Britain. The feature social event of the early colonial sporting calendar was usually the rowing regatta. This aquatic spectacle was held at specific times of the year as part of local expressions of empire loyalty – celebrating the British monarch's birthday, anniversaries of colonial settlement, and the like.[14] In short, rudimentary early colonial sporting events not only provided pleasure for free immigrants, emancipists, and their descendants, they also helped to transmit many of the social and cultural trappings of British civilisation abroad.

Established Settlers and New Immigrants

For colonists who sought to create a new Britannia in the Antipodes, the continuing flow of convicts to Australia made the evolution of a 'good' society problematic. After protracted debate between 1849 and 1851, the British government accepted local demands that transportation to eastern Australia be discontinued from 1852. Subsequently, by the late 1850s, each of the colonies (except for the new penal settlement of Western Australia) was granted responsible government under the auspices of empire. The colonies also grew in stature because of the discovery of gold in south-eastern Australia in the early 1850s; this brought new wealth to the settlers, as well as a flurry of immigrant speculators. Among them was a significant body of Chinese prospectors, as well as a much smaller volume of experienced gold diggers from the west coast of North America. By the late 1850s/early 1860s Chinese men constituted nearly 20 per cent of all males in Victoria (though only some 4.5 per cent of the colony's total population since there were only eight Chinese females compared with nearly 25 000 Chinese males). By comparison, fewer than 3000 American immigrants had settled in Victoria during this period.[15]

Aside from 'pull' factors towards the colonies with respect to land ownership, farming, and mining, there were also 'push' factors away from immigrant homelands. The Irish famine of the 1840s prompted the departure of hundreds of emigrant ships from Ireland: it is now commonly assumed that this was the era in which large scale movement of Irish people to Australia began. But the vast majority of Irish passenger vessels made their way to America during the 1840s, with just two per cent of all Irish emigrants (or a total of 23,000) making the much longer journey to Australia.[16] Nevertheless, during the 1850s gold rush decade, five times that many Irish people (or 8 per cent of the total volume of Irish emigrants during that period) travelled to Australia. In post-famine Ireland most emigrants received assisted passage to the Antipodes, but a significant minority also came, as had other immigrant groups, in search of gold. By contrast to these economic push-pull factors, hopes for freedom of religious worship were decisive in bringing emigrants from Central Europe. Most notably, Nonconformist Protestants in Germany were enticed to South Australia from the late 1830s. Local planners had openly advocated freedom of worship and, unlike other Australian colonies, South Australia had refused to take in convicts. This appeared to make Adelaide and its environs a more respectable destination for pious dissenters.[17]

Despite such varying push and pull factors by the mid nineteenth century, involving intakes of migrants from China, the United States, and Continental Europe, the most striking demographic feature of the Australian colonies was the preponderance of settlers from the British Isles (Britain and Ireland). Indeed, this numerical ascendancy of Anglo-Celts and their descendants continued throughout the next seven decades under focus. As Table 1 (p.44) indicates, in 1861 nearly 87 per cent of all foreign-born colonists were emigrants from the British Isles. Of this total the English were by far the most numerous, consistently comprising nearly half of all Australian residents who, between 1861 and 1921, had been born in the British Isles. The next largest ethnic group was the Irish who, for the second half of the nineteenth century, constituted around one quarter of all foreign-born Australians – though this figure was virtually halved between 1911 and 1921 as the world-wide flow of emigrants from Ireland slowed down by the turn of the century. The proportion of Scottish-born Australians was remarkably steady, at either 12 or 13 per cent for the same period; while the number of Welsh-born Australians, though similarly consistent over time, constituted a much smaller volume of immigrant Britons, rising almost imperceptibly from 1.3 per cent in 1861 to 1.6 per cent in 1921.

In the meantime, as indicated by Table 2 (p.45), the percentage of locally-born colonists was rising rapidly and regularly during the period under focus – from 37 per cent in 1861, to 77 per cent in 1901, and further again to 85 per cent in the census of 1921. Given the emigration patterns outlined above, the gradual exodus of a majority of gold prospectors from

China and the United States, and (as will be discussed later) a serious decline in numbers of Aboriginal people, it is not difficult to conclude that the vast majority of locally-born Australians during the second half of the nineteenth century were descendants of British or Irish settlers – whether first, second, or third generation. Indeed, according to Richard Cashman, by the turn of the twentieth century, 'Australia was 98 per cent Anglo-Celtic'.[18]

One outcome of this Ango-Celtic demographic dominance was that it soon became customary for Australian social commentators to use the generic term 'ethnic' to refer specifically to minority immigrant groups – particularly those from a NESB. This represented a departure from the original Greek notion of *ethnos*, which referred to an ethnic group broadly as 'a people' – not solely as a minority group.[19] In the Australian case, WESB observers used ethnicity as a means by which to differentiate and distance themselves from NESB European migrants. By labelling local Germans, Greeks, Italians, and so on as ethnic, they signalled that these groups were both numerically scant and culturally marginal. The term ethnic was, nonetheless, rarely used by WESB Australians to label non-white minority groups, such as immigrant Asians and Pacific Islanders, nor Aborigines. They were classified by white colonists as socially different – and inferior – by virtue of their 'race'. Such racial labels were laden with colonial assumptions about the inherent inferiority of non-whites in terms of their intelligence, behaviour, and even their blood. Racially 'determined' white/non-white characteristics were thought to extend well beyond differences in nationality, culture, and language – the basic hallmarks of ethnic identity among white colonists. In this respect skin colour was the quintessential indicator of race: white (European), black (Aboriginal and Pacific Islander), and yellow (Asian).[20] Additionally, though, white groups located themselves within the upper echelons of a hierarchical, European dominated racial 'order'. To colonial Britons, the vast British empire reflected the superiority of the Anglo-Saxon race; local Germans spoke proudly of the noble Teutonic race (though such heroic racial imagery turned sour for them during the First and Second World Wars); while resolute Irish nationalists (though very much a minority in Australia) spoke defiantly against British cultural imperialism, arguing for preservation of the Gaelic-Celtic race.

In terms of cultural heritage, Australians of English, Scottish, Welsh, or Cornish extraction handed down varying national customs and linguistic traditions to their children. Yet they shared a common bond of having emigrated from member nations of the United Kingdom, and by remaining subjects of the British monarch in the colonies. Some Welsh and Scottish Highland immigrants spoke Celtic languages more fluently than English, but these people could still be assembled symbolically beneath a Union flag that flew so prominently in Australia. Hence even though the Scots, Welsh, and Cornish were minority immigrant groups in Australia, they were also part of an overwhelming expatriate British majority. This Union membership, even if not 'de-ethnicizing' these rather small-scale immigrant groups, at least offered them the prospect of higher social status than non-British ethnic minorites or non-white groups.

The ethnic 'position' of Irish-Australians was, if anything, even more difficult to pin down given the linguistic, religious, and cultural diversity of emigrants from around the Emerald Isle. The Irish were a deceptively diverse group that included Protestants and Catholics, speakers of English and Gaelic, and political factions promoting different causes – such as Home Rule within the United Kingdom, or a republican Ireland independent of British authority. Ireland was officially part of Britain, though to many Irish – particularly its vast majority Catholic population – this relationship appeared to be ambiguous, dubious, and even unnatural, as this familial link also seemed to 'hardline' Ulster Protestants. As Geoffrey Partington puts it: 'The main obstacle to unity in the British Isles, whether before or after the Act of Union of 1801 ... arose from the refusal of many of the Protestant English and "Scotch-Irish" introduced into Ulster ... to extend Britishness to the native Irish Catholics and of the latter to accept it when on offer'.[21] There were small pockets of Protestant anti-unionism and Catholic pro-unionism but, as Oliver MacDonagh argues, 'the Act of Union had redrawn the Irish lines of battle in an essentially sectarian way. Henceforth political leaning ordinarily depended on religion'.[22] Despite this historical legacy, celebrations of Irishness in colonial Australia implied acquiescence to, or at least tolerance of, British rule. On 17 March each year, symbols of Erin took precedence over Union flags, but it was not incongruous (particularly from an Ulster Protestant perspective) for celebrations of Ireland and its patron saint to involve a toast to the British monarch and a rendition of God Save the Queen.[23] Suffice to say that in nineteenth-century Australia there were relatively few *demonstrably* anti-British Irish political activists, while reformist Irish patriots looked forward to the day when, as they expected, England would grant Home Rule to Ireland.[24]

The overall impression, then, is that while migrants to Australia from various parts of the British Isles were diverse in culture, language, and religion, most of them could be homogenized as British on the basis of having come from a homeland that had openly embraced the Union – in other words, if the immigrants originated from Scotland, Wales, Cornwall, (Protestant) Ulster, and (of course) England. Each of these ethnic groups was predominantly Protestant or Anglican, and they shared a lingering mistrust of, even animosity towards, the Church of Rome that had swept most of Ireland. Irish-Catholic emigrants to Australia were, therefore, most unlikely to identify themselves as British, since Britishness typically entailed a measure of antipathy towards Roman Catholicism. Other nineteenth-century Irish issues, such as wealthy absentee English landlords demanding the eviction of poverty-stricken Irish tenants, or the British Government's sloppy handling of relief measures during the Irish Famine of the late 1840s, also contributed to the characteristic unwillingness of many Irish people to be reconciled to their inclusion in the United Kingdom. Yet, as Patrick O'Farrell has shown, Irish-Catholics in colonial Australia did coexist relatively peacefully, albeit amidst some tension as a religious minority, with non-Catholic emigrants from various parts of the British Isles.[25]

Given such a diversity of ethnic groups and, indeed, relationships both within and between different ethnic groups, historians of sport have understandably been cautious when discussing ethnicity and physical culture in colonial Australia. This subject has been made even more difficult to analyse because, as mentioned previously, the term ethnic has typically been used narrowly in Australia – to label minority immigrant groups as 'others', particularly those from a NESB. In terms of Australian sport, this has commonly meant that the cultural practices of immigrant minorities – especially those from a non-British background – have been designated as ethnic. Reflecting on this problem, Cashman warns that '[local] definitions of some sports as "ethnic" represents a way of marginalizing certain sports and particular groups'.[26] He reminds us that 'in a sense, all Australian sport is ethnic because it has been (and continues to be) borrowed from a multitude of societies'.[27]

With these points in mind, this article takes a catholic approach to the term ethnicity, accepting the view that both majority and minority immigrant groups have shaped Australian sport by applying and adapting their imported cultural baggage according to local circumstances. In these respects ethnicity may be used not simply to label groups that have been numerically small and/or culturally marginal. Rather, the term ethnic may also be applied to immigrant groups that, historically, have been numerically large and/or culturally dominant in Australia.[28] This seems to accord well with Cashman's appended quote from Patrick O'Farrell – the doyen of Irish-Australian history – that the 'real history' of Australia, which has been 'monstrously neglected', is the 'history of the gradual growth and development, through confrontation and compromise, of a people of distinctive quality and character, derived from and produced by cultures – majority and minority – in conflict'.[29] Concurrently, though, we need to remember that the dominant immigrant group in Australia – the English – did not think of *itself* as ethnic. In other words, the relatively narrow framework in which the term ethnicity was applied in Australia meant that, in practice, groups classified as 'ethnic' (and particularly non-British) tended to have an ambivalent, or at best tangential, place in a sporting culture that lionized Englishness.

Embracing Englishness

English migrants and their descendants were by far the single most influential ethnic group in colonial Australia. Hence it is no surprise that English sports came to dominate colonial playing fields, setting an agenda for a dominant or so-called 'mainstream' Australian sporting culture. This involved explicitly amateur sports like rugby, rowing, athletics, lawn tennis, and (from c.1900) netball and hockey; as well as sports associated with gambling, prize money, and professionalism, such as horse-racing, cricket, boxing, sculling, pedestrianism, cycling, and (from 1907) rugby league.

Many of the customs and rituals associated with English sporting practices were taken up in the colonies. In particular, status-conscious settlers tried to emulate the distinctive style and structure of elite English sports. The Adelaide Hunt Club, for example, was an enclave for social exclusivity in early South Australia, with membership restricted to settlers of wealth and social prominence who commonly aspired to form a self-styled colonial gentry. They rode in traditional aristocratic sporting garb – hunting 'pinks' and English morning suits – which, although unsuited to a warm climate, symbolized social refinement. Sport was an important way for the 'better' class of English emigrants to 'keep up appearances'.

The local 'gentry' also used sport as a means by which to distance themselves from (or elevate themselves above) working-class colonists. When the Anglophile South Australian Jockey Club organized mid-week race meetings in the 1850s they certainly did not have the participation of local labourers in mind, while the fact that club membership costs five guineas effectively excluded Adelaide's working class from positions of influence in local racing.[30] Traditions of English 'refinement' and class privilege in sport were also apparent in colonial rowing. Elite private schools in Victoria took part in an annual Head of the River (1868–), with students in English-style blazers and straw boaters cheering on their colleagues to glory; the Universities' Cup (1870–) was presented to Australian college rowers by stalwarts of the Oxford–Cambridge Boat Race; while Melbourne's Henley-on-Yarra (1904–) was fully intended to be a glamorous, ostentatious social occasion in the tradition of the prestigious English boat race, the Henley-on-Thames. By involving themselves in sport, English immigrants were thus not making an overt statement about 'being' Australian. Rather, they were displaying publicly their Anglocentric cultural lineage.

Modifying Englishness

Although local adoption of various English games and pastimes affirms the highly derivate and imitative nature of Australian sport, the colonists introduced new norms of participation into such imported games. Most notably, Australian cricket did not follow the rigid, formal social segregation of English 'gentleman' amateurs and working-class professional players who, although in the same team, used different dressing rooms, entered the ground through separate gates, and had contrasting on-field responsibilities according to social status. The English professional was expected to bowl, as this task was considered a form of labour, while amateurs took to batting, an art form said to befit gentlemen. This type of explicit class prejudice was anathema to Australian cricket. Although at the elite level the game involved payment of players as part-timers, bowlers and batsmen were selected on the basis of cricketing ability, not by their occupational status or class position.[31] Similarly, in colonial rowing, manual-labour amateurs were accepted into the sport well before their counterparts in England, where traditions of social hierarchy and class privilege had excluded working-class membership of rowing clubs.[32] These differences are evidence of more flexibile norms of participation in colonial Australian sport, including a greater emphasis upon merit rather than social position as a basis for selection.

Despite such modifications to English influence in Australian sport, the colonists developed few games of their own during the second half of the nineteenth century – the very period in which sports were being codified and modernized in England. The only notable exception to this trend was Victorian (later Australian) Rules football. Yet we need to be wary about assuming that the birth of this game at Melbourne in 1859 was part of a concerted effort to create a unique local sporting culture. No definitive version of football existed in England at this time; so, when a group of four men (three of whom were very recently arrived immigrants with public school backgrounds) produced standard rules for a sport of football in the colonies, they had not set out to strike a blow for independence from English sporting traditions. Rather, Victorian Rules was constructed pragmatically by the game's founding fathers, who amalgamated what they took to be the best elements of various localized football practices in England.[33]

By the last quarter of the nineteenth century Victorian Rules was by far the dominant football code in the Australian colonies – except for New South Wales and, soon after, Queensland. In Sydney's elite private schools, several influential expatriate English schoolmasters had zealously promoted rugby football to their male pupils. Subsequently, standardisation of rugby rules in 1871 by the newly-formed English Rugby Football Union paved the way for the formation of the Southern Rugby Union in New South Wales in 1874. This development also enabled systematic rugby competition among clubs and between schools in north-eastern Australia. In each of the other colonies Victorian Rules was already entrenched in the sporting landscape, with this locally invented game even finding embryonic support in Brisbane and Sydney.[34] Association football (or soccer), was also played in the colonies by the 1880s, but as an essentially 'non-contact' sport it was fundamentally different to the already popular 'handling' and 'running' football games, both of which allowed tackling of a player's body.[35] So English rugby and Victorian Rules were the two main football codes and, as these sports vied for supremacy, their supporters and opponents engaged in vigorous debates about the respective merits of each game.

Victorian Rules football found detractors among some English immigrants. They argued that because rugby had imperial, rather than simply local importance, this made it a 'superior' sport. In Brisbane, for example, Victorian Rules was taken up before rugby spread north from Sydney.[36] To a number of newly arrived English migrants to Queensland, support for this Australian game seemed heretical in that it lacked an imperial dimension. As a report in the *Brisbane Courier* put it: '...the players who prefer the Melbourne rules have formed an association, and have given it the high sounding name of the Queensland Football Association – a title which it is hoped it will never be entitled to as long as there is any body of English-bred or English-born footballers in the colony.'[37] Doubts about Victorian Rules were also raised in Sydney. One rugby official declared: 'An Empire game for football appears to me to be far more desirable than an Australian game. One is universal; the other parochial ... Let us have England or Great Britain versus Australia. It has a relish that eclipses anything of a purely local character.'[38]

Because the colonial game was 'totally unknown at home' it was unable to function as either a source of imperial loyalty or as a form of Anglo-Australian rivalry. According to rugby supporters, this made Victorian Rules second rate.[39] Few people countenanced the notion that Australians should export *their* game to England. Yet Victorian Rules sides did play touring English rugby teams at both codes in 1888 – with one clash at the Melbourne Cricket Ground under local rules attracting a then huge crowd of 25,000 spectators. These contests were, however, not tolerated by Australian rugby authorities who saw the popularity of such contests as a threat to the future of the English game. So Victorian Rules enthusiasts in Melbourne were left to play among themselves and, on special occasions, against visiting teams from other colonies.[40]

Non-English Britons: Scots, Welsh and Cornish

Notwithstanding the pervasive Anglicisation of Australian physical culture, other Britons – the Scots, Welsh, and Cornish – were also part of an evolving colonial sports landscape. Scottish immigrants were culturally diverse: they ranged from avowedly Celtic Highlanders (many of whom spoke Scots Gaelic), to the more Anglicized Lowlanders from Edinburgh or Glasgow. Immigrants to Australia from these two key Scottish geographical regions tried to retain a sense of their distinct cultural heritage by forming Gaelic Societies (mainly Highlanders) and Caledonian Societies (mainly Lowlanders). With a relatively small volume of Scottish immigrants, though, societies for expatriate Scots tended towards merger. In Sydney in 1876, for instance, the newly formed 'Highland Society of New South Wales' elected a president (rather than a chief), while its Lowland/ Highland/Other Scots membership was committed, among other things, to 'promote Gaelic and Scots language with literature and music, Highland Games, ... and to commemorate Scottish [anniversary] days'.[41] In addition to this pride in matters Scottish, the vast majority of Scots and their descendants were staunchly loyal to both the British Crown and the British Empire. They were, in short, both cultural nationalists and political unionists. Some of the more parochial immigrant Scots were, however, wary of domination by the English. They objected, for example, to the reigning monarch being described by the colonists as Queen of England rather than Queen of Britain, while they were annoyed when Anglo-Australians used the term English to describe matters that were distinctly British or imperial. Hence Scottish heritage societies harboured a latent anti-Englishness, but their nationalist sentiment did not spill over politically to anti-unionism. Nostalgia for the culture of Scotland remained compatible with Scottish reverence for the power, security, and wealth of the British Empire.[42]

The influence of the Scots in Australian physical culture was most noticeable with the local establishment of golf. This game had been invented in Scotland, of course, so such an organisational connection in the colonies was no surprise. Golf courses were laid out by Scottish immigrants, their descendants helped to form golf clubs, and golfing equipment was imported regularly from manufacturers in Scotland. While golf had distinctly Scottish origins, the game had also spread to other parts of Britain – most noticeably England – by the nineteenth century. This regional expansion of golf had two major consequences for the development of the game in Australia. First, the Scottish custom of playing golf was now also a British pastime, so the game became more than simply a sporting practice for expatriate Scots, being taken up fervently in Australia by colonists from various national origins. Second, golf in England had developed as a preserve of 'well-to-do' players, both in terms of wealth or social status. A proliferation of private, rather than public, golf clubs in nineteenth-century England made the game a socio-economically extravagant, rather than accessible, sport. In Scotland the situation had been different: although private, member-based golf clubs were well established, local authorities typically laid out rudimentary golf courses on common land, with these areas set aside for public participation. Hence golf in Scotland was played regularly by 'the people', the middle classes, and the landed gentry (though not necessarily mixed together) on links courses that catered variously for golfing novices, aficianados, or professionals.[43]

Despite this Scottish heritage of wide public access to golf, the game's expansion to England provided a context in which the genesis of golf in Australia was shaped fundamentally by considerations of social class and status. Brian Stoddart summarizes varying Anglo-Scottish influences in golf this way: 'While [golf's] Scottish dimensions were relatively egalitarian, that was not the case south of the border [England] where clubs were established as exclusive environments in which the cultured society might congregate. Something of that atmosphere transferred to Australia and is most readily noticed in the creation of the "Royal" clubs.'[44] The prestigious prefix 'royal' was not, however, an exclusively English golfing label. The legendary 'home' of golf was, after all, the Royal and Ancient Golf Course at St Andrews, Scotland. Stoddart is, none the less, surely correct in stressing the exclusive nature of private golf clubs in Australia, but whether this elitism was a consequence of the Anglicisation of colonial golf is more difficult to discern.

Aside from golf, Scots are also credited with spreading lawn bowls to Australia. Yet the first bowling greens in the colonies catered for the English version of bowls, which was played on relatively rough, rather than smooth turf, and without clearly defined, uniform spatial parameters. Somewhat paradoxically, though, the clubs soon ceased to play the rather loosely organized English style of lawn bowls, instead opting for the more formally structured Scottish version of the game, which was played on enclosed rinks with specially mown greens and elaborate, yet uniform, rules. This decision appears to have been taken pragmatically by expatriate Scottish and English bowlers alike. For lawn bowls to flourish in Australia both local and inter-colonial teams needed to compete under common conditions. The rules for English bowls varied considerably between localities and venues; only Scottish rinks bowls offered the prospect of regulated and uniform standards of play in the colonies. Indeed, according to McCarthy, it was after a deputation to Britain by Australian lawn bowls officials in 1899 that 'the English adopted the more formal Scottish play'.[45] In a curious way, then, the

Scottish version of lawn bowls was taken up in various parts of the British Empire, and was championed as an imperial (and hence mainstream) more so than a distinctly Scottish (and hence minority) practice. So neither golf nor lawn bowls became exclusive or even distinctive Scottish pastimes in Australia. Rather, these games were taken up fervently across the ethnic spectrum, helping to establish them firmly within an evolving Australian sporting culture.

Association football (better known in Australia as soccer) was an English invention, but this sport gained considerable popularity in other parts of Britain during the late nineteenth century, though most of all in Scotland. This cultural diffusion of soccer in Britain had significant implications for the manner of its promotion in Australia. As Phillip Mosely and Bill Murray explain: 'At a time when Australian football and rugby were in the hands of locally-born organizers, soccer was generally run by British, especially Scottish, migrants often reflected in the plethora of Caledonians, Rangers and other teams of obviously Scottish inspiration. The Welsh and Irish influence was less pronounced, but ... soccer developed much later in those countries.'[46] English immigrants were, not surprisingly, also prominent in early colonial organisation of soccer, but like their Scottish-Australian counterparts they were usually working-class enthusiasts – coal-miners, factory workers, and the like. Middle-class and 'well-to-do' football aficionados from Britain tended to be rugby followers, particularly those who had graduated from elite public schools.[47]

While class was a key factor in determining which of the British football codes colonial men played, ethnic background was less significant. Soccer teams representing mining communities or factory workplaces in Australia contained immigrants from various parts of Britain. Yet there were local efforts to promote soccer teams along lines of ethnic origin – as was implied by the emergence of colonial clubs with distinctly Scottish or English names. However, this flew in the face of what Mosely and Murray describe as 'the peculiarly Australian organisation of sport whereby major teams are allocated a region and have first playing claim on all people resident in that district'.[48] Given the existing suburban structure of Australian team sports, clubs based on ethnic, rather than regional, lines was not readily accepted by local soccer authorities. Although a 'breakaway' group of ethnic-based clubs was formed in 1914, it lasted only a few years and the district system dominated again. Unlike in Britain, where soccer dominated winter playing fields, this game never seriously challenged the popularity of Australian rules nor the rugby codes. Hence soccer had the rather unusual status of being an emphatically British pastime, yet very much a *minority* sport in Australia. This was despite the fact that the colonists were overwhelmingly of Anglo-Celtic descent, and that their fascination with sport had been shaped fundamentally by the imported cultural baggage of British immigrants.

Thus far we have seen that the Scottish-invented games of golf and lawn bowls were a shared cultural domain for a variety of expatriate Britons, the Irish, and locally born colonists. Their commonality through sport was based on class: colonial golf clubs and bowls clubs were principally for individuals with sufficient financial means and adequate social status. Yet there was evidence of colonial Scots celebrating their own sense of cultural heritage through parochial group rituals. Most notably, various Scottish Societies organized Annual Highland Games, which involved Celtic dancing, playing of bagpipes, and traditional sporting contests like throwing the caber and putting the stone.[49] Significantly, though, these displays do not appear to have promoted a sense of ethnic tribalism among Scots in Australia.

While emigrant Scots were able to stamp some influence on the evolution of Australian sporting culture, the considerably smaller Welsh and Cornish populations were hardly in a position to do likewise. Cornish migrants were most noticeable in South Australia, particularly in the Yorke Peninsula mining towns of Moonta, Burra, and Kadina, some 50 miles north of Adelaide. Several hundred Cornish miners and their families had settled in this area, known colloquially as the 'copper triangle'. In terms of sport, these miners were renowned within their local communities for skill and bravado in Cornish-style wrestling. Significantly, though, some of the best Cornish wrestlers also competed for prize money in Adelaide pubs, where pugnacious contests between colonists from various national origins attracted enthusiastic audiences. In addition to the Cornish, there was also a small presence of Welsh miners in rural South Australia, many of whom were, like their Cornish neighbours, both religious Nonconformists and wrestling enthusiasts. Hence sport and religion became ways of promoting a sense of common purpose among these two groups of miners, despite their different ethnic backgrounds.[50] Eventually, though, local interest in wrestling relied too much on the combined efforts of the Cornish and Welsh. In the population centre of Adelaide, as with other Australian capital cities, bare-knuckle boxing (though often illegal) was a more recognized sporting spectacle. Prize-fighting involved protagonists from various parts of Britain and Ireland, as well as locals, so boxing was very much an ethnically plural form of colonial entertainment. Moreover, although it was a 'blood' sport, prize-fighting was given greater public legitimacy with the introduction, from c.1884, of gloved competitors and widespread acceptance of the Marquis of Queensberry rules.[51]

In summary, among non-English Britons only the Scots had a noticeable influence on the early development of Australian sporting culture.

Typically, they combined with other Britons to promote Scottish-invented games like golf and lawn bowls, while Scots were also prominent supporters of the English-invented games of soccer and rugby. Welsh and Cornish wrestling had little prospect of spreading widely because they were, for the most part, provincial sporting practices confined to disparate mining communities. Moreover, Welsh and Cornish immigrants of the late nineteenth century had already been introduced to English and Scottish sports, so they were more eclectic about their sporting pastimes than were a previous south-western British generation. Rugby, in particular, had become something of a passion to the Welsh. Among Britons, then, the colonial sporting culture was being shaped principally by Anglo-Scottish influences, and much less so by smaller population groups from Britain. But what do we know about the contribution of Irish sports to Australian popular culture? Or, for that matter, how did Irish settlers take to mainstream sports that were, for the most part, British in origin and spirit? These are complex questions, particularly in light of ongoing Protestant–Catholic sectarian tensions in Ireland, as well as troubling differences in Anglo-Irish political relationships during the late nineteenth and early twentieth centuries.

The Irish

Much like British migrants, Irish-born settlers brought their own sports to colonial Australia. Hurling and Gaelic football were common forms of physical activity for recently arrived Irishmen in the 1840s and 1850s, though as with British team games there were no uniform rules at the time. This meant that hurling and Gaelic football were generally played on an *ad hoc* basis – usually as a celebration of Irish culture rather than as a formal contest between organized clubs. Impromptu games of Irish football surfaced at Victorian gold-diggings in the 1850s, while exhibitions of hurling found their biggest audience during public celebrations on the colonial calendar. Tom Hickie notes that rejoicings in 1842 to honour Queen Victoria's birthday included a specimen of the game of Hurling, which was offered to the colonists by a number of Irishmen assembled in Hyde Park.[52] Tellingly, this was not solely a display of Irish sporting tradition and Celtic athletic prowess. It also signalled that local celebrations of Irishness could complement ceremonies of loyalty towards Britain and its monarch.

The Irish were the second largest ethnic group in colonial Australia, but they were not noticeably tribal either in location or vocation. O'Farrell accepts that there were pockets of major cities with a significant presence of Irish residents, but he argues that 'even in streets blazoning forth Irish allegiance – St Patrick's Lane, Shamrock Alley – there was no Irish monopoly, or endeavour to create one'.[53] Neighbours tended to be fellow workers – a mixed bag of English, Scots, Welsh, Irish, and Australian-born. O'Farrell also emphasizes that unlike their Celtic counterparts in the United States, Australia's Irish were 'intensely mobile', often moving in search of seasonal employment opportunities. This told against the formation of Irish ghettos, while it also worked towards Irish interaction with other ethnic groups.[54] What key factors, then, drove the experiences of expatriate Irish, and shaped their relations with other Australians?

The freedom of Catholic worship, coupled with the fact that Irish-Australians had rights to property and the franchise akin to other emigrant groups from the United Kingdom, meant that Irish-Catholics were not defined in colonial law as second-class British subjects – though in social practice they were often treated as such. O'Farrell points to a local employment 'atmosphere' where 'hiring, firing and promotion were open to continuous sectarian or racial interpretations'. He accepts that 'the area is shadowy and uncertain' but reckons that 'the general drift is clear: the Irish believed they were discriminated against, and to some extent they were'.[55] No wonder many Irish people looked to integrate into the wider society as soon as practicable. Even the Catholic church, though underpinned strongly by local Irish support, encouraged its flock to think of themselves as brethren and sisters of Australia rather than simply as expatriates of Eire. Leading the way was Cardinal Moran, the first Irish Archbishop of Sydney, who 'declared himself an Australian as soon as he arrived in 1884, and at once made plans to secure a supply of native-born priests'.[56]

This diminution of Irish cultural assertiveness was in stark contrast to developments in the Emerald Isle itself. McDonagh points to three key developments between 1884 and 1893: the formation of the Gaelic League, the Literary Revival, and the launch of the Gaelic Athletic Association. These movements were each concerned, albeit in different ways, with the erosion of Gaelic-Celtic culture and language in the face of Anglicizing forces extending throughout the British Isles.

O'Farrell argues convincingly that the Gaelic cultural revival in Eire had remarkably little influence upon the everyday lives of Irish-Australians. The Catholic church, which he describes as the 'arbiter of all things Irish', failed to see any local advantage in adopting Gaelic language and literature, arguing that such a move risked alienating Irish-Australians from the wider English-speaking colonial community.[57] In terms of sport there was a handful of Gaelic sporting teams, such as five hurling clubs in Sydney in the 1880s. But the GAA did not take root as a movement in the colonies. Irish-Australians were, by the time of the birth of the GAA in 1884, already prominent locally as boxers, cricketers, and rugby players. Intriguingly, O'Farrell describes colonial sport as a domain in which the principle of 'Australianize or perish' applied to the Irish. Yet many of these local sporting pastimes were already familiar to expatriate Celts: the nineteenth-century British games revolution had spread to Ireland before the GAA had revitalized (and indeed modernized) Gaelic games for popular consumption. O'Farrell tacitly acknowledges as much by stating that 'the popular aspects of the [Gaelic] movement in Ireland, in politics and sport, had no appeal in Australia because they sought to displace commitments firmly made, to Home Rule, and to *well-established* games'.[58] O'Farrell actually makes this point brilliantly in another context: in an article on St Patrick's Day he debunks any idea that the Sports Carnivals following the annual Irish parade centred on Gaelic Games. Instead, during the 1880s, there were mainstream athletic contests: high jumping, shot putting, hammer throwing, and foot racing; and, by the 1900s, cycling racing.[59]

On this evidence, the GAA's veneration of hurling and Gaelic football did not have much impact in an outpost of the British Empire that was fundamentally Anglocentric in terms of sport. As O'Farrell astutely points out, English sports like cricket and rugby 'were the avenue through which Catholic schools related to the rest of the sporting community. To drop them in preference for Irish games, would be to ... isolate such schools from the mainstream of Australian life'.[60] For Catholic parents this was an unacceptable risk. Just as significantly, there was little interest among local Irish-Catholics in the separatist Irish nationalism advocated by the GAA. On the other hand, a visit to the colonies in the early 1880s by the Irish Home Rule activists, the Redmond Brothers, attracted considerable support among Irish-Catholics, but determined opposition from many Anglo-Irish Protestants. Reprisals could be severe: McConville notes that '... two footballers in the Carlton Club were dismissed because they dared support the Irish visit'.[61]

Australian Rules football was not complicated by north-south class rivalries imported from England, nor was it associated with a particular immigrant tradition or religious denomination. This allowed the game to more easily accommodate players and fans from across the social spectrum. Some clubs, however, were said to represent the interests of either Catholics or Protestants exclusively. While this might have been true of schoolboy and local football – particularly in church-based competitions – it really amounted to hearsay in the big league. The Collingwood Football Club, for example, has long been characterized as 'essentially a Catholic institution in terms of supporters, players and officials'.[62] Richard Stremski, however, has shown that this assumption is based on myth, not fact: the team has always attracted ample proportions of both Catholic and Protestant supporters; around two-thirds of captains in the club's history have been Protestant; Freemasons were often influential in club affairs; and Collingwood did not have a Catholic club president until 1974.[63] A more general point arising from this is that top-level Australian sport has not sustained distinctive Protestant-Catholic club identities. There is nothing to compare, for example, with the historic Rangers versus Celtic rivalries in Scottish football.[64] We need to know more, however, about religious loyalties and sectarian divisions in local sporting clubs around Australia, particularly those involved in church-based or inter-school sports associations. This objective could be supplemented by studies of ethnic-based schools, a theme already raised for attention by Bob Petersen who, in a recent article, provides ideas about how historians might tackle what has been a largely overlooked subject in Australia.[65]

NESB White Immigrants: The Germans

During the nineteenth century the Germans were the largest and most influential non-English speaking white immigrant group in the colonies. They were especially recognisable as a distinctive regional community in South Australia. By 1851 the number of German-born people in the colony was 7130, or around 11 per cent of the total population.

German-named South Australian villages, such as Klemzig, Hahndorf, and Blumberg were settlements consisting mainly of German immigrants and their descendants. Their cultural baggage was evident through wine-making, Lutheran religious faith, and traditional folk dancing. Additionally, German physical culture was a feature of this community, though as with British-invented sports and games, these practices centred round men more so than women. Kegeln, for instance, was a popular game akin to skittles, but played on an alley around one-third the width of the British game, and about twice its length. Kegeln also used nine pins, unlike the customary ten in skittles. South Australian Germans commonly played kegeln after the Sunday morning had been spent at church, with participants and spectators separated along gender lines. As Ian Harmstorf and Michael Cigler report: 'The men, dressed in their Sunday best, challenged each other to games, while the women provided Kaffee and Kuchen, making the occasion an opportunity for relaxation and a break from hard work.'[66]

The male-centred nature of German sport was also apparent in the Annual Hunt. Men with rifles travelled by foot before dawn, camping out for two or three nights in the wilderness, depending on the length of the hunting competition. The most successful hunter was crowned Schützenkönig (King of the Hunt), and was adorned with a laurel wreath. Unlike British fox-hunting the emphasis here was upon the guile of the shooter, not his use of dogs to secure a kill. Additionally, the German hunt was not ostentatious in terms of social display: the accolade of Schützenkönig could be won by a competitor of modest means and humble community status, and his feats were achieved largely out of public view.[67] German hunting traditions were also reflected in the establishment of rifle and crossbow clubs in South Australia during the 1850s. These associations were organized specifically for locals of German extraction, as was suggested by the aptly named German Rifle Club, which was formed in the early 1850s. British settlers with a fascination for shooting had also established rifle clubs, so it could hardly be said that this sport was peculiar to the Germans. Moreover, although rifle clubs were typically organized along ethnic lines in South Australia, this did not prevent cultural exchanges between shooters of various national origins. John Daly has pointed to numerous 'trials of skill' between German and British riflemen in Adelaide during the 1870s, with the Teutons invited by the Anglo-Celts to join a representative body, the South Australian Rifle Association. The Germans were able to join, Daly emphasizes, while retaining membership of their original ethnic-based club, so this was not part of a process of 'de-ethnicization' on the part of immigrant Britons and their descendants. There was, at this time, no particular reason for jingoistic rivalry between these two national groups: Britain and Germany did not share an antagonistic relationship, while Australian-based Germans could plead allegiance to both a British and a Prussian monarch. The House of Windsor, after all, had distinctive German origins.[68]

The wider influence of German physical culture in South Australia was most apparent through gymnastics. In Adelaide a gymnasium was established as early as 1840, but few settlers had formal experience in this discipline and none were trained to teach it. This situation changed dramatically after the arrival in 1857 of the German physical instructor Adolph Leschen, who had been educated at the University of Kiel by the veritable 'father of gymnastics', Friedrich Ludwig Jahn. The local gymnasium became the site for Leschen's Adelaide Gymnastic and Fencing Club, though it was the turnverein (gymnastic) movement, more so than fencing, that captured most public interest. Leschen attracted many Germans to his classes, but he also instructed Anglo-Celts in the discipline of gymnastics.

Such was Leschen's public profile and self-confidence that he even argued, somewhat heretically for the time, that German gymnastics were a superior form of physical activity to British team sports: 'whatever can be said in favour of cricket, football and other games, they do not strengthen the body like the systematic training of the gymnasium does'.[69] While Leschen's claims about health promotion through gymnastics were not disputed, and were actively promoted in many schools, there were only small numbers of turnverein devotees among the wider community. Leschen's 'English' gymnastics classes typically involved Adelaide's 'well-to-do', who had appropriate social connections and sufficient leisure time by which to train together a couple of times per week. The elite status of these enthusiasts may also have been something of a disincentive to 'ordinary' people to join. Additionally, a relatively small number of regular members meant that annual subscriptions were required to sustain the gymnasium facility.[70] This, again, appears likely to have told against working-class participation. Daly also posits a cultural explanation for a typical lack of involvement in gymnastics by working-class colonists of British stock: 'The lower orders were never really attracted to an activity performed for its own sake and in terms of bodily vigour and health requiring a delayed gratification. Their preference was still for the tavern sports of billiards, skittles and quoits and the "new Australian game" of football.'[71] In other words, Anglo-Celtic labourers tended to view sport as a diversion from work routine, and hence as a form of *play* more so than an opportunity for physical and mental self-improvement. However, middle-class British colonists were more eclectic in their sporting interests. Through pastimes like horse racing they showed a fondness for sport that was recreational, entertaining, and speculative. And, as in England, expatriate British school masters lionized participation in organized team sports as a means of instilling self-discipline and moral improvement – particularly among boys. This functional view was shared by many of the churches which, in promoting Muscular Christianity, linked a healthy body and a lively mind to spiritual virtue.[72] When comparing these sporting models to turnverein, though, two significant cultural differences become apparent. First, while turnverein was motivated by a belief in physical activity as a cornerstone of human well-being, it was an essentially secular, rather than religious, movement. Second, the physical culture of turnverein was predominantly experiential and holistic, rather than competitive and aggressive – the latter of which was a central feature of most British-invented sports. Perhaps this helps to explain why some Germans saw turnverein as a cultural practice for their 'own kind'.

It would be simplistic to presume that the physical culture of colonial Germans rested solely with traditional activities from their former homeland. According to Ian Harmstorf, German adoption of British physical culture was but one of many examples of how readily they looked to integrate into the wider colonial community. In his view, wealthy and middle-class Germans were 'almost obeisant' to the dominant, British-centred culture. As prime evidence for this claim, Harmstorf points out that the once prestigious German Club (1854–), which was '... supposed to uphold German culture and traditions in South Australia', had closed down by 1907. Little wonder, remarks Harmstorf, that there had been no concerted effort on the part of Adelaide's Anglo-Celtic majority to demand assimilation of the Germans. This group had never seriously disturbed or questioned the colonial order, dominated as it was by Anglo-Celtic immigrants and their descendants. And, although English was their second language, the Germans accepted that this was the 'official' mode of communication in Australia.[73]

This study has not attempted to analyse the sporting experiences of other NESB European immigrants in colonial Australia. In this era they were far less numerous than the Germans, and they appear to have had little impact on wider local sporting practices. Nonetheless, historians of ethnicity in colonial Australia have basically failed to consider the significance or otherwise of imported physical culture *among* European immigrants (other than for the Germans). For example, social histories of Greek and Italian immigrants before the First World War make no mention of Greco-Roman traditions in sport, such as weight-lifting and Greek wrestling. These social activities may not have been publicly prominent in colonial Australia, but it seems reasonable to predict that among nineteenth-century Italian and Greek immigrants, such imported cultural baggage was a meaningful part of *their* way of life.

NESB Non-Whites: Aborigines

Although estimates vary, it is now widely argued by historians that several hundred thousand Aborigines died as a consequence of early European settlement.[74] This loss of life came about through violent conflict with settlers, isolation from traditional food sources, and most of all by the transmission of new, highly infectious, diseases to Australia. Given such stresses many tribal cultural practices ceased to be passed down to subsequent generations, among which – as is our focus here – were sporting customs. As we have seen, British and Irish colonists had brought their own sports to Australia, but these games were not originally intended for indigenous people. Some imported sports did become a part of Aboriginal lives, though very much on terms dictated by the settlers. To comprehend the ambivalent place of Aborigines in sport, we should first consider black–white race relations in colonial Australia.

Once British settlers had asserted territorial dominance over various Aboriginal hunting and fishing regions, they were faced with the 'problem' of a spatially dislocated and socio-economically deprived indigenous people in their midst. The Christian churches responded by offering refuge to Aborigines in their missions, most of which were located outside of colonial cities. These rural institutions intended benevolence, but their ethnocentric attempts to 'civilize' Aborigines were generally misguided. Missionaries failed to understand the significance and complexity of

Aboriginal culture and spiritual beliefs, but they at least fed and cared paternalistically for indigenous people, helping them to survive at a time when secular authorities had given them up as a 'dying race'.[75]

As part of their civilizing ideal the missions introduced codified forms of sport to local Aborigines. Most notably, cricket was promoted as a prime example of the importance of teamwork, obedience to rules, and respect for 'fair play'.[76] Aboriginal teams who conformed to these expected standards of conduct even had occasional opportunities to travel to the cities to play cricket, though matches against urban-based white teams were not generally accepted as serious contests. Rather, they were touted as good-will gestures towards the 'natives', as well as being a source of spectator amusement, for Aboriginal cricketers were renowned for playing in an unorthodox, yet spectacular, manner. This entertainment factor helps to explain why a team of Aborigines was organized by a colonial entrepreneur to make a gate-money cricket tour of England in 1867–68 (the first Australians to do so). These black-skinned men were objects of curiosity to the English, who came in large numbers to witness not only cricket, but boomerang throwing, and other 'native sports'. The Aboriginal players impressed by winning nearly half of their games, but they were exploited by organizers. The players were poorly compensated financially for their efforts, while several of them were ordered to continue touring despite having fallen ill.[77]

There were no further such Aboriginal cricket ventures, though not because of public concern about the condition of indigenous cricketers abroad. Rather, sports participation by Aborigines was less likely *generally* from the 1870s because colonial governments began to impose laws by which to officially distance Aborigines from white society. Racially-specific measures included restrictions on Aboriginal freedom of movement outside of reserves, outlawing of mixed-race marriages, and territorial segregation of races – black, 'half-caste', and white. This separation of groups was founded on the absurd notion that a person's character, morality, and worth were determined by blood: 'white' blood was claimed by colonists to be at the height of the 'scale of humanity', with 'black' blood deemed lowly. So-called 'mixed blood' was an enigma, said to produce the worst elements of constituent races. In other words, racial separatism was 'justified' by a mix of Social Darwinian and British imperial ideas. They helped to legitimize the dominance of 'progressive' white colonists, as well as the subjugation and expected demise of Aboriginal society. It mattered not that very few Australians had a grasp of evolutionary theory. The social 'implications' of Darwinism – as outlined by philosopher Herbert Spencer and others – were convenient and seemingly scientific bases by which colonial whites justified their *long-standing* treatment of indigenous people as not simply different, but inferior.[78]

With policies of racial separatism in place during the 1870s, team sport among Aborigines was restricted largely to rural government reserves or missions, where there were paltry playing resources. Despite predictions to the contrary, Aborigines survived the late colonial period, though their numbers had diminished considerably. Some nomadic tribes in central Australia remained oblivious to a white presence, but most Aboriginal groups had been affected fundamentally by colonialism, with many of them obliged to reside on reserves or missions. Between 1890 and 1911 further laws were passed to enshrine Aboriginal 'protection' through institutionalisation. With such wide-ranging controls over their lives, Aborigines had become subject to, and dependent upon, white overseers. Permission of white authorities was needed for Aborigines to marry, miscegenation was outlawed, while indigenous children could be taken from Aboriginal parents and made wards of the state. This trend of separation and marginalization was rarely interrupted, though Aboriginal men were recruited to work (often without pay) on outback sheep and cattle runs, where their knowledge of the bush and location of water holes made them valuable assistants – but certainly not social equals as far as white stockmen or jackaroos were concerned.[79]

Sport also offered occasional opportunities for black–white cultural connections. Most notably, some Aboriginal men were enticed into the white world of professional sport, particularly where their athletic talents could be exploited by promoters for financial gain. This was apparent in two sports centred on gambling – pedestrianism (foot-racing) and boxing. There were several outstanding Aboriginal sprinters during the 1880s, including the legendary Charlie Samuels, acclaimed officially as Champion of Australia (running 100 yards in 9.10 seconds in 1888); while in the 1890s Bobby McDonald invented the crouched start now taken for granted as standard technique in sprint races. Aborigines also produced stars of the boxing ring, with Jerry Jerome the first official champion, winning the Australian middle-weight title in 1912.[80]

Most Aboriginal athletes were not involved in elite-level sporting events. Typically, they took part in provincial rather than city games, and they were generally itinerant performers, contesting fights or footraces at various country shows, or competing in impromptu sporting 'entertainment' sponsored by local publicans to draw in punters. Perhaps the most familiar Aboriginal sportsmen in rural Australia were the black fighters who formed an integral part of Jimmy Sharman's Boxing Troupe. Sharman was a renowned prizefighter in the early 1900s, retiring in 1912 to manage a travelling 'circus' of boxers from various ethnic and racial backgrounds. Sharman, a white man, pitched the troupe's boxing tent in rural towns, and regularly at agricultural shows, around the country. He adopted the catch cry

'Who'll take a glove?' as a challenge for locals to try to defeat his fighters. Within Sharman's stable of boxers Aborigines were renowned as attacking fighters with little taste for defence. They proved capable of absorbing blows from bigger framed fighters, replying rapidly with a volley of well-timed punches to floor challengers.[81]

Although prize-fighting and pedestrianism were something of an Aboriginal 'passport' into white society this acceptance was ephemeral, usually lasting only so long as these sportsmen made money for backers and won the accolades of supporters. As Richard Broome and Colin Tatz have both shown, many prominent Aboriginal boxers ended their lives financially destitute, with their former star status in sport making no difference to their subsequent personal circumstances.[82] So even though many blacks dominated whites inside the boxing ring or the running track, outside of these spatial settings they were unable to call the shots. Not that they had free reign within sport or leisure environments: in many Australian country towns Aborigines were barred from swimming in public pools; they were segregated from whites in hotels and theatres; and (by contrast to today) indigenous footballers played little part in rural football teams. With such restrictions on black–white cultural connections it is no wonder that boxing and sprinting – both of which focused on individual performance, not teamwork – were sports that could be adapted to the socio-cultural constraints under which Aborigines lived.[83]

NESB Non-Whites: Chinese and Pacific Islanders

Arguments to justify the separation or marginalisation of Aborigines from colonial society were also used to support racial vilification of immigrant non-whites.[84] In this case, though, economic factors were cited as core reasons for such a position.

As mentioned previously, Chinese-born prospectors had competed with Anglo-Celtic fortune seekers at gold diggings since the 1850s. But the rush for gold was basically over by the late 1860s, with a majority of Chinese immigrants returning to their former homeland. During the 1870s most remaining Chinese-Australian residents were concentrated in urban areas as their employment and business opportunities changed; an unintended result of this relocation was an inflated impression among Anglo-Celtic colonists of the overall local Chinese population. Indeed, anti-Chinese feeling among whites remained as strong as ever by the 1870s, with reintroduction of hefty immigration fees and poll taxes (first introduced in the 1850s) as impediments to further Asian immigration.[85] There were now also vocal protests against Chinese business activities, including claims of 'unfair' economic practices in local industries. An array of restrictive workplace laws were passed, directed at the activities of Chinese manufacturers or Chinese labourers seeking employment.[86] Such economic arguments were, none the less, bolstered socio-culturally by a myriad of xenophobic anxieties, including claims of predatory sexual misbehaviour on the part of Chinese men, fears of miscegenation, and a general suspicion about Chinese customs and spiritual beliefs.[87]

In addition to the Chinese, the other major non-white immigrant group of the late colonial period was Pacific Islanders, known colloquially and pejoratively in Australia as 'Kanakas'. The vast majority of these immigrants were male, and of Melanesian or Samoan origin. Between 1862 and 1904 more than 62,000 Islanders were transferred voluntarily, or against their will, to Australia. Their import to the colonies owed much to the interests of north Queensland pastoral and plantation employers, who lured them under the premise that Pacific Islanders were better suited physiologically to work in the tropics than white colonists. These employers were also confident that Islanders would be a source of lowly-paid, essentially deferential labour – characteristics that attracted them to sugar cane-growers.[88] This situation threatened the position of white workers on the cane fields, so Australian trade unions called for repatriation of Pacific Islanders. Again, though, arguments to exclude these non-white workers were framed in terms of race, not simply economics. Queensland labourers stressed the threat to white Australian racial 'purity' posed by the import of Islanders. Their principal focus was the exclusion of Kanakas on the basis of racial 'inferiority'; seldom was there any explicitly humanitarian argument calling for protection for these men from workplace exploitation.[89] Admittedly, a tactic by employers of using non-whites as strike-breakers inflamed white working-class hostility towards Asian and Islander immigrants. But a pre-existing policy of 'white-only' unions reflected longstanding racist attitudes within labour ranks.[90]

Intercolonial Premiers' conferences of 1880–88 discussed a need for uniform legislation in terms of non-white immigration. By 1888 each of the colonies had agreed to exclude Chinese immigrants, though Queensland successfully pleaded a case to continue importing Pacific Islanders but conceded that their overall number be limited by Act of Parliament.[91] There were, in short, regional exceptions and variations, but by the mid 1890s most colonies sought to exclude all non-white immigrants and to refuse British citizenship to non-white residents.[92] Such was the breadth of this legislative regime that restriction of non-white immigrants was not even an issue in debates about federation during the 1890s. Central to the 'yes' campaign were claims that in a fragile post-depression era, federal union would streamline trade relationships between member states, and improve their collective position in terms of securing overseas borrowings. So despite the ceremony and pageantry associated with the birth of the Commonwealth in 1901, the decision to federate was pragmatic and, therefore, hardly a response to nationalistic fervour.

In the context of this paper, the most significant consequence of federation was that there was now an unprecedented opportunity to achieve national consensus on non-white immigration. Indeed, the newly elected Prime Minister Edmund Barton had correctly anticipated the attractiveness to voters (other than most north Queenslanders) of a White Australia policy. He thus received a mandate for his Commonwealth government to introduce the Immigration Restriction Act (1901), legislation that imposed draconian language and dictation tests intended to exclude non-white migrants entering Australia. A handful of non-whites did manage to overcome these tests, but non-white immigration was basically stifled. The sole consolation for existing non-white residents was that (aside from Pacific Island labourers) they were not required to leave Australia. But the swift repatriation of Kanakas in the Queensland sugar industry meant that by the end of the 1900s there were probably only about two thousand Pacific Islander residents still scattered around Australia.

Given such impediments to non-white immigration, together with hostility towards remaining Chinese/Islander residents, we might expect these two groups to have had little influence upon colonial sporting culture. Yet within the framework of such constraints, Chinese and Pacific Islander people still managed to leave a mark on recreational practices and physical activities in Australia. In the case of the Chinese, Eric Rolls' two volume study of Chinese-Australians, and John O'Hara's history of gambling in Australia, provide us with intriguing insights into cross-cultural sport and recreation – each of which cry out for follow up analysis.[93] Oriental people had a particular passion for games of chance, so in mid-nineteenth-century Australia it was hardly surprising that they continued a fondness for gambling, most commonly playing among themselves. As we have seen, the Chinese had an ambivalent place on colonial gold fields, being reviled by whites as economic competitors and, in many cases, labelled as racial 'vermin'. Yet Chinese prospectors showed interest in illicit gaming houses that were set up near gold fields, often as parts of hotel or 'sly-grog' premises. These 'dens of iniquity' attracted itinerant Anglo-Celtic gold diggers from various parts of Australia or the United States. But Chinese patrons could also be found among these white gambling throngs, since in houses of chance the colour of one's money was more important than the colour of one's skin.[94] Indeed, from the 1870s onwards, as the Chinese resided increasingly in the major cities, Asian-Australians set up their own gaming houses. These venues were theoretically illegal, but since they were patronized widely by white Australians, authorities were ambivalent about closing them down.

By comparison with Asian-Australians, Pacific Islander immigrants were few in number. As mentioned previously, the vast majority of Islanders worked in the north Queensland sugar industry, where their movements and activities were restricted by austere employer regimes. In Sydney, though, a handful of Pacific Islander residents were instrumental in the development of Australian swimming and surfing. Fittingly, it was a visitor from the Marshall Islands, Tommy Tana, who during the late nineteenth century inspired Manly beach-goers to try to emulate his feats of body-surfing. They were so taken with this new pastime that it become central to a local campaign which, by 1907, helped to overturn ultra-conservative laws that deemed bathing in the surf during daylight hours as indecent and hence illegal. Given this restriction on surf bathing the colonists had not been particularly innovative swimmers, so it seems ironic that the stroke now known as the 'Australian crawl' was pioneered by Alick Wickham, a young Solomon Islander boy residing in Sydney during the early 1900s. The next major innovation was surfboard riding, which took off after the visit of Hawaiian Olympic swimming champion, Duke Kanahomoku, in 1914–15. His presence was crucial because, beforehand, no-one in Australia had been able to surf properly. Only a few locals had tried to surf –whether on imported or home-made boards – but they had little success prior to the example set by Kanahomoku. In a magnanimous gesture, the Hawaiian offered his board to a local enthusiast, 15-year-old Claude West, who inspired by this gesture, went on to become Australia's first surfboard champion. Kanahomoku's visit was also significant because he surfed tandem with a local girl, Isabel Letham. She soon became a leading female board-rider, thus helping to pave the way for women to gain public acceptance (though this was slow in coming) as athletes of the surf.[95]

Once again it would be naive to expect that for Pacific Islanders, Hawaiians, and other black immigrants, issues of race played no part in the sporting culture of the newly proclaimed White Australia. At a time when Aborigines were barred from public swimming pools in various parts of the country, Duke Kanahomoku was given special dispensation by the New South Wales Swimming Association to compete in local championships. His status as an Olympic champion overshadowed the issue of the colour of his skin.[96] What was more, the Immigration Restriction Act notwithstanding, the ubiquitous Jimmy Sharman imported black fighters from overseas, including both Americans and Pacific Islanders. Boxing historian Peter Corris writes that '... race and colour played a large part in Sharman's approach' to promoting fights. Paradoxically, the wily promoter was able to claim no colour discrimination in his boxing tents: 'black fought black, white fought white and white fought black'.[97]

Majority/Minority Group Relations in Flux: Sport as Contested and Negotiated Cultural Terrain in Australia, c.1788–1918

As outposts of the British Empire, the Australian colonies were bound to import the cultural baggage of Anglo-Celtic immigrants. Yet the English, Scots, Welsh, and Irish shaped the local sporting culture in quite different ways. The English were the most dominant group, not only because of their numerical superiority in Australia, but because their homeland of England was the veritable birthplace of many modern, codified sports. Hence English immigrants brought a pre-existing cultural affinity for sport, combined with experience in organizing rules, clubs, and competitions. When amateur sporting associations were formed in England during the late nineteenth century, it was these bodies to which colonial sporting groups looked when framing local laws of cricket, boxing, and the like. Not that the colonists were simply derivative: with greater flexibility in terms of social class in Australia, hierarchical English models of 'gentleman' and 'players' in cricket, or barring of manual-labour amateurs in rowing, were considered inappropriate.

The Scots were instrumental in promoting golf in Australia, though in contrast to the previous point, the game was played predominantly on privately-owned courses with participation restricted largely to middle-class and well-to-do members. In this respect the elitist English model of golf proved most influential, while Scottish traditions of working-class participation on public courses was relatively uncommon. Not that this seemed to bother the Scots: they were feted as club professionals at private courses, while their experience in laying out courses was called upon regularly by propertied golfing enthusiasts. A further peculiarity was that although the Scottish version of lawn bowls was taken up uniformly in Australia, this was a consequence of the fact that the English game of bowls was (quite unlike other English sports) not standardized in terms of spatial parameters or equipment. So the colonists made a pragmatic, rather than 'Scottish-inspired' decision, to take up the northern British game of lawn bowls. Demographically smaller groups of Britons – the Welsh and the Cornish – had a negligible influence on Australian sporting practices. Their love of wrestling tended to be localized in their own communities, while by the late nineteenth century Welsh and Cornishmen were commonly taking part in mainstream sports, such as golf, cricket, rugby, and Australian Rules football.

It is difficult to generalize about the sporting experiences of the Irish in Australia. A variety of factors – for example, religious faith, political affiliation and so on – worked towards whether particular individuals took up rugby union or rugby league (from 1907); whether they embraced Gaelic

Games (particularly after the inception of the GAA in 1884); or whether, as O'Farrell has put it, they 'Australianized' in sport to avoid facing alienation from the British-Protestant majority. O'Farrell's thesis is persuasive: even St Patrick's Day had a paucity of Gaelic Games, while mainstream Australian favourites like athletics and cycling were features of Irish-Australian Sports Carnivals on 17 March. South Australia's German immigrants, perhaps because of their regional concentration in areas like the Barossa Valley and the Adelaide Hills, were better able to retain their traditional gymnastics, archery and hunts. Like the Irish, though, Germans also featured prominently in cricket and football, so they were not isolationist in terms of their sporting and cultural relationships with English-speaking 'others'. What the Irish and the Germans had in common, however, was that their loyalty to the British Empire was called into question during the First World War. Such wartime tensions moved many Irish, and almost all Germans, onto the margins of Australian sporting culture.

Aborigines had the most ambivalent place in colonial sport. Initially, the British Colonial Office ordered white settlers to protect Aborigines, and to encourage them to assimilate into colonial society. In that respect games like cricket were promoted to Aborigines on rural missions, where they were also taught the English language and Christian faith. By the 1870s, though, the now self-governing colonies showed their indifference towards the welfare of Aborigines by passing laws to separate blacks from whites. Institutionalization on reserves or missions was the preferred government policy, which in terms of their physical culture meant a diminution of Aboriginal development, and a loss of self esteem. Despite scientific predictions to the contrary, Aborigines survived the nineteenth century, with some black male athletes going on to become outstanding boxers and sprinters. But they were never independent of white manipulation: their exploits earned income for sports managers and financial backers, and when their transitory athletic careers finished, they were often 'finished' socio-economically too.

Non-white immigrants had a complicated place in Australian society, let alone its sporting culture. The Chinese were reviled as fortune seekers on gold-fields, while Pacific Islander labour was not so distant from slavery. Despite the dissimilarity of their social positions, these two non-white groups were both detested as economic competitors – the Chinese because of their gold-panning acumen, and the Islanders for their 'willingness' to work under servile conditions. Under these circumstances how could they be expected to contribute to, or involve themselves in, Australian sporting culture? Coincidentally, both Chinese and Anglo-Celtic Australians had a passsion for gambling (other than local Evangelical Protestants and

Wowsers). In this respect thay had a mutual interest in card-playing, lotteries, horse racing, and the like. Although racism against Chinese played a part in legal reforms over gambling, there was sufficient local support among white punters, business houses, and magistrates to allow Orientals to continue to play a significant role in Australian gaming and betting. As for Pacific Islanders, there were few outside of Queensland. But of those scattered south in New South Wales – who by their location were not the despised sugar cane labourers – a handful went on to pioneer surf bathing and surf-board riding. Hence these two non-white groups – Chinese and Pacific Islander – provided significant contributions to the local sporting culture, doing so in the face of an Anglo-Celtic dominated social structure that, by the turn of the century, proclaimed itself proudly as White Australia.

This study has raised more issues than it has resolved. The task awaiting historians of sport and ethnicity in Australia is to follow them up with detailed micro-analysis, as well as further synthesis studies which explore the changing relationships between majority/minority cultures in Australia. It is gloomy to admit, but we know virtually nothing of ethnicity and women in colonial sport – as the explicit focus on men in this article has reflected and, indirectly, reinforced. Surprisingly, Marion Stell's pioneering study of Australia's sporting females, *Half the Race*, does not even have an index listing under ethnicity, while a more recent publication, Mosely *et al.*, *Sporting Immigrants*, laments, as I have, the paucity of research on women, ethnicity and sport. The challenge is there to overcome these and other major shortcomings.

TABLE 1

PERCENTAGES OF BIRTHPLACES OF THE TOTAL IMMIGRANT POPULATION,
AUSTRALIA 1861–1921: MAJOR IMMIGRANT GROUPS FROM THE BRITISH ISLES
AS A PERCENTAGE OF TOTAL IMMIGRANTS

Year	England %	Scotland %	Wales %	Ireland %	Anglo-Celtic born %
1861	47.4	13.4	1.3	24.5	86.6
1871	45.4	12.9	1.4	27.6	87.3
1881	44.4	12.1	1.4	25.9	83.8
1891	44.3	11.9	1.5	22.7	80.4
1901	44.3	11.9	1.5	21.6	79.3
1911	46.0	12.4	1.6	18.5	78.5
1921	53.3	13.0	1.6	12.6	80.5

*Calculated from C. Price, 'Immigration and Ethnic Origin', in W. Vamplew (ed.), *Australians: Historical Statistics* (Sydney, 1987), pp.8–9.

TABLE 2
PERCENTAGES OF AUSTRALIAN BORN AND OVERSEAS BORN RESIDENTS IN
AUSTRALIA, 1861–1921*

Year	Australian born	Overseas born
1861	37.2	62.8
1871	53.4	44.6
1881	63.2	36.8
1891	68.2	31.8
1901	77.2	27.8
1911	82.9	17.1
1921	84.5	15.5

*Calculated from C. Price, 'Immigration and Ethnic Origin', in W. Vamplew (ed.), *Australians: Historical Statistics* (Sydney, 1987), pp.8–9.

NOTES

1. J. Jupp (ed.), *The Australian People: An Encylopaedia of the Nation, Its People, and Their Origins* (North Ryde, NSW, 1988); J. Jupp, *Immigration* (Sydney, 1991).
2. R. Cher and I.F. Jobling, 'Bocce', and R. Marsh, 'Wrestling', in W. Vamplew, K. Moore, J. O'Hara, R. Cashman, and I.F. Jobling (eds.), *Oxford Companion to Australian Sport* (hereafter OCAS), 2nd edn (Melbourne, 1994), pp.62–3, 385–6; P. Corris, *Lords of the Ring: A History of Prize-fighting in Australia* (North Ryde, NSW, 1980), pp.176–9.
3. See C. Tatz, *Obstacle Race: Aborigines in Sport* (Sydney, 1995).
4. See P.A. Mosely, *Ethnic Involvement in Australian Soccer* (Canberra, 1995).
5. Jupp, *Immigration*, pp.101–21, 128.
6. P.A. Mosely, R. Cashman, J. O'Hara and H. Weatherburn (eds.), *Sporting Immigrants: Sport and Ethnicity in Australia* (Crows Nest, NSW, 1997), Chs.11, 20.
7. See B. Harris, *The Proud Champions: Australia's Aboriginal Sporting Heroes* (Crows Nest, NSW, 1989); Tatz, *Obstacle Race*, Ch.15; Mosely *et al.*, *Sporting Immigrants*, pp.17–25.
8. Mosely, *Sporting Immigrants*, p.xv (emphasis in the original).
9. R.A. Howell and M.L. Howell, *The Genesis of Sport in Queensland* (St Lucia, Qld, 1992), pp.7–16; R. Schmelz, 'Ancient Australian Leisure', *Sport and Leisure*, No.5 (Sept. 1984), p.5.
10. See J.B. Hirst, *Convict Society and its Enemies* (Sydney, 1983).
11. C.R. Reid, 'Tracking the Immigrants: Assisted Movement to Nineteenth-Century New South Wales', in *Visible Immigrants 1: Neglected Sources for the History of Australian Immigration* (Canberra, 1989), pp.23–46; R. Haines, 'Shovelling Out Paupers?: Parish-assisted Emigration from England to Australia, 1834–1847', in E. Richards (ed.), *Visible Immigrants 2: Poor Australian Immigrants in the Nineteenth Century* (Canberra, 1991), pp.33–68; R. Haines, '"The Idle and the Drunken Won't Do There": Poverty, the New Poor Law and Nineteenth-Century Government-assisted Emigration to Australia from the United Kingdom', *Australian Historical Studies*, Vol.28, No.108 (April 1997), pp.1–21.
12. M. Hogan, *The Sectarian Strand: Religion in Australian History* (Ringwood, Vic., 1987); D. Adair, 'Respectable, Sober, and Industrious? Attitudes to Alcohol in Early Colonial Adelaide', *Labour History* (Australia), Vol. 70 (May 1986), pp.131–55.
13. D. Adair, 'Public-house Sports', in Vamplew *et al.*, *OCAS*, pp.282–3.
14. R. Waterhouse, 'Popular Culture and Pastimes', in N. Meaney (ed.), *Under New Heavens: Cultural Transmission and the Making of Australia* (Melbourne, 1989), pp.237–86; J.A. Daly, *The Adelaide Hunt: A History of the Adelaide Hunt Club, 1840–1986* (Adelaide, 1986), pp.1–8; D. Whitelock, *Adelaide: A Sense of Difference* (Adelaide, 1985), p.240; Adair, 'Rowing and Sculling', pp.172–3.

15. Sherington, *Australia's Immigrants*, p.66; Price, 'Immigration and Ethnic Origin', p.11; S. Wang, 'Chinese Immigration, 1840s–1890s', in Jupp, *The Australian People*, p.299.
16. See H.R. Woolcock, *Rights of Passage: Emigration to Australia in the Nineteenth Century* (New York, 1978); P. O'Farrell, *The Irish in Australia* (Sydney, 1987), pp.63–5.
17. See D. Pike, *Paradise of Dissent: South Australia 1829–57*, 2nd edn (Melbourne, 1967); E. Richards, 'The Peopling of South Australia', in E. Richards (ed.), *The Flinders History of South Australia: Social History* (Adelaide, 1986), pp.115–42.
18. R. Cashman, 'Ethnicity and Sport in Australia – Some General Reflections', in F. van der Merwe (ed.), *Sport as Symbol, Symbols in Sport*, Proceedings of the 3rd ISHPES Congress, Cape Town, 1995 (Berlin, 1996), p.147.
19. See Mosely *et al.*, *Sporting Immigrants*, p.xvii; D. Lucas, *The Welsh, Irish, Scots and English* (Canberra, 1987), pp.3–4.
20. See D. Adair, 'Declarations of Difference: Attempts to Exclude Non-Whites From Late Colonial Australia', *Flinders Journal of History and Politics*, Vol.16 (1993), pp.16–26.
21. G. Partington, *The Australian Nation: Its Irish and British Roots* (Kew, Vic., 1994), p.ix.
22. O. MacDonagh, *The Sharing of the Green: A Modern Irish History for Australians* (St Leonards, NSW, 1996), p.35.
23. O. MacDonagh, 'Irish Culture and Nationalism Translated: St Patrick's Day, 1888, in Australia', in O. MacDonagh, W.F. Mandle and P. Travers (eds.), *Irish Culture and Nationalism, 1750–1950* (Canberra, 1983), pp.69–82; K.S. Inglis, *The Australian Colonists: An Exploration of Social History 1788–1870* (Melbourne, 1974), Ch.6.
24. MacDonagh, 'St Patrick's Day, 1888', p.72; C. Kiernan, 'Home Rule for Ireland and the Formation of the Australian Labor Party, 1883 to 1891', *Australian Journal of Politics and History*, Vol.38, No.1 (1992), p.7.
25. See O'Farrell, *The Irish in Australia*.
26. R. Cashman, *Paradise of Sport: The Rise of Organised Sport in Australia* (Melbourne, 1995), p.151.
27. Cashman, *Paradise of Sport*, p.151.
28. This approach is similar to that taken by the Australian Institute of Multicultural Affairs in its report, edited by Lucas, *The Welsh, Irish, Scots and English*; and by the demographer Charles Price, editor of *Australian Immigration: A Bibliography and Digest*, Vol.4 (Canberra, 1979). For an Australian study that prefers to use 'the term "ethnic" for groups and cultures of non-Anglo-Saxon background', see J.I. Martin, *The Migrant Presence* (Sydney, 1978), p.16.
29. Cashman, *Paradise of Sport*, p.151, quoting from O'Farrell, *Irish in Australia*, p.10.
30. Vamplew, 'Sport: More than Fun and Games', pp.445–53.
31. For further discussion, see J. Bradley, 'Inventing Australians and Constructing Englishness: Cricket and the Creation of a National Consciousness, 1860–1914', *Sporting Traditions*, Vol.11, No. 2 (May 1995), pp.46–50.
32. Adair, 'Rowing and Sculling', pp.176–80.
33. See G.M. Hibbins, 'The Cambridge Connection: The English Origins of Australian Rules Football', in J.A. Mangan, *Cultural Bond* (London, 1993), pp.108–28.
34. For detailed analysis, see M. Phillips, 'Rugby', in W. Vamplew and B. Stoddart (eds.), *Sport in Australia: A Social History* (Melbourne, 1994), pp.193–6; M.P. Sharp, 'Australian Football in Sydney Before 1914', *Sporting Traditions*, Vol.4, No.1 (Nov. 1987), pp.27–46.
35. For further discussion, see P. Mosely and B. Murray, 'Soccer', in Vamplew and Stoddart , *Sport in Australia*, pp.213–17.
36. P. Horton, 'Rugby Union Football and Its Role in the Socio-Cultural Development of Queensland 1882–91', *International Journal of the History of Sport*, Vol.9, No.1 (1992), p.122.
37. 'Football', *Brisbane Courier*, 9 Oct. 1883, quoted in P. Horton, 'Dominant Ideologies and their Role in the Establishment of Rugby Union Football in Victorian Queensland', *International Journal of the History of Sport*, Vol.11, No.1 (1994), p.119.
38. *Sunday Times*, 26 April 1903; *Referee*, 23 Aug.1905, quoted in Sharp, 'Australian Football in Sydney ', p.38.
39. Horton, 'Dominant Ideologies', pp.119–23.

40. See Sharp, 'Australian Football in Sydney', p.35.
41. M.D. Prentis, *The Scots in Australia* (Sydney, 1988), p.198.
42. Prentis, *Scots in Australia*, pp.194–206.
43. J. Lowerson, 'Golf', in T. Mason (ed.), *Sport in Britain: A Social History* (Cambridge, 1989), pp.187–214.
44. B. Stoddart, 'Golf', in W. Vamplew and B. Stoddart (eds.), *Sport in Australia: A Social History* (Melbourne, 1994), p.79.
45. McCarthy, 'Lawn Bowls', p.299.
46. P. Mosely and B. Murray, 'Soccer', in Vamplew and Stoddart (eds.), *Sport in Australia*, p.216.
47. Mosely and Murray, 'Soccer', p.215.
48. Mosely and Murray, 'Soccer', p.217.
49. Prentis, *The Scots in Australia*, pp.202–4.
50. J. Daly, *Elysian Fields: Sport, Class and Community in Colonial South Australia* (Adelaide, 1982), pp.45–6, 162.
51. See P. Corris, *Lords of the Ring* (North Ryde, NSW, 1980), Chs.6–7.
52. T. Hickie, *They Ran With the Ball: How Rugby Football Began in Australia* (Melbourne, 1993), p.4, quoted in A. Hughes, 'The Irish Community', in Mosely *et al.*, *Sporting Immigrants*, p.76.
53. O'Farrell, *Irish in Australia*, p.156.
54. O'Farrell, *Irish in Australia*, p.157.
55. Quoted in O'Farrell, *Irish in Australia*, p.160.
56. Quoted in Inglis, 'Australian Catholic Community', p.10.
57. O'Farrell, *Irish in Australia*, p.178.
58. O'Farrell, *Irish in Australia*, p.178 (emphasis added to the original).
59. P. O'Farrell, 'St Patrick's Day in Australia', *Journal of the Royal Australian Historical Society*, Vol. 81, No. 1 (June 1995), pp.1–16.
60. Quoted in O'Farrell, *Irish in Australia*, p.187.
61. Quoted in McConville, *Croppies, Celts and Catholics*, p.83.
62. Quoted in R. Stremski, *Kill for Collingwood* (Sydney, 1986), p.207.
63. Stremski, *Kill for Collingwood*, pp.207–8.
64. See B. Murray, *The Old Firm* (Edinburgh, 1984). Also see the article by Joseph Bradley in this volume.
65. R.C. Peterson, 'Nurseries of Nostalgia: The History of Ethnic Schools', *Forum of Education*, Vol.50, No.2 (Nov. 1995), pp.47–58.
66. I. Harmstorf and M. Cigler, *The Germans in Australia* (Melbourne, 1985), p.85.
67. Ibid., pp.85–6.
68. J. Daly, *Elysian Fields: Sport, Class and Community in Colonial South Australia, 1836–1890* (Adelaide, 1982), pp.96–8.
69. Quoted in Daly, *Elysian Fields*, p.92.
70. Daly, *Elysian Fields*, p.92.
71. Quoted from Daly, *Elysian Fields*, p.92.
72. For detailed discussions, see D.W. Brown, 'Muscular Christianity in the Antipodes: Some Observations on the Diffusion and Emergence of a Victorian Ideal in Australian Social Theory', *Sporting Traditions*, Vol.3, No.2 (May 1987), pp.173–87; G. Sherrington, 'Athleticism in the Antipodes: The A.A.G.P.S. in New South Wales, *History of Education Review*, Vol.12 (1983), pp.16–28.
73. I.A. Harmstorf, 'God Ordered Their Estate', in I. Harmstorf and P. Schwerdtfeger (eds.), *The German Experience of Australia, 1833–1938* (Adelaide, 1988), p.51.
74. See J.P. White and D.J. Mulvaney, *Australians to 1788* (Sydney, 1987), pp.115–17; C. Price, 'Immigration and Ethnic Origin', in W. Vamplew (ed.), *Australians: Historical Statistics* (Sydney, 1987), pp.12–13.
75. Adair, 'Declarations of Difference', pp.16–26.
76. C. Tatz, 'Aborigines in Sport', in Vamplew *et al*, *OCAS* , p.3; J. Daly, '"Civilising" the Aborigines: Cricket at Poonindie, 1850–1890', *Sporting Traditions*, Vol.10, No.2 (May 1994), pp.59–67.

77. See Mulvaney and Harcourt, *Cricket Walkabout*.
78. K. McConnochie, D. Hollinsworth, and J. Pettman (eds.), *Race and Racism in Australia* (Wentworth Falls, NSW, 1988), pp.62–7; R. Broome, *Aboriginal Australians* (Sydney, 1982), pp.87–100; A. Mozley, 'Evolution and the Climate of Opinion in Australia, 1840–76', *Victorian Studies*, Vol.10 (June 1967), pp.411–30.
79. W. Thorpe, 'Archibald Meston and Aboriginal Legislation in Colonial Queensland', *Historical Studies*, Vol.21, No.82 (April 1984), pp.52–3; McConnochie *et al.*, *Race and Racism*, pp.81–6; R. Broome, *Aboriginal Australians: Black Response to White Dominance, 1788–1980* (Sydney, 1982), pp.87–100.
80. Since then Aborigines have claimed sixty-two professional titles, an astonishing feat by a group that has comprised around only 1% of the Australian population. Tatz, 'Aborigines in Sport', p.3; Tatz, *Obstacle Race*, pp.362–3.
81. G. Parker, 'Sharman, Jimmy (Senior)', in Vamplew *et al.*, *OCAS*, pp.310–11; Corris, *Lords of the Ring*, pp.78–84.
82. R. Broome, 'Professional Boxers in Eastern Australia 1930-1979', *Aboriginal History*, Vol.4, Nos.1–2 (June 1980), pp.49–71; C. Tatz, *Aborigines in Sport*, ASSH Studies in Sports History, 3 (Adelaide, 1987), pp.38–52; Tatz, *Obstacle Race*, pp.107–47.
83. For further discussions, see Tatz, *Obstacle Race*; Broome, 'Professional Boxers'.
84. McConnochie, *et al.*, *Race and Racism* , p.67.
85. R.A. Huttenback, 'No Strangers Within the Gates : Attitudes and Policies towards the Non-White Residents of the British Empire of Settlement', *Journal of Imperial and Commonwealth History*, Vol.1, No.3 (1972–73), pp.281–2.
86. R. Markey, 'Populist Politics: Racism and Labor in NSW 1880–1900', in A. Curthoys and A. Markus (eds.), *Who are our Enemies ? Racism and the Australian Working Class* (Sydney, 1978), pp.68–9. A. Markus, 'Divided We Fall: The Chinese and the Melbourne Furniture Trade Union, 1870–1900', *Labour History* (Australia), Vol.26 (1974), pp.1–10. Huttenback, 'No Strangers Within the Gates', pp.283–93.
87. A. Markus, *Fear and Hatred: Purifying Australia and California, 1850–1901* (Sydney, 1979), pp.78–81; Huttenback, 'No Strangers Within the Gates', pp.287, 294.
88. C. Price, *The Great White Walls are Built: Restrictive Immigration to North America and Australia, 1836–1888* (Canberra, 1974), pp.51–2; K. Saunders, 'Pacific Islander Recruitment', in Jupp, *The Australian People*, pp.722–5; Choi, *Chinese Migration*, p.24.
89. C.M.H. Clark, *A History of Australia*, Vol.V (Melbourne, 1981), pp.190, 201–4.
90. H. McQueen, *A New Britannia: An Argument Concerning the Social Origins of Australian Radicalism and Nationalism*, revised edn (Melbourne, 1976), pp.29–34; McConnochie *et al.*, *Race and Racism*, p.69.
91. M. de Lepervanche, 'Australian Immigrants, 1788-1940: Desired and Unwanted', in E.N. Wheelwright and K. Buckley (eds.), *Essays in the Political Economy of Australian Capitalism*, Vol.1 (Sydney, 1975), pp.73–81.
92. A.T. Yarwood, *Asian Migration to Australia: the Background to Exclusion, 1896–1923* (Melbourne, 1964), pp.5–18.
93. E. Rolls, *Sojourners: The Epic Story of China's Centuries-old Relationship with Australia* (St Lucia, Qld, 1992); E. Rolls, *Citizens: Continuing the Epic Story of China's Centuries-old Relationship with Australia* (St Lucia, Qld, 1996); J. O'Hara, *A Mug's Game: A History of Gaming and Betting in Australia* (Kensington, NSW, 1988).
94. See Rolls, *Sojourners*, Ch.6; O'Hara, *A Mug's Game*, Ch.3.
95. Cashman, *Paradise of Sport*, p.57; C. Dunshea, 'Surfing', in Vamplew *et al.*, *OCAS*, pp.342–3; P.A. Mosely, 'Australian Sport and Ethnicity', in Mosely *et al.*, *Sporting Immigrants*, p.37.
96. I. Jobling, 'Duke Kahanomoku – Hawaiian Olympian: Outcomes of his Visit to Australia in 1914–15', unpublished paper presented to the ASSH-NASSH Conference, Hawaii, 1993.
97. Corris, *Lords of the Ring*, pp.83–4, see also R. Broome, 'The Australian Recation to Jack Johnson, Black Pugilist', in R. Cashman and M. McKernan (eds.), *Sport in History* (St. Lucia, Qld, 1979), pp.343–63.

Croatia: Community, Conflict and Culture: The Role of Soccer Clubs in Migrant Identity

ROY HAY

Introduction

No-one who followed the European Football Championship finals in England in the summer of 1996 could be in doubt about the power of football to galvanise a nation and its people. For a brief period the performance of the English national team gave the country back its national identity and pride in a way that nothing since the World Cup win in 1966 had achieved. The bombing of the heart of its second city got far, far less media coverage, and as far as one can judge these things, less popular concern outside Manchester itself, than a football tournament. The miraculous escape from death involved may have had something to do with this. Damage was confined to bricks and mortar and a relatively few, though severe, injuries, but the contrast was overwhelming. This article is concerned with the role of soccer in the creation and moulding of migrant identity in Australia for that generation who arrived in the 20 years or so after the Second World War. The scale may be smaller than that witnessed in Europe, but the consequences are, in their way, equally profound.

It is evident, then, that the power of soccer to move and to mould has always been astonishing. Some of the claims as to its healing and divisive powers may be exaggerated or unprovable, but its salience is not fundamentally in doubt. Pierre Lanfranchi in his essay 'Italy and the World Cup: The Impact of Football in Italy and the example of Italia 90', wrote:

> Soccer clubs in Italy play the role of centres or 'nodes' around which social communities are formed. There have been numerous examples in the past where the fortunes of the local soccer club have generated a sense of communal identity and pride and a means for overcoming objective, socio-economic and political difficulties. Pundits have labelled soccer in Italy as the 'lay' religion.[1]

Davor Suker's account of what it means to him to play for his country, Croatia, shows how this passion translates itself at the individual level.[2]

Croatian migrants who arrived in Australia in the immediate post-war period faced major challenges in coming to terms with the new society in which they found themselves. Many were refugees from Yugoslavia, others came later under officially sponsored migration schemes. All faced the problem of establishing a form of identity in Australia. Croatian soccer clubs were among the first and the most wide-ranging institutions set up by migrants. They played a significant role in the creation and shaping of the self-conceptions of Australian Croatians and the attitudes of non-Croatian Australians from 1950 to 1995.[3]

The research derives in part from many interviews with Croatians and non-Croatians involved in soccer in Australia and a lifetime's involvement in the game in Britain and Australia. It is based on what several of that generation of migrants have revealed by their words and their actions and the interpretations which have been placed on them, by outsiders and by the migrants themselves. Many had not wanted to come to Australia in the first instance, but found it was either that or a return to a potentially hostile environment in Yugoslavia. Australia was accessible and it was cheap. Hence the Croatians were, on the whole, perhaps not quite as antipathetic about the prospect of Australia as the involuntary Jewish migrant aboard the *Dunera* who jumped overboard when he found that the destination was not Canada.[4]

The primary concern therefore is with questions of identity and identities in an historically specific time and place for a particular group of migrants to Australia, who arrived from various parts of Europe and who defined themselves as Croatians in the years after the Second World War, and the role which soccer clubs played in the negotiation of these identities with the host and other migrant communities.

A claim to a Croatian identity was always problematic for new arrivals to Australia for at least five reasons:

(1) No Croatian national state existed after the end of the Second World War. The 'independent' state of Croatia which was created between 1941 and 1945 was very much compromised by its relationships with Nazi Germany. The Croatian political leaders from that era, who fled abroad at the end of the war, were to be found in Argentina, Canada and Spain. So a claim to the name 'Croatia' raised many suspicions across the political and social spectrum in Australia.

(2) The nature of Croatia which existed prior to 1939 was very much contested over the previous centuries so that there was little agreement on what constituted Croatia in these years. Now it may be argued that the existence of an independent political unit is unnecessary for the assertion of a national identity.[5] The spirit may exist even though political independence

(*top*): Geelong Croatia Football Club, 1957; (*centre*): Geelong Croatia Football Club, 1950s/1960s; (*bottom*): Convoy of cars leaving Geelong, 1950s/1960s

(*top*): Croatia Melbourne take the field at Olympic Park in the 1960s; (*below*): Geelong Croatia, First Division North Champions, 1959

has long disappeared. As a Scot and an Australian the author is well aware that a species of nationalism has survived more than 300 years of absorption within the United Kingdom in the case of people from the area in which he was born, while an Australian nationalism preceded and underlay the tortuous road to the current 'independence' under the Crown.[6] People can feel and identify themselves as Scots, Irish, Australians or Croatians without an independent national political unit, or nation state. In other historical cases, it is arguable that an identification has followed, rather than preceded, the creation of political unification, as in the cases of Italy and Germany in the nineteenth century.

(3) In the case of Croatians in Australia the assertion of identity was made more problematic, and certainly more risky, because of the aggressive claim by the Yugoslavian state under Josip Broz Tito to represent the legitimate political aspirations of all persons from that part of the Balkans after 1945. To say you were Croatian, if you still had family in Yugoslavia or if you had plans or thoughts of returning there, was perceived to be, and, in some cases, demonstrably was, dangerous. Those who did return briefly often reported thoroughly well-informed grilling by officials of the Yugoslav state. There were enough horror stories about the ill-treatment of those who had gone back to fuel the imaginations of the migrant community.[7] Nikola Jurcic remembers a young fellow who went to Canada and then back home to Croatia who was jailed for 18 months for speaking out against the Yugoslavs while in Australia.[8] Croatian migrants were thus unlike their Italian, Greek, Dutch or British counterparts who could count on some support at least from the government of the country they had left. They were similar to migrants from the Baltic states, Lithuanians, Estonians and Latvians, the original 'Balts', or those from the Ukraine or Macedonia, who had to cope with varying degrees of passive or active opposition from the regimes then in power in or over the original land from which the migrants came. Regularly immigration officials would overwrite 'Yugoslav' on the forms on which immigrants had used 'Croatia' as the country from which they came. Steve Horvat, soccer player, Geelong businessman and several times President of North Geelong Soccer Club, remains convinced that Yugoslav agents and agents-provocateurs infiltrated the Croatian community, its clubs and political organisations in the 1950s to 1970s. They stole soccer club minutes, organized the expulsion of Croatian clubs from the Victorian soccer competition in 1972, and killed Croatians, in Australia and overseas.[9] Whether all these charges could be sustained in a court of law is immaterial, they were believed by a significant number of members of the Croatian community in Australia and coloured their views and expectations.

(4) To say you were Croatian, rather than Australian, was also to offend against the official Australian ideology and policy of assimilation in the post-war years. The notion was that on arrival immigrants should learn the language, drop as much cultural baggage as possible and become Australians. Though Australia desperately needed the labour and skills of the new migrants, members of the host society believed that they were offering newcomers a great opportunity and doing them a favour, and the price for this was to try to become 'good Australians' as soon as possible. 'Croatian' was thus a risky political statement in Australia as soon as it was uttered.[10]

(5) There had been Croatian migrants to Australia before the Second World War. Many of these were socialist or at least inclined to the left and thus not

necessarily hostile to the concept of a socialist Yugoslavia, in which Croatia had a degree of autonomy. Croatian migrants arrived in Australia in numbers between the wars mainly settling in Western Australia, and also formed a small but significant community in Broken Hill. The leadership of this group was said to be strongly socialist, and its influence over Slavs in Australia claimed to be profound.[11] Some of their number were involved in soccer and the Alagich family in particular were to carry this interest through into the post-Second World War period.[12] Probably the earliest post-war Croatian soccer club was set up in Sydney in 1945 by Marin Alagich from Broken Hill. It was called Lola.[13] So the post-Second World War migrants had to contend with other Croatians in Australia, who did not necessarily share their views.

Croatian Migrants to Australia

Establishing the number of Croatian migrants to Australia in the post-war period is not easy. Australian Census data did not discriminate between the various groups which constituted the former state of Yugoslavia. 829 Yugoslav-born were recorded in the 1921 census, 3,969 in 1933 and 5,866 in 1947. By 1986 the number of people born in what was Yugoslavia had risen to 150,012, and there were a further 105,723 people born in Australia who had one or both parents born in Yugoslavia. In the 1986 census, for the first time, questions were asked about ancestry and language spoken at home. In these 18 per cent (27,265) of the 150,000 people from the former Yugoslavia gave Croatian as their ancestry and 23 per cent of those over the age of five spoke Croatian at home.[14] In the fifties however, even in the large urban centres of Australia, the number of Croatians was very small. Branko Filipi indicated that there were 300 Croatians in Adelaide when he arrived in 1953. Regina Groher said that there were eight families and six single men in Geelong in 1952. Frank Burin talks of one hundred or so families in Melbourne in 1957. So in the early fifties there were few Croatian migrants, no community organisations existed and there was a vacuum which the soccer clubs were often the first to fill. The dates of foundation of Croatian Soccer Clubs in the various states are given in Table 1. Soccer clubs are virtually ignored in the history of migrant communities in Australia, apart from odd ritual reference to migrant interest in the game. An exception is Rachel Unikoski's sensitive study of migrant organisations in Melbourne.[15]

Many of the new arrivals came from refugee camps, others by way of Italy, Austria, Germany and Trieste. The majority of this group is said to have come from Lika, Slavonia, Bosnia and Hercegovina. Ideological and nationalist in outlook, and often strongly anti-communist, their views were commonly at variance with those of the earlier arrivals. The subsequent history of Croatian organizations in Australia was often punctuated by struggles between them for the right to represent a Croatian identity. Later migrants in the 1960s and 1970s, probably the majority, came from Yugoslavia with the agreement of the government under migration programmes negotiated with Australia.

The majority of the new Croatian arrivals were Roman Catholics. The Catholic church of course existed as an institution in Australia but, at least initially, it was not geared to the reception of the mass of immigrants of varying ethnic and cultural backgrounds who arrived in Australia after 1945. Used to dealing with the descendants of Irish immigrants to Australia, it took time for it to come to terms with the new demands, which often were for a native of the particular European homeland to act as priest to the newcomers in Australia. Croatian priests did arrive in Australia and very quickly began to minister to their congregations. Often they found it in their interests to work through the soccer clubs as places where the often unattached young men and the families could be found. Churches and refugee aid organisations often processed the papers of young aspiring migrants. For example, the church in Trieste identified 50 young Croatian single men in 1953–54 and asked Branko Filipi to sponsor them which he did through the Adelaide Croatia soccer club and his business. This was so successful that a further 50 were sent by the same means. On arrival similar linkages between churches and soccer clubs were evident. In another study I have shown how Joe Radojevic, in the company of a Slovenian priest, met immigrant ships arriving in Melbourne and sought out soccer players among the new arrivals. In all he claims to have brought 350 people to Geelong, many of whom were not much use at soccer, but he brought them nevertheless.[16]

When I began this research I had a mental picture of the sequence of actions likely to be pursued by the new immigrant to Australia in these years. He, since most were males, would first seek out at job, a house, get himself married and have a family, then find himself some recreation. The reality for a significant minority is that they went down to the soccer club, which often got them the other three elements - the job, the house, the family. Harry Mrksa, Franc Bot, Steve Horvat, Frank Burin and many more speak of their involvement in soccer within days of arrival in Australia. The same applies to many other migrants from the United Kingdom and elsewhere, it is not just a Croatian phenomenon.

In his study of sport in industrial America at the end of the nineteenth century, Steven A. Reiss argues that immigrants from south and east Europe, came from pre-modern (hence by implication pre-sporting) communities. Only the second generation became heavily involved in American sports.[17] Croatians did come from rural society, but not quite pre-modern and certainly not pre-sporting, even though involvement with sport may have been less than the Australian norm. Stephanie Dew has shown that immigrants to the Geelong area had a lower sports participation rate than Australians, though she noted a higher involvement on the part of Yugoslav migrants.[18] My own data on soccer players in Geelong suggests that Croatians have a higher participation rate than any other group of immigrants in the late 1980s. We have no equivalent information for the 1950s and 1960s though I would hazard a guess that even then the Croatian participation rate in soccer was well above average for immigrant groups.

Folkloric, cultural and most political organizations were formed after rather than before the soccer clubs and the churches, or the soccer clubs were significant offshoots of these bodies where they existed. Later I will look in more detail at the relationships between the political organizations and the soccer clubs, for the moment I just want to assert that the claim made by the political groups that they were the inspiration for the soccer clubs needs to be thoroughly tested. There has been a tendency to read history backwards through periods when political involvement was very significant, the late 1960s and early 1970s, for example. The fact that many of the early post-war immigrants were fervent anti-communists does not necessarily mean that they were completely susceptible to any kind of right-wing or fascist political appeal, as will become clear later. However, there was a Croatian on the New Australian Council set up in 1958 by the Democratic Labour Party to attract migrants to become naturalised and register as voters for the DLP.[19] Later the Ethnic Communities Council emerged in Melbourne and Sydney in 1974. It acted as an umbrella organisation for migrant community groups including Croatians and Serbians, Arab and Jewish organisations and it is claimed that it operated without the sectarian strife feared by many Australians.[20]

There were institutions in Australia specifically to assist the new migrants to settle and to come to terms with their new home. First, there were the migrant camps and hostels set up for the reception of migrants and designed to tread the very fine line between meeting the demand for labour after the war and not upsetting local labour markets and offending trade union susceptibilities. The camps were located up country, like Bonegilla near Wondonga on the Victoria–New South Wales border, while hostels were to be found in urban centres including Geelong, in the suburb of Norlane within walking distance of the Ford Motor Company. Providing some rudimentary instruction in English language and in Australian institutions, they were very much temporary staging posts, though a few migrants spent substantial periods in the camps.[21]

The Good Neighbour Councils were designed to build bridges between host and immigrant groups. The process was not always smooth. Other similar bodies like Apex were involved. Some of the tensions and issues in contention were spelled out at an Apex Convention in Ballarat, when the National President, Gordon Murray of Geelong, was quoted as follows: 'There were two dangers, caused by large-scale emigration which had to be guarded against – the formation of national groups and the growth of the new element to such an extent that the Australian way of life was swamped'.[22] In reporting this speech the *Geelong Advertiser* went on to mention language difficulties and social differentiation (which it was not prepared to enlarge on) which made the absorption of migrants into existing institutions difficult: 'The migrants as a body will have to learn English – or bear the consequences.'[23]

This provoked what appears to have been a considerable response among migrant groups.[24] A week later the *Advertiser* returned to the subject and put the case for the national groups. After pointing out that the Irish and the Scots already had their national organizations and that fair play demanded that all have the same opportunity, the paper then mentioned the positive side of the national groups. These helped bring individuals out of potential cultural isolation, particularly migrant women. The migrant organisations also allowed the ways and customs of the old society to be passed on to children, something which many migrant parents desired.[25] Then it went on to say:

A sharp line of distinction was made by many migrants between national groups and the various clubs affiliated with them. There is in Geelong quite a number of clubs which pursue a variety of aims. The Italians have their Soccer Club which is a fountain of pride to them, but which has no other aims but to play first class soccer. Again there is the Hungarian Sport Club Toldi which accepts anybody to its membership, and there are many other clubs and organisations which pursue similar aims.[26]

Interpretations of the role of the soccer clubs in these early days vary. The Croatian soccer club in Geelong has been said to have been a meeting ground for the different factions of the Croatian community.[27] On the other hand one of the prime movers, Joe Radojevic, has been identified with one particular political group and his dynamic personality did have considerable influence on the way the club developed. Radojevic, as mentioned already, made a practice of meeting boats arriving in Geelong and Melbourne in the company of a local Slovenian priest and selecting Croatians who could play soccer to join his team.[28]

The involvement of politics in sport is now established as fairly commonplace. Reiss, whose work has already been cited, writes about Irish nationalist associations involved with sport in the USA from the 1870s.

Gaelic football was first played in New York in 1858. The German turners used sport to promote ethnic identity and for political purposes. Some socialist turners were active in left wing politics.[29]

The use of soccer clubs for political purposes is appreciated in Europe, in the Basque country and Catalonia in Spain, to take only two well-known examples.[30] Athletico Bilbao and Barcelona were, and are, the flagships of Basque and Catalan nationalism. The same was true in many parts of the Soviet Union, where Dynamo Kiev performed a similar role for Ukrainians. But in these cases the football club had to carry the nationalist flag only, it did not have to perform the socialising and integrating roles of the Australian Croatian clubs. It did not have to teach the language, as some migrant soccer clubs did in Australia.[31]

Three groups have 'claimed responsibility' for the foundation of Croatian soccer clubs in Australia in the post-war period – the politicians, the church and concerned migrant businessmen and aspiring community leaders. These groups often overlapped and were linked, which makes analysis difficult at times. As the then President of Melbourne Croatia put it in his introduction to the nineteenth Croatian soccer tournament, 'In a time when the place of the Croatian community was yet to be established in Europe, the tournaments provided the Croatian people and soccer clubs a chance to unite with a common purpose, to compete'.[32] The claims of the politicians have been advanced by Philip Mosely, who has drawn attention to links with the Ustashe and emphasized the fascist and anti-Serbian elements in Croatian soccer clubs.[33] Church and community leaders are championed by Branko Filipi.[34] For Melbourne at least both these claims raise the question of reading history backwards from subsequent developments.

The founders of Croatia Melbourne seem to have been a group of youngsters who wanted to play football. The same was true in Geelong. The first soccer uniforms the players wore were not the Croatian colours of red, white and blue, but green, because a friend of the players, who was a tailor, happened to have some material available, from which he agreed to make up the shirts. When the Melbourne Croatians entered a team in the Victorian 'World Cup', a competition for ethnic teams, including those from the four home countries, started in the early 1950s, it is claimed they came up against political opposition. The appearance of a team labelled Croatia was opposed by JUST (Jugoslav United Soccer Team) and its Yugoslav backers. On the other hand, according to Ivica Marin, the entry of Croatia was supported by Hakoah, the Jewish club, and Kurt Defris, its secretary. Croatia Melbourne had many difficulties in its early days. On one occasion it had to appeal to colleagues in Geelong to send players to make up the numbers for a key match against the Greeks. Seven players and a goalkeeper were needed in all! Sometimes it had to use people off the street to form a team, including non-Croatians and, according to two people who should know, even Serbians on occasion. Only after the club began to move up through the leagues did political support kick-in.

There was also a strong denial of political involvement from within the club. Joe Radojevic said of the Geelong Croatian club, 'I started it so my son could play' - his family, not politics, was at the centre of things. In this he was to be disappointed as his elder son became one of the finest full forwards in Australian Rules with the VFA club Geelong West.[35] In the case of another Croatian club in Melbourne there is a more political story to tell, but it is somewhat ambiguous. Hajduk Melbourne was formed after the tour of Hajduk Split in 1949 as a name likely to be known and understood by the Australian people. But Tito's claim that Hajduk players had enlisted *en masse* in the partisans gave rise to problems within the Croatian community. In fact the Hajduk club did not last long. The Australian pronunciation of the name made it sound like a Walt Disney character. Little support was given by the community. The club struggled to field players and folded in 1958.

In 1957 the Croatia Melbourne club moved to Geelong, away from the political centre in Victoria, largely because there were more Croatians in Geelong, with Ford as a large employer of labour. Frank Burin talks about slave labour in the car factories, work that native Australians would not touch. This was said with a smile because he later worked for the Commonwealth Employment Service placing people in just such jobs. In 1962 the club moved back to Melbourne and this has been associated with the establishment of the Croatian Liberation Movement's headquarters in Footscray, but demographics now favoured Melbourne as far as Croatian numbers were concerned, and the newly-formed Victorian Soccer Federation had made it clear it did not want Geelong clubs in metropolitan competition. Besides, major clubs in the capital did not want to travel to Geelong for matches. All the Geelong clubs were banished from Melbourne competition in 1963. So one can take these pieces of evidence and interpret them according to demographic, political or internal soccer arguments.

When talking about Croatian politics and soccer in Australia it is necessary to distinguish between a common resistance to Serbian nationalism and aggrandisement and the internal political groupings within Croatian politics. The latter spans groups on the far right, neo-Nazis in some respects, to those on the far left, who are Croatian communists. In between are a whole range of groupings – nationalists, democrats, the labour movement, peasant parties, religious groups and so on. It is said that there are 52 political parties in Croatia, one for every week of the year.

According to Mistilis the political learning process takes about 20 years whether you are migrant or native born.[36] Hence there was little political activism by migrants in Australia in the 1960s because the migrants were still learning. The Croatians must have been precocious because they were very active. 'Australian ethnics have generally kept their heads down and remained "invisible" people politically.'[37] Jupp's focus is on activity within mainstream Australian politics, but the activism of the Croatians is virtually excluded since it did not lead to national political involvement or leadership: 'The structure and behaviour of ethnic community organisations have been relatively well investigated. A lot of ethnic politics is byzantine and arguably irrelevant in understanding relationships with the broader political society. However such pressures as ethnics do exercise are frequently produced by ethnic organizations.'[38] Yet by any test, except national political party involvement, Croatians were highly active politically, in and through organizations, and without them, in the 1960s and 1970s. This needs to be understood and explained.

Political differences are also seen as underlying the violence associated with soccer from the 1950s to the 1970s. The chain of causation runs from the political groups to the behaviour and role of the soccer club. Furio Radin provides a modern example from Croatia itself.[39] But many of the people within the club argue strenuously that soccer was kept clear of politics, that the soccer club was neutral ground where all sections of the Croatian community could meet. They talk of successful avoidance of a political take-over of the club, whether it be in Geelong, Adelaide or in Melbourne. Yet these same people are often the most fervent of supporters of the idea of Croatian identity and independence. Joe Vucica talks of his sense of personal responsibility that he has not done more to promote Croatia and its struggle for independence in Australia.

As we have seen, the politicians claim credit for the foundation of the clubs, but the sources for this are the memories of people who were not necessarily around at the time and the book by Mato Tkalcevic, which relies heavily on oral testimony. If they did found the club, then the politicians did little to help it in the early days, when it struggled even to put eleven players on to the park on a regular basis. Moreover, numbers of non-Croatians and even a few Serbians played with the club until the late 1960s. The claims of the politicians have been uncritically accepted by some subsequent writers. There is no doubt that later in its development the club did become a major political asset. At a time when the mainstream media was virtually closed to Croatian nationalist propaganda, a soccer club, at the highest level, kept the Croatian name before the public. Prior to reaching the State League in Victoria or later the national league there was little value in a Croatian soccer club in terms of media coverage. Apart from the Croatian papers, games involving Croatia were not reported until the team was playing at

State League level. At best a score might be recorded, or a violent incident would be reported, but there was no regular coverage or reports, and very few news stories.

In an attempt to reconcile these differing views I propose that in the early days there was relatively little political involvement in the soccer club and that it was only after it rose to prominence in the State League that its value as a political asset was appreciated and attempts were made to exploit it, sometimes successfully, sometimes, more often, not. Since there is such heavy reliance on oral memory, it is tempting to read the early activities of the club back through the lens of later political involvement and hence attribute a greater role to the political groups in the 1950s than was the case. This interpretation remains to be tested.

What have been the gains and losses for the Croatian community in Victoria of having Croatian soccer clubs? There is a strong argument that soccer has contributed to the sense of identity and cohesion of the community. It has maintained the Croatian name at a time when other avenues for the legitimate expression of nationality were inhibited. It has certainly been a major source of fund raising for Croatian causes, most recently during the Homeland War. The clubs have on occasion provided a focus for interaction where other divisions existed within the Croatian community.

Branko Filipi, former President of Adelaide Croatia, and now President of the Melbourne Knights, stressed that the soccer club was the first community organization set up in Adelaide. With the church, it proved a major formative influence on the lives of young Croatians arriving in Australia, often sponsored by the two organizations. Filipi said he paid special attention to the development of the youngsters, pointing out that Croatia would be known in Australia by their behaviour. He noted how many of them had gone on to become model citizens of this country. Filipi himself is one of the largest builders in south east Australia, having built over 3,600 houses, more than anyone except Jennings. At times he employed half the Adelaide Croatia team in his business.[40] The degree of control which a Branko Filipi exerted over these young men might be looked at somewhat askance by those brought up in a more liberal, individualist tradition, but Filipi would defend his role in terms of the absence of a family to pass on the correct moral values, and the ease with which unsupervised young men could go wrong.

These gains have not been without price. The clubs may have contributed to an embattled siege mentality among Croatians in Australia, limiting the extent to which they have integrated into the broader community. Such integration as there has been, it might be argued, was despite the existence of the soccer clubs, rather than because of them, as was the case with many other so-called ethnic teams. The existence of the clubs and their behaviour has aroused the distrust and enmity of other groups. There is a lack of wider community support for Croatian interests because of a perceived clannishness by Croatians in the past. There have been splits within groups which may have been exacerbated by divisions within and between clubs.

Mato Tkalcevic says that Croatians are often reluctant to accept decisions which go against them. They tend to protest through legal and other systems and are aggrieved when decisions are then upheld by the appellate bodies. Tkalcevic also stresses the importance of *Zadruga*, the extended family, and its honour, which must be defended at all costs. Revenge may be extracted for perceived wrongs and the head of the family would suffer a catastrophic loss of face were he not to uphold the family name and honour. Events in 1972 and 1997, connected with soccer, seem on the face of it to support such an interpretation. In 1997 Sydney United fought a protracted battle in the courts against Soccer Australia which had threatened to expel the club from the Ericsson Cup (the national soccer league) after a brawl in which some of its supporters and players were involved.[41] Harry Mrksa, on the other hand, argues that the class composition of Croatian migrants has militated against effective political influence on the soccer authorities in Australia. Croatian clubs have tended to be composed of working class, peasant or small businessmen and there have been relatively few professional people able to lobby articulately and effectively to promote Croatian interests. Greek and Italian migrants by contrast have always had a cadre of professionals available to advance their cause.[42]

One may conclude by arguing that for the Croatians as for Asian migrants in the United Kingdom:

> This study, then, shows how ethnic identity, far from being some primordial stamp upon an individual, is a plastic and changing badge of membership. Ethnic identity is a product of a number of forces: social exclusion and stigma and political resistance to them, distinctive cultural and religious heritages as well as new forms of culture, communal and family loyalties, marriage practices, coalitions of interest and so on.[43]

Modood and colleagues go on:

> Our research shows, we believe, that the emerging and evolving plurality on the ground, especially when allied to developments in mixed ethnicity relationships which we have not explored, belies those who argue that the infusion of new cultural groups is disruptive

to social cohesion and British identity. It challenges those who think in terms of the simplistic oppositions of British–Alien or Black–White. A significant population on the ground is living in ways which refute these dualisms. It is time for social analysts and policy makers to catch up. We need a new vision of Britishness which allows minorities to make a claim upon it, to be accepted as British regardless of the their colour and origins, and without having to conform to a narrow cultural norm.[44]

Substituting Australian and Croatian for British and Alien or Black would make my point about the plasticity of Croatian-Australian identity in 1997.

TABLE 1
CROATIAN SOCCER CLUBS IN AUSTRALIA[45]

Name	Location	State	Founded	Ended	Tkalcevic
Metropolitan	Perth	Western Australia	1968		165
Croatia	North Perth	Western Australia	1969		165
Croat	Preston	Victoria	1960	1963	84
Croatia	Ballarat	Victoria	1959		116
Croatia	Geelong	Victoria	1954		82-87
Croatia	Melbourne	Victoria	1952[46]	1972	82-87
Dinamo	St Albans	Victoria	1977		98
Dinamo	Morwell	Victoria	1979		115
Hajduk	Melbourne	Victoria	10 Jan 56	1958	87
South Parkmore	Dandenong	Victoria	18 March 79		CT 19
HNK Hajduk	Chelsea	Victoria	1981		99
HNK Mostar	Sunshine	Victoria			99
Zagreb	Geelong	Victoria	1958	1960	111-2
Zagreb/AR Split	Melbourne	Victoria	1975		97
Zagreb	Mildura	Victoria	1978		116
Essendon Lions		Victoria	1974		82-87
Essendon Croatia		Victoria	1978		
Melbourne Croatia		Victoria	1984		
Melbourne CSC		Victoria	1992		
Melbourne Knights		Victoria	1993		
Croatia	North Geelong	Victoria	1967		112-3
HNK Osijek		Victoria	1984		CT 18
HNK Split	Glenroy	Victoria	1976		CT 19
HNK Vukovar	Melbourne	Victoria	1975/1981		CT 19
Croatia	Glenorchy	Tasmania	1957		219 CT 18
Croatia	Launceston	Tasmania			221
Croatia	Adelaide	South Australia	1952		172
Croatia	Mount Gambier	South Australia	1960		180 CT 19
Croatia	Port Lincoln	South Australia	1970		179
Zadar	Port Lincoln	South Australia	After 1970		179
Croatia	Whyalla	South Australia			179-80
Zagreb	Renmark	South Australia			181
Adriatic	Adelaide	South Australia	After 1960		174

TABLE 1 (cont.)
CROATIAN SOCCER CLUBS IN AUSTRALIA

Name	Location	State	Founded	Ended	Tkalcevic
Dinamo	Adelaide	South Australia			175
Croatia Old					
Boys	Adelaide	South Australia	15 April 90		CT 19
Croatia	Brisbane	Queensland			209
Sunny Side		Queensland			210
Blue Adriatic		Queensland			45
Croatia	Sydney	New South Wales	15 March 58		137-8
King Tomislav	Liverpool	New South Wales	6 Oct 72		145
Mladi Hrvati	Blacktown	New South Wales	1972		153
Zagreb	Botany	New South Wales	20 Feb 70		152
Istra		New South Wales	Post 1975	1983	152
Napredak	Broken Hill	New South Wales	1939		48-50
Lola		New South Wales	1945		53
Jadran-Hajduk	Bonnyrigg	New South Wales	1969		54
Dalmatinac	Cabramatta	New South Wales	1957		55
Yugal	Cabramatta	New South Wales	11 Dec 60		55
South Coast	Illawarra	New South Wales	1984		CT 19
Croatia	Werrington	New South Wales	1982		CT 18
Croatia	Deakin	ACT	1968		200

NOTES

1. John Sugden and Alan Tomlinson, *Hosts and Champions: Soccer Cultures, National Identities and the USA World Cup* (London, 1994), p.141.
2. Jason Crowley, 'Playing for the Ghosts of Croatia', *Times*, 20 June 1996, Features, p.19.
3. Roy Hay, 'British Football, Wogball or the World Game? Towards a Social History of Victorian Soccer', in John O'Hara (ed.), *Ethnicity and Soccer in Australia* (Studies in Sports History Number) Australian Society for Sports History (Campbelltown, 1994), pp.44–79; Roy Hay, '"Making Aussies" or "What Soccer is all about": Soccer and European Migrants to Australia, 1945–93', Bradman, Balmain, Barellan and Bocce, Australian Culture and Sport Conference, Australian Sports Commission/ Australian Defence Forces Academy conference at the Australian Institute of Sport, Canberra, 8–9 Oct. 1993.
4. Youngsters in Europe saw Australia as a land of snakes, venomous spiders and kangaroos, America as the land of fast cars and consumer goods, Martin Groher, interview, 13 Aug. 1992 (tape recording in the possession of the author). When the Jewish migrants aboard the *Dunera* arrived at camps in Hay, New South Wales, one camp specialized in handball, the other in soccer. K.G. Loewald, 'A *Dunera* Internee at Hay, 1940–41', *Historical Studies*, Vol.17 (1969), pp.513 and 518.
5. For a useful discussion of the ideas of the nation and the state and their relationships, see Anthony Smith, *National Identity* (London, 1991), pp.1–18, esp. 14–15.
6. This was written before the 1997 Referendum produced a majority in favour of a Scottish parliament with limited tax raising powers.
7. Interview with Joe Vucica (notes in possession of the author).
8. Notes on interview at Frank Bot's funeral.
9. Interview with Steve Horvat, tape recording in possession of the author.
10. The DLP recruited central European refugees from Communist totalitarianism in their campaign against the Labour Party. See Janet McCalman, *Struggletown* (Melbourne, 1984), p.284.

11. Mato Tkalcevic, *Croats in Australia: An Information and Resource Guide* (Burwood, 1988), p.17.
12. Brian Murphy, *The Other Australia: Experiences of Migration* (Melbourne, 1993), pp.186–91.
13. Tkalcevic, *Croats in Australia*, p.53.
14. *Community Profiles. Yugoslav Born* (Canberra, 1990), pp.vii, 7, 31 and 37.
15. Rachel Unikoski, *Communal Endeavours: Migrant Organisations in Melbourne* (Canberra, 1978).
16. Hay, 'British Football, Wogball or the World Game?', p.58.
17. Steven A. Reiss, *Sport in Industrial America, 1850–1920* (Wheeling, IL, 1995), pp.97–105.
18. Stephanie Dew, 'Ethnic Involvement in Sport in Geelong, 1945–1990', MA thesis, Deakin University, 1992.
19. Lyn Richards, 'Displaced Politics', in James Jupp (ed.), *Ethnic Politics in Australia* (Sydney, 1984), pp.152–6.
20. James Jupp, 'Power in Ethnic Australia', in Jupp (ed.), *Ethnic Politics in Australia*, pp.186–7.
21. It has been suggested that the rural location of many of the camps was designed to encourage migrants to settle in the area near them. Like most European Australians since 1788 however the new migrants preferred urban settings. See Sol Encel (ed.), *The Ethnic Dimension: Papers on Ethnicity and Pluralism by Jean Martin* (Sydney, 1981), p.19.
22. *Geelong Advertiser*, 4 July 1955, in the New Australian column, under the headline 'National Groups Endanger Assimilation'.
23. Ibid.
24. 'Dutch Disclaimer', letter from W. L. Melai, publisher of *De Nieuwe Wereld*, *Geelong Advertiser*, 12 July 1955, p.11.
25. As Jean Martin pointed out as early as 1953, 'if we are not prepared to accept the development of immigrant groups, then we must be willing to forgo the continuance of immigrant cultural traditions', Encel (ed.), *The Ethnic Dimension*, pp.20–21.
26. *Geelong Advertiser*, 11 July 1955.
27. Interview with Joe Radojevic, 8 July 1991 (tape recording in possession of the author).
28. Ibid. This is confirmed by Frank Bot who arrived in 1961 from Slovenia via Trieste. Being of independent mind Bot decided to go to the camp at Bonegilla. On returning to Melbourne some three weeks later his taxi driver, who was also Croatian, took him to the Preston club. Interview with Frank Bot, 31 Jan. 1994 (tape recording in possession of the author).
29. Reiss, *Sport in Industrial America, 1850–1920*, pp.88–9 and 94–7.
30. Jesus Maestro, 'Football and Identity in Spain', Paper to the Football in Europe Conference, Leicester, June 1996.
31. 'Making Aussies: A Vital Role for Soccer', *Sun-Herald*, Sydney, 30 March 1958, p.76.
32. And(j)elko Cimera, *19th Annual Croatian Soccer Tournament Programme*, Melbourne Croatia Soccer Club, 1993, p.7. These tournaments started in 1975, after Croatian teams had been expelled from Victorian soccer, which was twenty years after the arrival of the early wave of Croatian migrants and the formation of the first Croatian soccer club in Melbourne. For details see Roy Hay, *The Croatia Story* (forthcoming).
33. Philip Mosely, 'A Social History of Soccer in New South Wales, 1880–1956', University of Sydney, Ph.D. thesis, 1987; Philip Mosely and Bill Murray, 'Soccer', in Wray Vamplew and Brian Stoddart (eds.), *Sport in Australia: A Social History* (Cambridge, 1994), pp. 213-230; Philip Mosely, *Ethnic Involvement in Australian Soccer, 1950–1990* (Canberra, 1995); Philip Mosely, 'European immigrants and soccer violence in New South Wales, 1949-1959', *Journal of Australian Studies*, Vol.40 (March 1994), pp.14–26.
34. Interview with Branko Filipi, 2 Feb. 1994 (tape recording in possession of the author).
35. VFA is the Victorian Football Association which at the time ran the second level Australian Rules football competition in Victoria.
36. Nina Mistilis, 'The Political Participation of Immigrant Electors', *Politics*, Vol.15, No.1 (1980), pp.69–71.
37. Jupp (ed.), *Ethnic Politics in Australia*, p.8.
38. Ibid, p.12.

39. Furio Radin, 'The Supporters of Dinamo Zagreb, now Croatia: From Nationalistic to Political Dissent', Football in Europe Conference, Leicester, 30-31 May 1996, translation by Pierre Lanfranchi.
40. Interview with Branko Filipi, 2 Feb. 1994 (tape recording in possession of the author) and cuttings from Adelaide papers.
41. Ray Gatt, 'United win key points over SA', *The Australian*, 24 Sept. 1997, p.23; *Australian and British Soccer Weekly*, Vol.844, 23 Sept. 1997, p.6; Media releases by Soccer Australia, 23-4 Sept. 1997.
42. James Jupp, *Immigration* (South Melbourne, 1991), pp.79–80.
43. Tariq Modood, Sharon Beishon and Satnam Virdee, *Changing Ethnic Identities* (London, 1994), p.119.
44. Ibid., p.120.
45. Sources: Mato Tkalcevic, *Croats in Australia: An Information and Resource Guide* (Burwood, 1988); And(j)elko Cimera, *19th Annual Croatian Soccer Tournament Programme*, Melbourne Croatia Soccer Club, 1993; *18th Annual Croatian Tournament Programme*, 1992.
46. This date is almost certainly incorrect. It should be 1953. See Roy Hay, *The Croatia Story* (forthcoming).

Basketball as Cultural Capital: The Original Celtics in Early Twentieth-Century New York City

MURRY R. NELSON

Pierre Bourdieu and Cultural Capital

The playing of sport is usually a conscious decision initially entered into for reasons of pleasure. At first it is physical – the exhilaration of play; then there is the added dimension of mental acuity which fuels the competitive drive; later in professional sport comes the economic pleasure – the acquisition of economic capital to make the play a vocation and to make the pleasure of sport pay for one's well-being and that of one's family.

Embedded within this framework, particularly for immigrants or the children of immigrants, is the establishment and retention of cultural capital. Since the term was popularized in the 1970s by Pierre Bourdieu, cultural capital has most often referred to education. However, cultural capital can be established in a variety of ways. This contribution will discuss how the sport of basketball became cultural capital for many New York City immigrants in the early 1900s. Particular focus on the Original Celtics professional basketball team will illustrate the notion of basketball as cultural capital.

The theory of education and reproduction essentially provides that schooling, as reflective of the dominant class or culture, will favour members of that dominant class for greater school success since they bring the accepted, lived experience of that class to the school. These then serve to reproduce the existing dominance. For those not of that dominant class, success comes through assimilation and acculturation.

Harker explains: 'Just as our dominant economic institutions are structured to favor those who already possess economic capital, so our educational institutions are structured to favor those who already possess cultural capital, in the form of the habitus (i.e. disposition) of the dominant cultural faction.'[1] The acquisition of cultural capital, then, acts as a screen – a filter in the reproductive scheme of a hierarchical society. The challenge for members of the non-dominant classes is to determine what appropriate cultural capital is and how to acceptably obtain it since *how* one acquires such capital is as important as the acquisition itself.

In his article 'Sport and Social Class' Bourdieu specifically addresses radically new sporting activities such as volleyball and basketball which almost immediately moved from amateur game to professional, spectator sport. Usually, this transition took place in the 'educational establishments reserved for their elites of bourgeois society' where folk art in fields like dance and music were gradually transformed into high art forms.[2] Basketball did not follow this institutional path. The time between basketball's invention and its practice as a game or amateur sport was relatively short – less than ten years before the establishment of professional teams and a professional league (the National Basketball League located around Philadelphia in 1898). The theory of amateurism, one championed by aristocrats like Baron Pierre de Couberin, largely 'incorporates the most essential assumptions of the bourgeois ethic of private enterprise … and is brought to fruition in the major private schools intended primarily for the sons of the heads of private industry'.[3] As members of the lower or middle classes age beyond adolescence, the likelihood of practicing a sport decreases, particularly when the sport is a team sport like basketball (popular among working-class and lower middle-class adolescents).[4]

Although Bourdieu is more knowledgeable about soccer and rugby, his hypothesis seems to fit the early years of basketball. Professional basketball was produced by 'the people' and it 'returned to the people in the form of spectacles produced for the people … as one branch among other of show business'.[5] This describes the pro-basketball scene in the 1920s, performed in armories, small church gyms, or make-shift courts throughout the Northeast. The spectacle of sport became one 'produced by professionals for consumption by the masses'.[6] This aptly describes the state of professional basketball at the time.

Although sport was originally developed for the elite, it became useful to the dominant classes as a divertissement for the masses of immigrant youth. 'When the pupils are on the sport field, they are easy to supervise, they are engaged in healthy activity, and they are venting their violence on each other rather than destroying buildings'[7] or committing other crimes. This is the logic behind the funding of 'Midnight Basketball Leagues' in some inner-city youth programmes in the United States. Institutions such as schools, churches, and settlement houses were competing at the turn of the century in struggles 'totally or partly organized with a view to the mobilization and symbolic conquest of the masses and therefore competing for the symbolic conquest of youth'.[8]

To many immigrant groups, a sports career was a contradiction in terms, but to many poor youth from among these groups, it represented a potential for lifting them out of their impoverished existence. Basketball's invention in 1891 caused a restructuring of the space of sporting practices and a more

Standing—WITTE, DEHNERT, CONNOLLY (Referee), TRIPPE, BARRY, SMOLICK
Sitting—J. FUREY (Mgr.), REICH, BECKMAN, T. FUREY (Asst.Mgr.)

(*top*): 'Why Jews Excel in Basketball'; (*bottom*): The Original Celtics Basketball Team

or less complete redefinition of the meaning attached to the various practices.[9] It was fortuitous that basketball's creation coincided with the beginning of the largest influx of new immigrants to the US ever. The purpose and use of sport, in this case basketball, is viewed differently by different classes or groups. Basketball, particularly professional basketball, was largely a working-class, ethnically-based sport.

To some groups success in sport, as in education or schooling, may 'imply an individual's rejection of their social origins'.[10] Perception of success, then, is very much a factor of the structural location of the perceiver and 'the highest form of cultural capital can be acquired only from the family'.[11]

Yet in many cases in the 1920s, the immigrant family was unfamiliar with new American sports, particularly basketball. Harry Litwack, who first attended and later played games for the South Philadelphia Hebrew Association (Spha) basketball team, recalled that his parents were too busy to keep close tabs on him and that they were glad that his basketball interests kept him in the neighbourhood. In response to a question about being out late at basketball games when he was barely a teenager, he said: 'It was only a block ... It was a matter of about maybe three or four, minutes, that's where the (team) originally played and that's how I got the job with a friend of mine setting up the chairs. My mother knew where I was. I'd come home and have something to eat and about 7:30 I'd go back' (Litwack, interview with author, Cheltenham, PA, 31 July 1996). Families, then, were tolerant of 'alternative' forms of education, culturally and intellectually. One may choose other forms of cultural capital than sport but the family as culture remains vital to the banking of such capital. Many families encouraged these sporting endeavours since they provided 'the opportunity to add a well paid breadwinner to the family'.[12]

The establishment of cultural capital may accrue in a variety of ways that produce consonance within the family and the ethnic group. One is economic capital as cultural capital, the acquisition of money. Many groups have seen this as the *ne plus ultra* of 'acceptance' at least on one's own terms, if not necessarily that of the dominant class. How one acquires such money may be more or less important, depending upon the culture and family. At one extreme is the belief that acquisition (means) is inconsequential to possession (ends). At the other extreme, the ends are inconsequential unless means are appropriate, which often meant reflecting the stated mores of the dominant classes, even if those mores are more mythological than actual when applied to the dominant classes themselves.

A way of judging the successful accumulation of cultural capital is through fame or notoriety. In some groups or families this may mean *negative* capital because the habitus (as Bourdieu uses the term) may imply hubris which may bring shame and derision to the family rather than admiration and fame. Still, fame in an appropriate forum may be deemed a successful form of cultural capital, especially among the youth of the classes involved.

A third form of cultural capital is acquired through education. As Bourdieu repeatedly notes, education tends to perpetuate the dominant class as the current social order reproduces itself in successive generations. Education is viewed by cultural groups and families as offering cultural capital through the acquisition of intellectual credentials. It is then up to the individual to struggle with the realization of class dominance that exists, yet which can be tempered, modified, or ignored by the crucible of schooling and education.

In some families or ethnic groups, another form of success and cultural capital may be acquired through what I shall term dignity and respect. This can exist in conjunction with fame, money, or education, or may exist without such descriptors. Some of the qualities of this form of cultural capital may be honesty, reliability, leading a 'good' life, easily assimilating or *refusing* to assimilate. One may, thus, be held in high esteem, despite one's status, for this type of cultural capital.

Returning, then, briefly to sport which may reflect some or all of these criteria, it is clear that professional sport can lead to fame, economic success, and respect. The examples of today are easy to behold and need not be discussed here. Of even greater concern is the way that sport was viewed in the 1920s *vis-a-vis* the accumulation of cultural capital, particularly among the Irish, the Germans, and the Jews of America, particularly in New York City and the Northeast.

Immigration and the Celtics

Between 1820 and 1930, over 15 million immigrants came from Germany, representing the largest number of members of one nationality arriving in the United States. These Germans came in various waves – pre-Civil War, post-Civil War (to 1900), pre-First World War, and post-First World War – though the latter number was significantly reduced for obvious reasons.

These arriving Germans represented various religious affiliations. Many German Jews, who identified themselves as German as much as they identified themselves as Jews, were included in some of the earlier waves of German Protestants. The post-Civil War émigrés were largely German Catholics from Bavaria and Southern Germany. The large number of German Catholics rivalled the entrenched Irish Catholics for power in the American Catholic Church. Constant agitation among the German Clerics and a boiling sense of outrage among the Irish bishops ensued.[13]

Amelioration was achieved through the ascension of James Cardinal Gibbons to the position of Cardinal of New York City in 1887. Ultimately, the two groups were reconciled and the Germans and Irish 'ruled the 'rooftop' [of the church] together to the notable exclusion of the Poles and the Italians'.[14]

By the beginning of the First World War, anti-German sentiment was common but there were some notable exceptions. The newly arrived Jews from Russia and Poland 'were overwhelmingly pro-German. All of them had come to America to flee the pogroms'.[15] Thus, these were pro-German if only because they were so violently anti-Russian. The seemingly unlikely alliance of Germans, Irish, and Jews seen on the Celtics was emblematic of these same alliances being played out on the larger stage of New York City.

The athletic fields and arenas, indeed, reflected these alliances in various ways. O'Connor noted this pattern and the effect it had on a number of ethnic groups, particularly Germans:

> One way for a minority to win acceptance in the American scheme, among its generally sports-mad fellow citizens, is on the athletic field, baseball diamond, or in the boxing ring. Thus, the Irish, and later the Italians, were tremendously uplifted by the example of the prize fight champions that they produced. Germans, however, showed little aptitude for fighting with fists padded. But baseball, the 'American pastime' as it once was, with its geometric order, its requirement of technical skills as well as brute strength and quick reflexes, its disciplined pattern, appealed to something in the German psyche.'[16]

So, too, with basketball, though its court size was not exactly standardized then. It was a rough, though appealing, game in the manner which the Celtics performed. It did not hurt that the Celtic success was inextricably linked to the Germans on the Celtic team: Leonard, Beckman, Dehnert, Reich – all German Catholics.

Like their German Catholic counterparts, the Irish Catholics of New York viewed sport as a wise investiture of cultural capital. 'Like religion and politics, sports offered possibilities to the Irish, who were excluded from business and professions by the Anglo Protestant establishment. And athletics provided the Irish community with badly needed heroes.'[17]

Sport, however, also stigmatized the Irish, who were seen as strong but dumb – good for digging ditches, building railroads, pounding criminals, and playing athletics. Strong backs indicated weak minds. 'The association of Irish Americans with baseball, the great national game, indicates that they accepted the United States more than it did them.'[18] Riess saw baseball as 'a good source of vertical mobility for Irishmen, the ethnic group at the bottom of the job hierarchy in the late nineteenth century'.[19] Athletic competition unleashed bottled up anger and resentment. 'The Irish role in sports expressed alienation as well as assimilation.'[20]

Getting the Irish in America interested in sport was not very difficult. After all, these were a people with a great fondness for sport – football, hurling, Gaelic football, billiards, boxing, track, walking – and for talking about sports as the many Irish sports writers were wont to do.[21]

The Irish were linked to the Jews in other obvious ways – through their prominence in show business and their associations with trade unionism. The lower class status of both groups made them easy allies in labour and show business and, ultimately, in sport.

The Celtics, after all, had been founded originally as an Irish Settlement House team on Manhattan's West Side with players like Morrisey, McArdle, Barry, Whitty, Calhoun, McCormick, and Kennedy. The team had appeal among the local Irish populace before the First World War. After the war, the Celtic name would initially attract Irish spectators. Would they stay to support basketball on a team with only two of the original Celtics?

From 1921 to 1926, Nat Holman was the only Jewish member of the Celtics. In 1926 the Celts obtained Banks, also Jewish, and a prolific scorer from New York City who had arrived back in New York after performing for the Sphas in Philadelphia and in the Metropolitan League for Brooklyn among others.

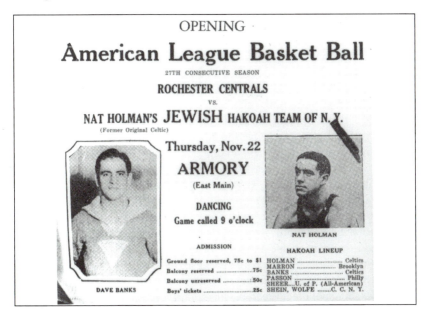

Rochester Centrals *versus* Nat Holman's Jewish Hakoah Team of N.Y.

As a Celtic player, Holman was aware of the esteem that Jews held for him. In a 1974 letter he stated: 'During my career as a professional basketball player – especially when I was the only Jewish player on the Celtics – I was very much aware of the Jewish following that supported me in a number of cities on the circuit. While I always played at my very best, I tried even harder when I knew the Jewish community was rooting for me'.[22]

In his thorough and insightful history of sports and the American Jewish experience, Peter Levine examines and explains this phenomenon in general as well as regarding basketball in particular. He questions the exclusively scholarly stereotype by noting that immigrant Jews by their actions were obviously more adventurous and less tied to the stereotype of Jews as exclusively people of the book. To many embracing American opportunity and experience, this included a love of sport:

> The growth and acceptance of sport as a new way of spending leisure time hinged on its promotion as an activity full of social purpose, one even capable of transforming immigrants into competent workers replete with new American values and character. Consciously emphasized as a mechanism of Americanization, especially for the children of Jewish immigrants and other outsiders, it was, from the outset, a critical melting point where majority and minority people intersected and, as such, a special place for illuminating the on going process of assimilation.'[23]

Through sport, one could be more American and not any less Jewish. This was especially noteworthy in New York City where, by 1920, almost half of all American Jews lived (constituting 30 per cent of the population of 4.3 million New Yorkers).[24] The lower East Side held 75 per cent of the Eastern European Jews in the city.

At about that same time, nearly 10 per cent of the Germans in the US and over 12 per cent of the Irish lived in New York City's five boroughs. These groups lived in contiguous neighbourhoods largely in Southern Manhattan from 14th Street South. What today is the East Village, which abutted the Lower East Side, was largely German at the turn of the century. The Lower East Side which abutted that area held 75 per cent of the Eastern European Jews in the city. Although the bulk of Irish lived uptown and in Brooklyn, 40 per cent of the populations of the wards below Canal Street were Irish.

A large segment of the Jewish media encouraged Jews to take part in athletics to be more American and because 'athletics and morality go hand in hand'.[25] It was recognized that athletics were a powerful opportunity to overcome the bookish stereotype mentioned earlier, the belief that Jews neglected physical development because of their deep devotion to intellectual and spiritual development.

Map of Lower Manhattan, *c.*1900–1920

Of the athletics entered into, none were received with more enthusiasm than basketball. An early University Settlement House team (1903–5) – with members known as the 'Busy Izzies' – won the New York Settlement House Championship. This provided early role models for Jewish youth in the persons of Barney Sedran, Marty Friedman, Lou Sugarman, Harry Brill, and others.[26] Nat Holman noted that 'thanks to the Settlement Houses we always had a place to play basketball ... It was not a new game on the Lower East Side (in 1905). It was very popular'.[27] Levine claimed, 'Jewish children flocked to the sport making it a significant part of everyday community life'.[28]

As Jewish players excelled, the Jewish community became greater fans of basketball and, by doing so, they 'became more "American" in turn, by watching their own kind transform it into a Jewish majority sport. These Americanizing experiences unfolded in ways that encouraged ethnic pride and identification.'[29]

The investment in basketball by Jews was seen as not just an American experience, but one consonant with Jewish culture, a suitable and respected source of cultural capital. Thus, 'long before basketball became a national entertainment vehicle, it was local sport, operating on amateur and professional levels, that provided a cheap and available form of amusement totally integrated into the local community's social fabric'.[30]

Levine's assertion is complemented by that of Nat Holman, the original Jewish player on the Celtics. In a letter to Buddy Silverman in 1974, Holman stated: 'Excellence in sports helps Jews to be even prouder of their great heritage so they can keep their heads high without feeling inferior to any other group. It helps non-Jews to understand that Jews are not only "people of the book"; but that they also share in the wholesome activities and interests of all their fellows.'[31]

This understanding by non-Jews was not always apparent, even to 'sympathizers' of this issue. Paul Gallico, the famed sports essayist, felt that basketball was a natural sport in which Jews would excel because 'it is a game that above all others seems to appeal to the temperament of Jews ... I suspect, that it appeals to the Hebrew with his Oriental background (because) the game places a premium on an alert, scheming mind and flashy trickiness, artful dodgery, and general smart aleckness'.[32] Ed Sullivan also thought Jews were ideally suited to basketball. Using Holman, Chick Passon of the Sphas, Banks, and Borgeman as examples of Jewish youngsters who are 'crackerjacks', Sullivan noted: 'Jewish players seem to take naturally to the game. Perhaps this is because the Jew is a natural gambler and will take changes. Perhaps it is because he will devote himself more closely to a problem than others will.'[33]

The Celtic Composition

The original Celtics were begun as a settlement house team in the Chelsea district which is located on the West side of Manhattan from the area just north of today's Greenwhich Village to just south of Penn Station, a distance of roughly two miles. At the turn of the century this neighbourhood was already one of transition, a characteristic that seems to still be prevalent in the 1990s. The neighbourhood had been Irish and held other recent immigrants in the mid to late 1800s, but was changing as native New Yorkers and later immigrants moved out of the city to Brooklyn, which did not become incorporated into New York City until 1898. The growth in New York City in 1870 and 1880 was largely the result of large-scale immigration from Germany and Ireland.[34]

The Chelsea neighbourhood, acknowledged as a 'tough' area,[35] was still a neighbourhood with a large number of Irish families. These young Irish lads constituted the Celtic teams of 1914–17, but the reconstituted Original Celtics after the First World War retained only two of these Irish Americans, John (Pete) Barry and Johnny Whitty. Whitty never played very much, serving as seventh man on seven man clubs. He also doubled as club manager, unofficial road manager and sometimes coach. These latter functions allowed him to retain his position on the Celtics through 1928 when the team disbanded. Although there is no explicit evidence to support this, it is not unlikely that Whitty also served as a kind of community liaison promoting the Celtics and preserving ties with the Irish American community.

Pete Barry probably served this latter function also, and he too stayed with the Celtics until 1928. Barry's assets, however, were more noticeable on the court where his six-foot frame and versatility allowed him to play all positions well.

In 1921, Barry and Whitty were joined by a third Irishman, George Haggerty, the only non-native New Yorker to log significant time (more than one year) with the Celtic Squad. Haggerty was a native of Springfield, Massachusetts, a small city. When he travelled to Reading, Pennsylvania, to play for the Reading Bears at the behest of former Springfield resident and Reading Star, Andy Sears, Haggerty felt at home in the city. In fact, after playing for more than 100 teams in 20 years, Haggerty returned to Reading and resided there from his basketball retirement until his death in 1961 at the age of 60. Haggerty was less comfortable in New York City, despite the large Irish population and his popularity every place he played. His presence certainly was an asset in the Celtics' appeal to the Irish communities of New York City and other cities of northern New Jersey and southern New York. Eddie Burke, a Metropolitan League star, played on the

Celtics from 1922–25. Though never one of their starters or stars, his Irish good looks and native New York City roots could not have hurt the Celtics' appeal to the Irish Community.

The Celtics achieved universal acclaim for their basketball excellence only after three German Americans joined the squad from 1920 to 1921. Beckman, Reich, and Leonard first met as teenagers and began playing together about 1907 for the St. Gabriels, an independent club in New York City that won the National Middleweight Championship during that time. (It should be remembered that basketball division for youngsters was done on the basis of weight, rather then height or age, much like some youth football teams are organized today. This division gives some insight into the nature of the play of the game itself where weight and bulk were seen as key factors in discriminating abilities.)

Over the period from 1905 to 1921 when all were reunited on the Celtics, the three German Americans played together for various teams including the Metropolitan Big Five in 1913–14 (Beckman, Leonard, and Reich), Paterson of the Interstate League in 1915–16 (Beckman and Leonard), Newark in 1916–17 (Beckman and Leonard), Norwalk in the Connecticut League in 1917–18 (Beckman, Reich, and Leonard), Bridgeport of the Interstate League in 1919–20 (Reich and Leonard).

Henry 'Dutch' Dehnert, another young German American, joined the Downey Shipyard team along with Reich in 1918. The next year, Dehnert played with Reich and Leonard in Bridgeport as well as with Beckman on Nanticoke of the Penn State League. In 1920–21, they played together with Thompsonville of the Interstate League. Also a native of New York City, Dehnert and the other three young players of German origin – Beckman, Reich, and Leonard – gave the Celtics great popularity with the German population of New York City. The most recent German immigrants were German Catholics, most of whom still lived in Manhattan. All four Celtics were German Catholics, children of the immigrant wave of the 1870s and 1880s. Reich was emblematic of the German Catholic/Irish Catholic alliances that began to be formed in the late 1800s in New York City. He married Mary Murphy, an Irish Catholic, whom he widowed at his death in 1922.

Both the Celtics and Tex Rickard's Whirlwinds achieved success in the early 1920s by eschewing a team based solely on ethnicity and instead strengthening their teams by signing players of outstanding ability, regardless of ethnicity. The Whirlwinds had Barney Sedran, Marty Friedman, and Nat Holman, all Jews from New York's Lower East Side. When Holman joined the Celtics in 1921 as their first Jewish player, he not only made them a much better squad, he also attracted a whole new legion of Celtic supporters – the Jewish American community in New York City.

Davey Banks, who was beginning his professional career with the Visitation team in the Metropolitan League, was among that audience. Banks joined the Celtics in 1927 after making a name for himself as a top scorer for teams in both the New York and Philadelphia regions. In Philadelphia, Banks led in scoring with the South Philadelphia Hebrew Association team and endeared himself to the local Jewish Community there. In the early 1920s, Holman had led Germantown to the Eastern League title and Scranton to the Penn State league crown. As a result, Jewish communities in these Pennsylvania cities could also identify with the Celtics in the 1920s.

Solidifying, to some extent, the Celtics' popularity in the Jewish communities of the Northeast was the presence of Benny Borgmann of Paterson, New Jersey. Although only a Celtic regular in 1925–26, he had appeared a few times in a Celtic uniform earlier in the decade.

Czechs were the final ethnic group represented by a Celtic regular. Joe Lapchick, native of Long Island, did not have significant effect on ethnic support of Celtic games, since Czechs constituted a much smaller number of people in the city and the region than the huge numbers of Germans, Irish, and Jews. Nevertheless, his excellence as a player and his contribution to the team's success overall not only improved the team's performance but also exemplified possibilities for other eastern European immigrants to successfully assimilate and acquire cultural capital.

The Media and Ethnicity

The newspapers made much of the backgrounds of professional basketball players in an apparent effort to exploit interest along ethnic lines and, ultimately, to sell basketball along with newspapers. The newspaper articles were often casual in their reliance on truth and therefore often inaccurate in their information. One example occurs in Hugh Bradley's 1927 New York article which states that Dave Banks 'is not a native New Yorker. He comes from Philadelphia', which was absolutely incorrect.[36] Another New York City writer, 'Lank' Leonard, referred to Lapchick and Banks as the 'tall Pole and the little Jew'. In his story, he notes that Banks is also known as 'Rabbi'.[37] Lapchick was, of course, not Polish, and though Banks was Jewish, the constant religious referencing would not have been tolerated were this to be written today.

Banks was commonly referred to as the 'young Hebrew' or the 'Hebrew star' by the *Philadelphia Inquirer*'s Gordon MacKay in 1926–27, but this may have also been in reference to his previous employment in 1924–25 and 1925–26 with the Spha squad. In a 15 March 1928 account in which Banks was battered in a Philadelphia/Celtics game, the *Inquirer* noted that

'Banks got a deep gash in his forehead and the blood spurted out and his face crimsoned.' After being attended by a physician, 'The young Hebrew, dizzy but courageous, returned to the battle' ('Celts Win ... ').[38] Lapchick was often referred to as Polish, 'that lengthy and troublesome Pole',[39] although he was Czech. Leonard was called Irish, though he was German. Dehnert was called a Dutchman because of his nickname which was probably anglicized from 'Deutsch' as in 'Pennsylvania Dutch'.

These labels were not done in malice, but to identify the players as representatives of ethnic groups, to break or to extend stereotypes of such groups. The reporters reflected the feelings of the times rather than attempting to set ethnic groups against one another. After all, it was the teams themselves which chose such appellations as sources of pride and identity. Names of teams reflected vocations and symbols (Shoe Pegs, Electrics, Potters, Glassblowers, Miners) as well as ethnicity (Buffalo Germans, Hebrews, Celtics, Jew(el)s, Busy Izzies, Knights of St. Anthony) so being referred to as a Hebrew, a Catholic, a German, followed rather naturally.

The Celtics became successful by drawing on diverse ethnic groups for their players and fans. This led to success on the court because of the quality of the players and success at the box office because of the cultural capital that different groups 'invested' in the basketball successes of their young ethnic group members.

Levine noted that 'For both adults and children, appreciation of and connection to Jewish basketball encouraged assimilation to unfold within the rich fabric of the ethnic, Jewish world in which they lived'.[40] He also notes in a postscript the parallels between the Jewish experience of sporting success/assimilation and that of American blacks. Although the success he chronicles is less dramatic because of historically embedded racism, the analogy of establishing cultural capital through the investiture of basketball or sport generally is validated to a large degree.[41]

Basketball served as cultural capital for a number of immigrant groups, particularly the Irish, the Germans, and the Jews (who constituted most of the émigrés from Russia and Romania in the early 1900s). The game was an investment in both American culture and a modified re-investment in these immigrant cultures.

The Celtics' greatest successes came when they went against popular practice by composing a squad of men from more than one ethnic group. The rationale was that these were the best players in the game; but coincidentally, they also brought along the support of ethnic groups that they represented. Diverse support brought cultural and economic success to the team both individually and collectively. As a result, basketball was seen as an appropriate venue for the growth of cultural capital.

NOTES

1. R. Harker, 'Bourdieu – Education and Reproduction', in *An Introduction to the Work of Pierre Bourdieu* (London, 1990), p.87.
2. P. Bourdieu, 'Sport and Social Class', *Social Science Information*, Vol.17, No.6 (1978), p.823.
3. Ibid., p.835.
4. Ibid., p.828.
5. Ibid.
6. Ibid., p.830.
7. Ibid., p.831.
8. Ibid.
9. Ibid., p.833.
10. Bourdieu, 1974, quoted in Harker, op. cit., p.91.
11. Harker, op. cit., p.94.
12. S. Riess, *City Games, the Evolution of American Urban Society and the Rise of Sports* (Urbana, IL, 1989), p.185.
13. R. O'Connor, *German Americans* (Boston, MA, 1968), p.355.
14. Ibid., p.359.
15. Ibid., pp.395–6.
16. Ibid., p.309.
17. L. McCaffrey, *Textures of Irish America* (Syracuse, New York, 1992), p.27.
18. Ibid., p.28.
19. Riess, *City Games*, p.185.
20. McCaffrey, *Textures of Irish America*, p.27.
21. C. Wittke, *The Irish in America* (New York, 1956, revised 1970), p.264.
22. B. Silverman, *The Jewish Athletes Hall of Fame* (New York, 1989), p.73.
23. P. Levine, *Ellis Island to Ebbets Field* (Chicago, IL, 1992), p.6.
24. I. Rosenwaike, *Population History of New York* (Syracuse, NY, 1972), p.111.
25. YMHA, 1912, quoted in Levine, *Ellis Island to Ebbets Field*, p.14.
26. B. Postal, J. Silver and R. Silver (eds.), *Encyclopaedia of Jews in Sports* (New York, 1965), pp.83, 92.
27. J. Healy, 'Nat Holman Player and Coach'. Copy in Holman File, Naismith Memorial Basketball Hall of Fame (no date), p.1.
28. Levine, *Ellis Island to Ebbets Field*, p.27.
29. Ibid., p.38.
30. Ibid., p.72.
31. Silverman, *The Jewish Athletes Hall of Fame*, p.73.
32. P. Gallico, *Farewell to Sport* (New York, 1938), p.325.
33. E. Sullivan, 'Ed Sullivan's Sports Whirl', *New York World*, 1926; Joe Lapchick Scrapbooks (1926).
34. Rosenwaike, *Population History of New York*, p.56.
35. Z. Hollander, *The NBA Official Encyclopedia of Pro Basketball* (New York, 1979), p.272.
36. H. Bradley, 'Dempsey to Open Basketball Duel by Tosssing Sphere', 1927, in Joe Lapchick Scrapbooks. Richard Lapchick, Boston, Massachusetts.
37. '"Lank Leonard", Joe Lapchick and Davey Banks are "Mutt and Jeff" of Profesional Basketball', in Joe Lapchick Scrapbooks, 1927. Richard Lapchick, Boston, Massachusetts.
38. 'Celtics Win and Take Eastern Division Title ...', *Philadelphia Inquirer*, 15 March 1928, p.22.
39. E. McAuley, 'Rich has Edge on Collegian for Pivot Job', 1927, Joe Lapchick Scrapbooks.
40. Levine, *Ellis Island to Ebbets Field*, p.73.
41. Ibid., pp.281–4.

Race, Nation and Authenticity of Identity: Interrogating the 'Everywhere' Man (Michael Jordan) and the 'Nowhere' Man (Ben Johnson)

STEVEN J. JACKSON, DAVID L. ANDREWS and CHERYL COLE

Introduction

This is the tale of two men, two athletes. Both of these men are black, both have reached the pinnacle of their respective sports, departed and then returned, and both are destined to figure prominently in any history of sport. Moreover, Michael Jordan and Ben Johnson emerged within a post-industrial, post-modern, era where their celebrity, racial and national identities were manufactured by an ever expanding media network. However, it is at this juncture that most similarities between Michael Jordan the 'everywhere' man, and Ben Johnson the 'nowhere' man, end.

Michael Jordan has become a 'global hero of a global show'[1] partly because people believe that, at least compared to we mere mortals, he can fly. The number of books written about this 'all-American hero',[2] not to mention an entire special edition of the *Sociology of Sport Journal* entitled: 'Deconstructing Michael Jordan: Reconstructing Post-Industrial America', are testimony to his apparent invasion of both popular and academic circles. If there was any doubt that he is one of, if not, the most known people in the world, then the global launch of his movie Space Jam should remove any scepticism about the veracity of the everywhere man label.

Michael Jordan's revered celebrity status is a stark contrast to former Canadian sprinter Ben Johnson. If indeed Michael Jordan is the everywhere man then Ben Johnson, whose name circulates with each successive steroid scandal and each ensuing black athletic achievement in Canada, and whose seemingly exiled existence renders him invisible, might be referred to as the nowhere man. Once the fastest human being on earth (a title he still proclaims), Johnson gained infamy by becoming the ex-fastest human being alive for testing positive for the use of steroids, twice. A two year ban followed the 1988 Seoul Olympics, with his lifetime banishment handed down in Canada in 1993, an involuntary exile currently under appeal with the IAAF. Ben Johnson did achieve what can be described as hero status in Canada at one time but it is doubtful he could ever have achieved the global icon status of Michael Jordan. The reasons for this are many and varied but likely include the fact that he was involved in a less than high profile spectator sport but also because he lacked the telegenic qualities of a Michael Jordan. Jordan appeals to many corporate sponsors because of his family oriented, wholesome, all-American image, the antithesis of the stereotypical threatening black masculinity so often represented by the media. Ben Johnson, despite obtaining some extremely lucrative endorsements, may have held less commercial appeal because he did display aspects of this threatening black masculinity. In part this was signified through his ultra mesomorphic black body but it was likely compounded by his 'foreign', slightly impeded speech, and his location within a much smaller Canadian market.

Jordan's success and the emergence of his racially transcendent, authentic, American identity is in part explained by his rise within the context of new right politics in America.[3] The result was the expansion of specific cultural spaces that afforded the opportunity for a successful black athlete, embodying the right characteristics to bridge the existing gap between a racist and a white-dominated, corporate America. To this extent it has been suggested that Michael Jordan, despite his explicit racial minority status, symbolically transcended his race because to be an all-American or alternatively authentic American almost by definition subordinates any sense of being an African or other hyphenated American.[4]

The case of Ben Johnson's authenticity and identity is quite different. Unlike Jordan, Johnson was born in Jamaica, immigrated to Canada, and later became a 'naturalized' Canadian. Johnson was first heralded as a great Canadian in 1987 when he defeated Carl Lewis at the World Athletics Championships and then again when he won the gold at the 1988 Seoul Olympics. However, Johnson may never have achieved all-Canadian status, perhaps because the concept is somewhat foreign in Canada. In part this stems from historical differences between Canada and the US with respect to the politics of racial and national identity, as well as the more explicit philosophy of Canadian multiculturalism. Commenting on the former, Wilson and Sparks note that:

> Canada is widely acclaimed to be one of the most tolerant and pluralistic societies in the world, although there exist notable institutional and structural disadvantages (as opposed to overt discrimination for visible minorities) ... This is in contrast to the American system, which is widely characterized as a society where widespread segregation and disadvantage exists, as well as continued

racial violence and political ambivalence over state aid to Black urban poor.[5]

Moreover, whereas the US espouses a popular notion of the melting pot, where different cultures exist but are subservient to a dominant American one, in Canada the very existence of the 1988 Multicultural Act suggests the recognition, at least through legislation, of difference. Thus, while one can achieve both official and popular all-American status in the US (it would be interesting to ascertain how many foreign born college athletes have attained this title) a corresponding title would have a different connotation in Canada, which is not to suggest that the term all-Canadian has never been used.

Although Michael Jordan and Ben Johnson represent different nation states and have led very different public and private lives, it is our intention to demonstrate that these individuals are instructive of many important contemporary debates related to identity politics. Stated somewhat more generally Michael Jordan and Ben Johnson are 'vehicles for developing progressive understandings of the broader social and cultural concerns'[6] related to racial and national identity politics. By excavating the careers and discourses which surround these two men we hope to provide insights into how identities are defined, contested and reproduced particularly through the media. We begin by examining Michael Jordan as a signifier of transcendence with respect to racial identity in contemporary America. In turn, we discuss Ben Johnson and the politics of racial and national identity in Canada. Although the two case studies differ in their specific focus they share a common desire to explore the notion of race, nation, and authenticity.

The Everywhere Man and the Politics of Transcendence

In the Nike commercial featuring Michael Jordan which debuted on American television in late 1996, the ubiquitous 'commodity, pop star, all-African American guy'[7] drives, ascends, and executes one of his signature dunks. The greatness of the act being witnessed is framed, and affirmed, by the commercial's angelically voiced accompaniment. Interspliced with this engaging slow-motion faux footage of Jordan's performance (purportedly taken from a Chicago Bulls and Los Angeles Lakers NBA game), are vignettes of a deliberately diverse consuming populace. In an effort to characterize how Jordan appears and, more importantly, how he is seen, each consumer is depicted as being transfixed by Jordan's mediated image, whose power is derived from its referent: a body which knows no limits.

'Common culture' and 'collective experience' are established as we watch 'the people' in a shared moment defined by the witnessing of greatness: the eyes of a multi-racial assemblage of fitness club members are uniformly directed to the screen above their treadmills which features Jordan's dunk; a solitary white male becomes so engrossed – while in the midst of shaving – by Jordan's exploits, that the water in his sink begins to overflow; a racially ambiguous mother and child, as well as their dog (shaking the water from its coat), stare intently at the televised image in their low rent apartment; a small African American boy reverentially gazes at the mediated bodily presence in a shop window; a small white boy, distracted by the televised Jordan, in slow-motion, allows his bicycle to fall onto the driveway of his suburban home; a pair of elderly men are caught in a moment of jaw-dropping stupefaction when confronted with Jordan's image traversing the cinematic screen; the hypnotized expression of an Hispanic boy fills the screen, whilst Jordan appears as a reflection in his eyes; lastly, the visual narrative briefly returns to the African American boy before Jordan completes his dunk. This profound cultural experience – imagined in relation to abstract, yet concrete, spaces and identities – is summarized by the final image of Jordan, in yet another incarnation of his promotional form. Against a black background, a red version of Nike's Air Jordan jumpman logo appears, silhouetted and centred. Significantly, this trademark is perhaps the most familiar means by which Jordan has entered into public culture. The aforementioned commercial represents the familiar configuration of Jordan and contemporary America: it 'captures the USA's fascination with the athlete' who is seemingly everywhere and admired by everyone.[8] Particularly in relation to the chronic absence of African American celebrities in American history, Jordan's privileged location as an 'iconic minority subject'[9] marks alleged advances in the tortuous race relations associated with the installation and maturation of the modern American nation. Moreover, as a relatively young African American male, Jordan's intelligible distance from conventional popular media representations through which members of that demographic group are routinely pilloried, subtly demonized, or painfully caricatured, would seemingly signal widespread cultural accomplishment and progress.[10] According to the cultural critic Michael Eric Dyson: 'Despite the mixed messages they send, the cultural meanings that Jordan embodies represent a remarkable achievement in American culture. We must not forget that a six foot six inch American of obvious African descent is the dominant presence in a sport that twenty years ago was belittled as a black man's game, unworthy of the massive attention it receives today.'[11]

In response to Dyson's assertion, care should be taken to neither understate Jordan's contemporary cultural significance, nor overstate his importance as a signifier of social and racial cohesion. With regard to the former point, and as Dyson is keenly aware, Jordan's domineering presence and influence has reached far beyond the boundaries of the National Basketball Association, he is 'bigger than basketball: he's a pop icon'.[12] In response to the latter point, we believe it is important to problematize the pervasive common sense and utopic reading of Michael Jordan as a figure who 'transcended the negative meanings of race to become an icon of all-American athletic excellence'.[13] Necessarily focusing on the context of contemporary American racial politics, our main interest is to highlight the political significance of Jordan as an American sign of transcendence. Thus, this discussion is intended to demonstrate the pressing need to develop new ways of talking about and visualizing race in, and through, Michael Jordan. In this very real sense, and paraphrasing both Cornel West and Judith Butler, Michael Jordan matters in America, particularly with regard to late twentieth-century American formations of black masculinity and American identity.[14]

According to Berlant, and as a 'ligament of sociality', the national stereotype – in this case the Jordan version of the All-American hero – must be understood according to its specific context and effects.[15] It is impossible to understand Michael Jordan's cultural and political significance without recognizing his relationship to the 'new cultural racism' which underpinned the American New Right's pernicious agenda within the Reagan and Bush administrations.[16] Embracing prescient moral panics surrounding the issues of urban crime, violence, drug abuse, and welfare dependency, the New Right targeted an essentialised model of the irresponsible, indolent, deviant, and promiscuous non-white urbanite as representing a virulent 'enemy from within'[17] whose very existence threatened the core values of Reagan's America.[18] Renouncing the profound and chronic influence of centuries of systemic racial discrimination, the New Right appropriated Patrick Moynihan's view of the African American family as 'a tangled web of pathology'[19] and efficiently pathologized the African American population through pronouncements and policies within which 'Unemployment, poverty, urban decay, school crises, crime, and all their attendant forms of human troubles were spoken of and acted upon as if they were the result of individual deviance, immorality, or weakness'.[20]

In a seemingly contradictory twist, the populist cultural politics of the New Right also vilified the African American population through the 'right-wing appropriation of the celebrated media achievements of a handful of prominent African American 'individuals' – Bill Cosby, Whoopi Goldberg, Arsenio Hall, Michael Jackson, Michael Jordan, Eddie Murphy, Keenan Ivory Wayans, and Oprah Winfrey'.[21] The circulation of these popular embodiments of achievement not only authorized American narratives of utopian possibilities, they also managed the contradictory relations between American identities and the lived conditions of vulnerable urban populations.

The celebration of African American success stories graphically substantiated Reaganite explanations of the genesis of America's urban problems, by directing popular attention to a perceived lack of personal resolution, will, and enterprise, as being the underlying reason for the lack of achievement of America's struggling urban inhabitants. Perhaps more than anything, Jordan is a key figure in America's management of paradoxical claims and practices, and a towering instance of the New Right's re-articulation of America's utopian narrative within the guise of the colourblind ideology which dominated Reagan's popular cultural politics. This populist ideology can be characterized in Reagan's own words:

> We hear much of special interest groups. Well our concern must be for a special interest group that has been too long neglected. It knows no sectional boundaries or ethnic and racial divisions, and it crosses political party lines. It is made up of men and women who raise our food, patrol our streets, man our mines and factories, teach our children, keep our homes, and heal us when we're sick – professionals, industrialists, shopkeepers, clerks, cabbies, and truckdrivers. They are, in short, 'We the people', this breed called Americans.[22]

Reagan's comment appropriated 'special interests' in ways that rendered appeals to the profound problems (or indeed their catastrophic manifestations) experienced by minority populations, as divisive and distinctly un-American activities. In this way, 'People in trouble were reconceptualized as people who make trouble'.[23] By conflating the American population into a homogenous grouping which shared the same problems, anxieties, and experiences, Reaganism's colourblind credo thus denied the continued existence of race-based discrimination. This cynical politicking justified savage cuts in the social welfare programme, much of which was designed to address systemic race-based inequities and injustices that were deemed to no longer exist. De-funding social welfare thus allowed the Reagan administration to re-direct monies into financing vote-winning populist policies, such as tax reform and increased crime prevention strategies, which were designed to placate the predominantly white suburban American masses.[24]

While masquerading behind a purported egalitarianism, it is evident that Reaganism's colourblind agenda was profoundly embedded in norms which favoured America's white middle class. Given Jordan's location in this context, we contend that his popular presence was, and remains, implicated in ways of thinking and seeing that deny, and yet extend, the subordination of the American racial Other. The strategic exclusions and depictions of race which characterized the Reaganite agenda, were reproduced through Jordan's invasive presence in the mass public sphere. Whilst Jordan's phenotypical features could not be overlooked, as with those African American sporting figures touted as possessing 'crossover' appeal who preceded him (i.e. Arthur Ashe, Julius Erving, and, ironically, O.J. Simpson),[25] Jordan was manufactured as a 'race-neutral'[26] or 'colourless'[27] celebrity.

The widely felt need for African Americans to disavow any overt expression of, or reference to, their blackness as a strategy for securing – as opposed to alienating – popularity, was indicative of the ingrained racism which informed and was manufactured by the American culture industries. As Arthur Ashe shrewdly noted, 'if you're going to be a genuine sports hero in this country, a Ruth, DiMaggio or Palmer, you have to keep your political *views* to yourself. Advertisers want somebody who's politically neutered. That's unspoken, but it's understood'.[28] Within the context of Reagan's America, overt expressions of racial difference were unquestionably discomforting, and were hence studiously avoided within promotional strategies aimed at nurturing a commodity-sign's widespread popular appeal. Thus, the numerous corporate concerns forefronted by Nike and the National Basketball Association, who had vested interests in accentuating Jordan's popular appeal, strategically distanced his image from the highly suggestive signifiers of racial difference which dominated popular representations of African American males.

With reference to Joan Copjec's *The Unvermogender Other: Hysteria and Democracy in America*, 1991, Sandell notes that 'to participate in the American democratic process requires not so much a positive American identity as it does the ability to shed one's particular identity in order to become a 'disembodied' citizen of America'.[29] As Clarke noted, the forms and imagery of the American identity have historically been steeped in the changing manifestations of white middle class culture.[30] Within the popular imaginary there exists a naturalized relationship between the discursive location of Americanness as a site of cultural dominance, and that of whiteness as a site of racial dominance.[31] Thus, providing Jordan with a means of seductively disembodying his imaged existence from its potentially troubling connotation of racial Otherness required articulating his imaged identity in, and through, the white myths of America. David Falk, Jordan's agent and the individual recently described as the 'man behind Michael Jordan',[32] devised a project intended to promote Jordan as having an 'All-American image ... Not Norman Rockwell, but a modern image. Norman Rockwell values, but contemporary flair'.[33] Jordan's mediated rendition of the American odyssey centred on a late twentieth-century rugged individualism: a 'striving for agency, self determination, differentiation from others and freedom from control'[34] which provided a largely undeviating narrative backdrop linking his multitudinous, yet consistent and highly predictable, televisual incarnations.

Within NBA game commentaries, personal profile segments, home videos, Nike commercials, and those for the myriad of other products he endorses, Jordan was routinely portrayed as someone whose wholesomeness, humility, inner drive, personal responsibility, and perhaps uppermost his sterling successes, 'allow us to believe what we wish to believe: that in this country, have-nots can still become haves; that the American dream is still working'.[35] In this way, Jordan acts as a symbolic representation of the American project; the virulently guarded national fantasy revolving around myths of origin, consensus, and imagined community.[36] Casting Jordan as a vindication of the reassuring persistence of America's founding categories such as freedom, liberty, rights, justice, responsibility, and agency,[37] Breskin noted, 'In fact, for some folks he has come to represent America – as in, we may not make cars or televisions too well, but we turn out a helluva Michael Jordan'.[38]

Breskin's comment would appear to be disturbing given the apparent incommensurability of consumer goods and Michael Jordan. Yet, the comment is perhaps apropos because it registers: Jordan's location in a mass public culture; ways of thinking and seeing America and American progress; and, the continual denial of the social relations, and manifestations, of post-industrial production. Jordan's location in mass public culture, then, can never be reduced to his exceptional embodiment. Instead, his location is inextricably bound to signs of a new and improved America, and to America's ability to produce commodities that function to stimulate and satisfy consumer desire. Michael Jordan matters because he was made in and by America and serves as a public form of the successes and achievements of the American political formation. Fabricating 'American Jordan'[39] occludes the social and, most pertinently, racial realities of both Jordan and the American project: both are made abstracted, transhistorical, and seemingly apolitical entities. That distance from the historical context in which he is made (as well as the ongoing anxieties around the possible recognition of those conditions) are expressed in the rhetorical strategies, and repetitions, in which Jordan's race-neutered American identity is celebrated through the category of transcendence.

Examples abound of the ways Jordan has been represented as a transcendent being: 'Michael Jordan ... has a charisma that transcends his sport. He belongs in a category with Arnold Palmer or Arthur Ashe';[40] 'For one thing, he's nearly transracial';[41] 'He's the first modern crossover in team sports. We think he transcends race, transcends basketball';[42] 'Down-to-earth hero: Middle-class and apolitical, he breaks down nearly all racial boundaries';[43] 'Jordan's allure transcends not only race but gender, age, politics, socioeconomics and the cola wars as well'.[44] The rhetoric of transcendence appears to distance Jordan from the historical conditions, including the semiotic field, that locate and position other (non-transcendent) African American males. As Berlant noted: 'As iconic minority subjects, they prove the potentialities of the marginal mass population to the hegemonic public; as minority exceptions, they represent heroic autonomy from their very identity; as "impersonations" of stereotyped minority identity, they embody the very ordinary conditions of subjective distortion that characterize marginality'.[45]

Mobilized in such a fashion, the meaning of Michael Jordan, and that of the stereotypically deviant black male urbanite against which his identity is defined, arose from an interweaving between presence and absence, 'Nothing, neither among the elements nor within the system, is anywhere ever simply present or absent. There are only everywhere, differences and traces of traces'.[46] While Jordan's achievements are represented as so momentous that they transcend any relation to the social relations in which they were produced, the trace of the stereotypical black male is an ever-present and telling absence within the promotional discourse which fabricated Jordan. Thus, as a sign of transcendence, Jordan works as an agent of displacement. Jordan's exceptional black body works in concert with pejorative racial codes that render visible unexceptional black bodies: those who cannot shed their particularity. Jordan's popular presence thereby precludes America's recognition of, and facilitates the continued denial of, its innate racism. Consequently, the exceptional Jordan emerged as the type of figure whose transparent success legitimated the reactionary colourblind shift in American racial politics by vindicating the existence of an 'open class structure, racial tolerance, economic mobility, the sanctity of individualism, and the availability of the American dream for black Americans'.[47] As an embodiment of Reaganite virtue, and akin to his celebrity bedfellow Bill Cosby, Jordan thus functions as a mechanism for reconciling the distance between American fantasy and materiality, and for 'throw[ing] the blame for black poverty onto the impoverished'.[48]

In summary, Michael Jordan is a culminating example of the extent to which the long-term project of the American New Right fashioned a politics of the popular[49] which both raided from, and contributed to, the expanding inventory of the American promotional culture industries. In this respect, Jordan is an effect and instrument of an ever more reactionary, late twentieth-century expression of the racist credo which dominated the American advertising industry in the decades immediately following the end of the Second World War: 'Advertising firms, reacting to research demonstrating that commercials overwhelmingly focused on and appealed to whites, stridently maintained that advertisements should not "look like America" but should look like what advertisers thought white mainstream audiences thought America should look like.'[50] Jordan's racially transcendent (displacing) image distanced his promotional identity from that of the hyper-mythologized, and indeed hyper-pathologized, black male urbanite; which is evidently how the promotional media thought white mainstream audiences imagined the African American Other. Furthermore, Jordan's status and influence as a faithful Reaganite replicant[51] (a black version of a white cultural archetype, the quintessential American hero) expressed advertisers' sense of how they wished the African American Other would look. Thus, as well as subverting, submerging, and subordinating the African American racial Other,[52] Jordan's popular presence has simultaneously further normalized America's white mainstream culture. The benevolence shown by the American public in such statements as 'We must be good people – we love Michael Jordan',[53] or 'Jordan to me is an icon of reconciliation and good will every which way … Everybody likes him and nobody seems to notice any racial implications to anything he does',[54] is thus wholly narcissistic and self-serving.

As we hope to have demonstrated, America's common culture is dialectically implicated within, and therefore inseparable from, the identities that it confers and manages. The disavowal of the problems and effects of racism, the elision of immediate contradictions, and by extension the evasion of social and historical context, are integral to the mediated management of late modern American identity. Out of such forces, Michael Jordan emerged under the sign of transcendence as both a national and commercial spectacle. Jordan, whose potential is represented as being without limits, is thus the sign of infinite transport: the sign of the inevitable progress of [trans]national capitalism. As such, representations of Jordan are based on a primary elision of America's history, which nurtures an uncritical acceptance and blithe celebration of the products and practices of contemporary American racism. Consequently, America's social and psychic loyalty to Michael Jordan is an effect of a regulatory loyalty to America's ethnopolitical fantasy of itself.

The Nowhere Man and the Politics of Racial and National Identity

Although it would be impossible to argue that Ben Johnson has attained the same global notoriety as Michael Jordan, he will no doubt be long remembered in the annals of Olympic history. Although the use of performance enhancing substances in sport has a long history, arguably the genesis of the modern sport-steroid controversy begins with Ben Johnson. What was it about this particular Jamaican-born, black Canadian sprinter that made him the focal point of international pity and disdain as well as the scapegoat of the multi-million dollar Dubin Inquiry in post-1988 Canada? What was so significant about one athlete's disqualification for the use of steroids that, almost ten years later, he still haunts the new generation of Canadian and foreign-born black athletes, including double gold medalist and world record holder Donovan Bailey? We suggest that the Ben Johnson affair is a complex story that is as much about the meaning of being black in Canada, and of defining an authentic Canadian identity, as it is about the politics of the Olympics and the illegal use of steroids. We begin with a brief overview of Johnson's rise to national hero, a discussion of the specific context within which he attained his success and then an analysis of some of the various ways in which his racial and national identities were constructed by the media before, during and following his disqualification.

Benjamin Sinclair Johnson, Jr., who at the height of his career became affectionately known in Canada as 'Big Ben', was born on 30 December, 1961 in Falmouth, Jamaica. Sharing his older brother Edward's interest in athletics, Johnson's early track career consisted primarily of running in little races through his neighbourhood, sometimes with small bets on the side.[55] Slightly more formal, but still very limited athletic participation commenced when he became a member of the Conquerors, a local Falmouth track club. Arriving in Canada in April, 1976 the quiet, shy, 97 pound Johnson was to become one of Canada's and sport's most famous athletes not to mention minority immigrants. Johnson officially became a Canadian citizen in 1980 at the age of 18, eight years prior to the 1988 Seoul Olympic scandal. He first started attracting attention in the track world in 1981 when he finished second in the World Cup Finals in Zurich, Switzerland. In 1984, he won bronze finishing third behind Carl Lewis and Sam Graddy, respectively, in the Los Angeles Olympics. Then, in 1985, he beat Carl Lewis for the first time on the European track circuit in the Weltklasse meet at Zurich. From this point onward the rivarly between Lewis and Johnson intensified although Ben was continually overshadowed by his American counterpart. Even in Canada it is evident that despite the rapid improvement during his career, he did not really receive any 'national' recognition until about 1987.

A key turning point in Johnson's career occurred on 30 August, 1987 when Johnson defeated Lewis and set a world record in Rome. The headline read 'Big Ben has struck his finest hour'. Subsequently, Johnson's status in Canada began to flourish as evidenced in the list of national honours bestowed upon him including: Member of the Order of Ontario (1987); Member of the Order of Canada (1987); Associated Press Male Athlete of the Year (1987); Top International Sport Story of the Year (1987); Track and Field News Indoor Athlete of the Year (1987–88); World Champion Award (1987); The Jesse Owens International Trophy (1988) and, medal performances in the Olympics, World Championships, Commonwealth and Goodwill Games. These awards are testimony to Johnson's success and provided a platform for him to serve as an important symbolic representative of Canada. However, in conjunction with his emerging athletic success several interrelated processes unfolded that influenced the popular representation of Ben Johnson's racial and national identity. It would appear that as Johnson's profile ascended and he was increasingly located within contexts wherein Canada's success could be reified, the hyphenated signifiers of race and ethnicity that characterized his early career began to disappear. In the course of about a decade the initially 'Jamaican immigrant', then 'Jamaican-Canadian' was suddenly being referred to as just 'Canadian'. Moreover, as Johnson's national identity as a Canadian was confirmed his racial-ethnic identity as Jamaican, or even Caribbean-Canadian, although it could not be completely obscured, was to some degree subverted. Notably, these transformations did not occur in a social vacuum and they cannot be dissociated from the wider political and cultural climate of Canadian society and some understanding of Canada's relationship with the United States.

The context of Johnson's most famous victory and subsequent disqualification is central to any understanding of the issue of authenticity and racial and national identity in Canada. A key feature of that context is Canada's reputed insecurity and inferiority in comparison to its dominant southern neighbour, the United States. Consider the following sample of book titles which reflects both Canada's preoccupation with its identity and how it is influenced by the United States: *Canada and the Canadian Question, The Americanization of Canada, Life With Uncle, Neighbors Taken For Granted, From Nation to Colony*, and, *In the Eye of the Eagle*.[56] Many of these books examine the historical struggles Canada has faced living next to the world's most powerful economic and cultural nation. However, some address more contemporary issues which are important considerations in understanding the context of Johnson's story in 1988. For example, in the same year that Ben Johnson was disqualified from the Olympics, Canada was in the midst of signing a Free Trade Agreement (FTA) with the US which many critics argued signalled the cultural and political end of Canada as a nation.[57] The debates between pro and anti-FTA parties became so strong that it served as a major political platform during the Canadian federal election held in November 1988. In combination, the previously noted historical, economic and political factors contributed to what some have characterized as a crisis of Canadian identity and established an important framework within which it is possible to understand the overall significance of sport and sport heroes, such as Ben Johnson, in constructing a national identity.

Historically, Canada has never had a reputation as an international sporting power although official government policies emerging in the late 1960s certainly recognized the important role of sport in promoting national identity. These state initiatives suggested that sport ' … has an important role to play in any government attempt to promote unity and a unique Canadian identity',[58] and ' … in countering the threat to Canadian identity of the pervasive mass culture of the United States'.[59] The success of these policies is open to debate but in 1988 the events surrounding one particular athlete, often described as Canada's prodigal son, Wayne Gretzky, provide some evidence of the significance of sport in defining Canadian identity 'out of difference' to the US Jackson, for example, notes that Gretzky's marriage to American actress Janet Jones and his subsequent trade from the Edmonton Oilers to the Los Angeles Kings became fully articulated within the Canada–US free trade debates such that the media, politicians, and nationalists linked one individual's fate with the threat of Americanization.[60] The Gretzky crisis played an important role in shaping the national mood that pervaded Canada in 1988, a mood of uncertainty and anxiety. Likewise, there is every possibility that the Gretzky crisis, as it was articulated to the debates about the threat of Americanization, served to augment the meaning and significance of Ben Johnson as illustrated in the following note that one member of the Canadian public addressed to the Americans: 'We haven't in Canada, in recent years, had many international sports heroes … We've got 25 million people; you've got more than 250 million. You've got lots of international athletes. We've got Wayne Gretzky and Ben Johnson, and now you have Gretzky.'[61] Such sentiments also help explain the key role that Carl Lewis played in establishing Ben Johnson as Gretzky's replacement as the premier national hero in 1988 and why the Seoul disqualification was so devastating.

The intense rivalry between Lewis and Johnson provided a stage upon which differences between Canada and the US could be highlighted, thereby defining and confirming a distinct Canadian identity. To this extent the intense rivalry with Carl Lewis was an important factor in the social construction of Johnson's national and racial identities. Consider the following remark appearing in the Canadian media which described the victory as 'as a triumph over Carl Lewis, a superb athlete whose arrogance, glitter and artifice reminded so many Canadians of what they find objectionable in their mighty neighbour to the south'.[62] The relatively quiet, humble, reserved, perhaps stereotypically Canadian, demeanour ascribed to Ben Johnson provided a point of contrast to his American counterpart. Yet, this superficial contrast may mask some deeper differences between Canada and the US that account for their respective views on identity and authenticity.

Like Michael Jordan, Carl Lewis has been referred to as an all-American. The term has both an official (for example, college all-American) and a popular connotation which tends to infer that, like Michael Jordan, an individual embodies idealized American characteristics and values: a clean-cut, wholesome appearance, obedient to authority and, even if unsuccessful, perennially in pursuit of the American Dream. The stereotypical conceptualization of America as the 'melting pot' suggests that although foreign individuals and their cultures may have an influence, the all-American identity remains paramount. In Canada, although the term all-Canadian sometimes emerges with respect to particular athletes, for example, Wayne Gretzky, it does not hold the same cultural significance. Again, referring to a stereotypical, although popular, conceptualization of culture, Canada is often symbolically referred to as a 'salad bowl'. Although it no doubt represents the issue far too idealistically, in Canada, the metaphor of the salad suggests that each element of culture contributes to the overall appearance and quality of the nation as an entity, but distinct flavours are maintained. Hence, immigrants, while certainly being encouraged to enjoy and contribute to Canadian culture, are also encouraged to maintain and celebrate their own cultural traditions and practices.

Although the spirit of this sentiment has long been espoused in Canada in 1988 it was taken one step further when Prime Minister Brian Mulroney announced the institutionalization of The Multicultural Act (formally labelled the 'Act for the Preservation and Enhancement of Multiculturalism in Canada'). Thus, multiculturalism as a popular Canadian ethos became something that was not only encouraged but legislated. However, it is not difficult to see how this provides the basis for a very complex notion of national cultural formation with the Parti de Quebecois' fight for an independent state serving as a prime example. The notion of an all-Canadian, whether in appearance or philosophy, almost defies description. Moreover, The Multicultural Act, while serving to foster cultural uniqueness, in part, legislates the notion of otherness. Although he was not referring to Ben Johnson or Canada, Miles identifies the significance of the social construction of otherness in the context of nationalism and national identity formation asserting that: 'nationalism is a means to sustain a sense of commonality, particularly in periods of conflict and crisis within a nation … the state's admission of citizens of another nation … admits a population which, at least potentially, may be identified as a threat to the imagined community'.[63] The Ben Johnson affair was constituted by, and constitutive

of, a national crisis in Canada in 1988, a crisis emerging out of a complex
intersection of political and economic forces which were represented as
playing a major role in defining Canadian culture and the basis of a unique,
purportedly authentic, Canadian identity.

The reactions of the Canadian State, members of the Canadian public,
and key media commentators following the Ben Johnson steroid scandal
illustrate the politics of race, nation and authenticity. For example, in what
has become one of the most blatant, yet widely accepted, rituals Canadian
Prime Minister Brian Mulroney telephoned Johnson immediately after his
100 metre victory at Seoul expressing his pride and gratitude on behalf of
all Canadians. Through his actions the Prime Minister is able to achieve
several self-serving objectives including: basking in the reflected glory of
Johnson's victory in an attempt to capture the people's attention during a
moment of heightened nationalism and patriotism; aligning himself with
'the people' by translating Johnson's victory into a triumph for the nation;
subtly demonstrating his support of visible minorities within the Canadian
social structure; and, justifying the excessive government expenditure on
elite sport in Canada by showing that its policies had finally paid off. In
sum, Mulroney utilized the media and a popular sporting hero to
strategically position himself before the Canadian electorate only two
months prior to the federal election. However, as if seeking refuge from any
guilt by association immediately following the disqualification the Prime
Minister referred to the incident as a 'personal' tragedy for Ben Johnson and
his family. Johnson's fame and celebrity as an embodiment of Canadian
nationalism had become a political liability.

The Prime Minister's spineless, if unsurprising, manoeuvre
notwithstanding, what is increasingly clear was the manner in which
Johnson's racial and national identities had been constructed, deconstructed
and reproduced by the media. As previously alluded to, and although it no
doubt oversimplifies the process, it would appear that early in his career
Ben Johnson was a Jamaican-born immigrant and with each small step up
the ladder of success he was slowly redefined as a Jamaican-Canadian. With
his 1987 victory over Carl Lewis and particularly his gold medal victory at
Seoul Johnson attained the status of 'Canadian'. Then, following his failed
urine test Johnson was again relegated to Jamaican immigrant or Jamaican-
Canadian status.[64] Arguably the signifiers 'immigrant', 'Jamaican-born',
'Jamaican-Canadian' and 'Canadian' provide the basis for defining,
confirming and authenticating Johnson's racial and national identities
within particular cultural specificities. The subtle use of the hyphen in
defining Johnson's identity clearly identifies him as black and despite 'full'
citizenship, serves to signify his otherness within Canada. If there is any
validity to these statements then it could be suggested that Ben Johnson's

national identity had to be achieved through athletic success which provided international recognition for Canada, whereas his racial/ethnic identity was ascribed. Support for this contention is provided by Cecil Foster, Jamaican-Canadian author and journalist, who notes how Johnson, like all black Jamaicans in Canada, is defined first and foremost by his race:

> ... we knew that he was paying the price for the so-called double burden of being black: that you rise to fame as an individual but you crash back to earth as a representative of your race; that several times Johnson had mounted the medal podium as a Canadian hero, but when – the world records were erased, he was merely a Jamaican, reduced in the eyes of the mainstream to his most common denominator, to his base.[65]

In addition to the use of the hyphen to construct Johnson as an immigrant, there were a variety of racial stereotypes and discourses that emerged following his disqualification that served to confirm his status as an other. Included in these racially-based, if not racist, discourses were those related to animals,[66] intelligence,[67] and racist humour.[68] Some writers were even more openly critical in their claims about racism in Canada. Hampson, for example, castigated Canadians for their about-face in the aftermath of the Johnson affair: 'After hailing Johnson as one of Canada's own after his record-breaking triumph, there was a disconcertingly rapid tendency to disown him after his fall. Far too many Canadians instantly transformed him into a Jamaican or an immigrant in his disgrace – an attitude which smacks of the worst sort of racial intolerance.'[69] According to Hampson, Canadians had 'transformed' Johnson into a Jamaican. Other writers, for example Levine, even suggested that irrespective of the steroid incident, Johnson was never accepted as an equal in Canada. She argues that, even at the peak of his success, many Canadians were actually hoping for Johnson's downfall because they could not bear the thought of a Jamaican, which she argues is simply a euphemism for black in Canada, providing Canada's long awaited moment in the international sporting limelight.[70]

The emergence of various media discourses which redefined Ben Johnson's national and racial identities, along with those reproducing negative stereotypes, provide some support for Levine's claim of racism in Canada. Yet, there is also evidence of pride, support and adulation for Ben Johnson. In one instance, Ben Johnson, like Michael Jordan, is described as transcending his race as reflected in the following statement made prior to the 1988 Seoul Olympics: 'That's what Ben Johnson represents to many Canadians, beyond black and white. It's more of a national identity'.[71] Such a statement represents the contradictory nature of the salad bowl or multicultural conceptualization of culture and identity in Canada. The espoused uniqueness or authenticity of Canadian culture and identity, and indeed its popular mediated representation, is based upon the celebration of difference. Yet, it would appear from the preceding statement that Canada's 'national' identity supersedes any other type of identity, for example, racial/ethnic identity. The complexity and dynamics of this issue demands much more attention than we can fairly devote to it here. Yet, what is evident is that Ben Johnson's national and racial identities were subject to varying popular representations all of which can be linked to power relations being exercised and negotiated within specific contexts in Canada.

It has been suggested that Johnson's national identity was achieved, whereas his racial identity was ascribed. Arguably, the same statement could be made about Michael Jordan with some qualification. Because he was an immigrant with particular overt significations of difference, particularly skin colour, Johnson's national identity appeared to be contingent upon his ability to succeed within the constraints of the existing Canadian social structure and to contribute positively to the national profile of Canada through sport. By contrast, although Michael Jordan certainly attained all-American status based upon his extraordinary achievements in sport, his national identity was never in question. Yet, despite his all-American, hence more than African-American identity, there were particular times when Jordan's racial identity was more overtly signified, for example, when he was accused of having a gambling problem and when his father was brutally murdered. At this stage we can only guess at how Jordan's racial and national identities might be influenced by a scandal which compares in magnitude to that of Ben Johnson. Would, for example, there be a shift in Jordan's popular representation as an all-American to an African American? Likewise, if Ben Johnson was born in Canada and devoid of a 'foreign, speech impeded' accent, would his status have been different? These are hypothetical questions at best but the very fact that they can be raised identifies the complex, shifting terrain of identity within contemporary society.

Conclusion

It is increasingly clear that the notion of identity requires some reconceptualization in light of many factors, particularly the politics of representation, which reveal the fluid and unstable nature of identities. As such, our analyses of Michael Jordan and Ben Johnson have heeded Stuart Hall's advice that: 'Precisely because identities are constructed within, not outside, discourse, we need to understand them as produced in specific historical and institutional sites within specific discursive formations and practices, by specific enunciative strategies'.[72] By specifying the historical, political, economic and popular cultural contexts of the US and Canada respectively we have endeavoured to locate the politics of racial and national identity for the everywhere man (Michael Jordan) and the nowhere man (Ben Johnson). Although the signification of transcendence is much more pervasive in the case of Michael Jordan, we should not ignore some of the related, in some cases parallel, processes accompanying the social construction of Ben Johnson's identity. Jordan's individual achievements, as articulated within a new-Right America, contributed to a dynamic reconfiguration of his racial and national identity. Jordan's all-American status was suggested to have transcended, if only metaphorically, his racial identity. Ben Johnson was also, at least on one occasion, characterised as transcending his race. However, several factors including his Jamaican origins, his impeded and accented speech, his link to drugs, and his highly publicized shaming of both Olympic sport and Canada, contributed to Johnson's representation as a demonized racial Other.

We would like to suggest that any notion of authentic identity, whether national, racial, gender or other demands careful consideration and critical analysis. The very idea of an authentic identity, particularly a national one, has been challenged and criticized. However, this is not to suggest that analysis, discussion, and debate about the concept has no value. It would be both naive and counterproductive to ignore the powerful, yet taken for granted, sentiments and ritualized expressions that are at the vanguard of the search for an authentic basis of national identity. Hence, while we may reject the basis of the concept, it does provide a point from which we can investigate the politics and power relations of identity within contemporary cultural settings. In conclusion, we once again draw upon Stuart Hall who effectively captures the crux of the identity and authenticity debates advising us that: 'identities are about questions of using the resources of history, language and culture in the process of becoming rather than being: not "who we are" or "where we came from", so much as what we might become, how we have been represented and how that bears on how we might represent ourselves'.[73]

NOTES

1. D. Halberstam, 'A Hero for the Wired World: In the Satellite Age, Michael Jordan has Become the Global Hero of a Global Show', *Sports Illustrated*, 23 Dec. 1991, pp.76–81.
2. See R. Equinas, *Michael and Me: Our Gambling Addiction, My Cry for Help* (San Diego, 1993); B. Greene, *Hang time: Days and Dreams with Michael Jordan* (New York, 1992); B. Greene, *Rebound: The Odyssey of Michael Jordan* (New York, 1995); J. Naughton, *Taking to the Air: The rise of Michael Jordan* (New York, 1992); S. Smith, *Second Coming: The Strange Odyssey of Michael Jordan from Courtside to Home Plate and Back Again* (New York, 1995).
3. D.L. Andrews, 'Deconstructing Michael Jordan: Reconstructing Postindustrial America',

Sociology of Sport Journal, Vol.13. No.4 (1996), pp.315–18; M.G. McDonald, 'Michael Jordan's Family Values: Marketing, Meaning, and Post-Reagan America', *Sociology of Sport Journal*, Vol.13, No.4 (1996), pp.344–65.

4. D.L. Andrews, 'The Fact(s) of Michael Jordan's Blackness: Excavating a Floating Racial Signifier', *Sociology of Sport Journal*, Vol.13, No.4 (1996), pp.125–58.

5. B. Wilson and R. Sparks, 'It's Gotta be the Shoes: Youth, Race, and Sneaker Commercials', *Sociology of Sport Journal*, Vol.13, No.4 (1996), pp.398–427.

6. D.L. Andrews, 'Deconstructing Michael Jordan: Reconstructing Postindustrial America', *Sociology of Sport Journal*, Vol.13, No.4, (1996), p.316.

7. N. George, *Elevating the Game: Black Men and Basketball* (New York, 1992), p.236.

8. D. Enrico, 'Nike Commercials Score with Consumers', *USA Today*, 20 Jan. 1997, p.6b.

9. L. Berlant, 'America, "Fat", the Fetus', *Boundary 2*, Vol.21, No.3 (1994), pp.145–95.

10. C.L. Cole and D.L. Andrews, 'Look – Its NBA ShowTime!: Visions of Race in the Popular Imaginary', in N.K. Denzin (ed.), *Cultural Studies: A Research Volume*, Vol.1 (Greenwich, CT, 1996), pp.141–81; H. Gray, *Watching Race: Television and the Struggle for 'Blackness'* (Minneapolis, 1995); J. Lule, 'The Rape of Mike Tyson: Race, the Press and Symbolic Types'. *Critical Studies in Mass Communication*, Vol.12 (1995), pp.176–95.

11. M.E. Dyson, *Between God and Gangsta Rap: Bearing Witness to Black Culture* (New York, 1996).

12. M. Snider, 'Michael Jordan's Bigger Than Basketball: He's a Pop Icon', *USA Today*, 19 July 1996, p.3d.

13. Dyson, *Between God and Gangsta Rap*, p.13.

14. C. West, *Race Matters* (Boston, MA, 1994); J. Butler, *Bodies that Matter: On the Discursive Limits of 'Sex'* (New York, 1993).

15. Berlant, 'America, "Fat", the Fetus', p.156.

16. N.K. Denzin, *Images of Postmodern Society: Social Theory and Contemporary Cinema* (London, 1991); H. A. Giroux, *Disturbing Pleasures: Learning Popular Culture* (New York, 1994).

17. S. Hall, C. Critcher, T. Jefferson, J. Clarke and B. Roberts, *Policing the Crisis: Mugging, the State, and the Law and Order* (London, 1979); K. Mercer, *Welcome to the Jungle: New Positions in Black Cultural Studies* (New Yorke, 1994).

18. S. Jeffords, *Hard bodies: Hollywood Masculinity in the Reagan Era* (New Brunswick, NJ, 1993).

19. Department of Labor, *The Negro Family: The Case for National Action* (Washington, DC: US Government Printing Office, 1965).

20. C. Reinerman and H.G. Levine, 'The Crack Attack: Politics and Media in America's Latest Drug Scare', in J. Best (ed.), *Images of Issues: Typifying Contemporary Social Problem* (New York, 1989).

21. J.L. Reeves and R. Campbell, *Cracked Coverage: Television news, the Anti-Cocaine Crusade, and the Reagan Legacy* (Durham, NC, 1994).

22. From Ronald Reagan's inaugural speech, January 1981, in *Public Papers of the Presidents of the United States: Ronald Reagan, 1981* (Washington, DC, 1982), pp.1–2.

23. Reinerman and Levine, 'The Crack Attack', p.127.

24. See J. Clarke, *New Times and Old Enemies: Essays on Cultural Studies and America* (London, 1991); S. Diamond, *Roads to Dominion: Right-wing Movements and Political Power in the United States* (New York, 1995); J.L. Reeves and R. Campbell, *Cracked Coverage: Television News, the Anti-Cocaine Crusade, and the Reagan Legacy* (Durham, NC, 1994); L.J.D. Wacquant, 'The New Urban Color Line: The State and Fate of the Ghetto in Postfordist America', in C. Calhoun (ed.), *Social Theory and the Politics of Identity* (Oxford, 1994), pp.231–76.

25. E. M. Swift, 'Reach Out and Touch Someone: Some black Superstars Cash in Big on an Ability to Shed Their Racial Identity', *Sports Illustrated* (1991), pp.54–8.

26. K.W. Crenshaw, 'Color-Blind Dreams and Racial Nightmares: Reconfiguring Racism in the Post-Civil Rights Era', in T. Morrison and C.B. Lacour (eds.), *Birth of a Nation 'hood : Gaze, Script, and Spectacle in the O.J. Simpson Case* (New York, 1997), pp.97–168.

27. L. Johnson and D. Roediger, '"Hertz, Don't It?" Becoming Colorless and Staying Black in

the Crossover of O.J. Simpson', in T. Morrison and C.B. Lacour (eds.), *Birth of a Nation'hood: Gaze*, pp.197–239.

28. Swift, 'Reach Out and Touch Someone', pp.54–8.
29. J. Sandell, 'Out of the Ghetto and into the Marketplace: Hoop Dreams and the Commodification of Marginality', *Socialist Review*, Vol.25, No.2 (1995), pp.57–82.
30. J. Clarke, *New Times and Old Enemies: Essays on Cultural Studies and America* (London, 1991).
31. R. Frankenberg, 'Whiteness and Americanness: Examining Constructions of Race, Culture, and Nation in White Women's Life Narratives', in S. Gregory and R. Sanjek (eds.), *Race* (New Brunswick, NJ, 1994), pp.62–77.
32. *New York Times Magazine*, 17 Nov. 1996.
33. G. Castle, 'Air to the throne'. *Sport*, Jan. 1991, p.30.
34. L. Langman, 'From Pathos to Panic: American Character Meets the Future', in P. Wexler (ed.), *Critical Theory Now* (London, 1991), pp.165–241.
35. J. Naughton, *Taking to the Air: The Rise of Michael Jordan* (New York, 1992), p.7.
36. S. Bercovich, *The Rites of Assent: Transformations in the Symbolic Construction of America* (New York, 1993).
37. W.E. Connolly, *The Ethos of Pluralization* (Minneapolis, 1995).
38. D. Breskin, 'Michael Jordan: In his Own Orbit', *Gentleman's Quarterly*, March 1989, p.322.
39. C.L. Cole, 'American Jordan: P.L.A.Y., Consensus, and Punishment', *Sociology of Sport Journal*, Vol.13, No.4 (1996), pp.366–97.
40. Donald Dell, head of ProServ, quoted in P. Patton, 'The Selling of Michael Jordan: Uncanny Move Son the Court and a "Charisma that Transcends his Sport" have Created Basketball's most Lucrative Property', *New York Times Magazine*, 9 Nov. 1986, p.49.
41. C. Kirkpatrick, 'An Orbit all his Own', *Sports Illustrated*, 9 Nov. 1987, p.88.
42. Ibid., p.93, quote by David Falk.
43. J.E. Wideman, 'Michael Jordan Leaps the Great Divide', *Esquire*, Nov. 1990, p.144.
44. C. Kirkpatrick, 'Up, Up and Away', *Newsweek*, 18 Oct. 1993, p.64.
45. Berlant, 'America, "Fat", the Fetus', p.156.
46. J. Derrida, *Positions* (A. Bass, trans.), (Chicago, IL, 1981), p.26.
47. H. Gray, 'Television, Black Americans and the American Dream', *Critical Studies in Mass Communication*, Vol.6 (1989), p.376.
48. H.L. Gates, 'TV's Black World Turns – But Stays Unreal', *New York Times*, 12 Nov. 1989, p.40.
49. L. Grossberg, *We Gotta Get Out of This Place: Popular Conservatism and Postmodern Culture* (London, 1992).
50. Johnson and Roediger, 'Hertz, Don't It?', p.201.
51. S. Willis, *A Primer for Daily Life* (London, 1991).
52. Ibid.
53. Marvin Bressler quoted in Swift, ' Reach Out and Touch Someone', p.58.
54. Jack Christ quoted in Snider, ' Michael Jordan's Bigger Than Basketball', p.3d.
55. J.R. Christie, *Ben Johnson: The Fastest Man on Earth* (Toronto, 1988).
56. G. Smith, *Canada and the Canadian Question* (Toronto, 1971); S.E. Moffett, *The Americanization of Canada* (Toronto, 1972); J.W. Holmes, *Life with Uncle* (Toronto, 1981); L. Merchant (ed.), *Neighbors Taken for Granted* (New York, 1966); M. Scott, *From Nation to Colony*, (Lindsay, Ont., 1988); J.F. Lisee, *In the Eye of the Eagle* (Toronto, 1990).
57. M. Bowker, *On Guard for Thee: An Independent Review of the Free Trade Agreement* (Hull, 1988); R. Davies, 'Signing Away Canada's Soul: Culture, Identity, and the Free Trade Agreement', *Harper's*, Vol.278 (1989), pp.43–7; L. Lapierre, *If You Love This Country: Facts and Feelings on Free Trade* (Toronto, 1987); M. Scott, *From Nation to Colony* (Lindsay, Ont., 1988).
58. D. Macintosh, T. Bedecki and C.E.S. Franks, *Sport and Politics in Canada* (Kingston, 1987), p.186.
59. Ibid., p.174.
60. S.J. Jackson, 'Gretzky, Crisis and Canadian Identity in 1988: Rearticulating the Americanization of Culture Debate', *Sociology of Sport Journal*, Vol.11 (1994), pp.428–46.

61. J. Longman, *The Philadelphia Inquirer*, 26 Feb. 1989, p.D-1.

62. 'Truth at the Finish Line', Editorial in *The Globe and Mail*, 28 Sept. 1988, p.A-6.

63. R. Miles, *Racism* (London, 1989), p.121.

64. S.J. Jackson, 'Disjunctural Ethnoscapes: Ben Johnson and the Canadian Crisis of Racial and National Identity', Paper presented at the Crossroads International Cultural Studies Conference, July 1–4, 1996, Tampere, Finland.

65. C. Foster, 'Captain Canada: But Will Media Allow Bailey to Escape Johnson's Shadow?', *The Toronto Star*, 10 July 1996, p.D-3.

66. A. Fotheringham, 'The Johnson Saga in Perspective', *Maclean's*, 10 Oct. 1988, p.64; B. Levin, C. Wood, H. Quinn, J. Bierman, N. Underwood, A. Finlayson, T. Tedesco, M. Clark, and M. Stuart-Huarle, 'The Steroid Scandal', *Maclean's*, Vol.101, No.42 (1988). pp.50–3; M. Janofsky, 'Johnson Loses His Gold to Lewis After a Drug Test', *The New York Times*, 27 Sept. 1988, p.D31.

67. L. Siegel, 'Ben Johnson Case Questions Validity of IQ Tests', *Toronto Star*, 20 June 1989, p.A-15.

68. D. Boyd, 'Canada Waits for Ben to Say It Ain't So After Steroid Controversy', *The Vancouver Sun*, 27 Sept. 1988, p.A-3.

69. A. Hampson, 'Press Made Poor Showing in Johnson Affair', *The Financial Post Daily*, Vol.1, No.148 (1988), p.16.

70. M. Levine, 'What If He'd Kept the Gold?', *The Globe and Mail*, 13 Oct. 1988, p.A-7; M. Levine, 'Canadians Secretly Relieved at Johnson's Fall', *New Statesman and Society*, Vol.1, 7 Oct. 1988, p.8.

71. Sue Wilson, quoted in Christie, *Ben Johnson*, p.144.

72. S. Hall, 'Introduction: Who needs identity?', in S. Hall and P. DuGay (eds.), *Questions of Cultural Identity* (London, 1996), pp.1-17.

73. Ibid., p.4.

Global Sports and Patriot Games: Rugby Union and National Identity in a United Sporting Kingdom since 1945

JOSEPH MAGUIRE and JASON TUCK

Introduction

The aim of this contribution is to investigate the nature of media representation relating to sport, national culture and national identity in the British Isles. For the purposes of this study, this exploration has been restricted to reports related to rugby union in Britain between 1945 and 1975 as cited in a single daily national newspaper, *The Times*. A central theme of the substantive part of this study was therefore how to make sense of the media discourse relating to the construction of 'common-sense' notions of national belonging. This study forms just part of a wider project which will provide a sociologically-driven account of the dynamic relationship between sport, national culture and identity in the British Isles in the post-war period with specific reference to rugby union. In this project we examine official records of the 'Home' Rugby Unions, conduct interviews with current international players and undertake an in-depth analysis of the 1995 World Cup competition held in South Africa.[1] In this context we begin with a discussion of sport, national identity and globalization processes. Attention is then directed to the substantive case study that highlights several of the key features raised.

The theoretical framework underpinning this wider study is based on a figurational approach to issues surrounding national identity. Its principal roots lie in two of the most recently re-published and translated works of Norbert Elias, specifically *The Established and The Outsiders* (1994) and *The Germans* (1996). This approach is concerned with several key issues: the multiple characteristics of personal identity; the place of national identity within the 'globalization debate'; the balance between invented traditions and habitus construction; the formation and employment of 'I-', 'we-' and 'they-images'; and the emergence of wilful nostalgia.[2]

In the introduction to *The Established and The Outsiders* the processes at work between established (the 'we' element) and outsider ('they') groups are explored. The 'problem' in which Elias was interested was: '... how and why human beings perceive one another as belonging to the same group and include one another within the group boundaries which they establish in saying "we" in their reciprocal communications, while at the same time excluding other human beings whom they perceive as belonging to another group and to whom they collectively refer as "they".[3] In *The Germans*, Elias intertwines theoretical reasoning and substantive evidence to produce an investigation of the deeply embodied aspects of German habitus, personality, social structure and behaviour and how these features (the 'we'-image of the Germans) can be seen to have grown out of the nation's history. The central question which Elias addresses throughout this book is how the fortunes of a nation have become sedimented, over many years, into the habitus of its citizens. Our work here represents a small contribution to this school of thought and attempts to relate the processes involved to the arena of sport.[4]

It is not possible here to accomplish a similar task to Elias as to what it means to be 'English', 'Scottish', 'Irish', 'Welsh', or even 'British'. It is, however, necessary to provide a working definition regarding the concept of 'identity'. Mennell views the formation of identity (or 'I/we' images) as a social process through which various categories of people come to share a collective cultural consciousness.[5] This 'consciousness' is built up, over time, both within and between increasingly interdependent social groupings.[6] However, individuals do not simply find themselves shackled to one consciousness. Each individual possesses multiple and complex identities that are continually developed and shaped, through time, by social networks of interdependencies.[7] These identities are constructed through a process of cultural representation which can be viewed as an exchange of dominant, emergent and residual views. The dominant notion of identity tends to 'invent' traditions, recall 'common' events and stress those who 'belong' and those who do not. This much a figurational account shares with writers such as Klein and Bairner, who have drawn inspiration from the work of Hobsbawm and Ranger.[8]

Let us try to develop our own position a little more. National cultures are commonly regarded as a state of being into which an individual is born (and thus have little control over) and they provide one of the main sources of collective cultural identity. Elias stated that:

> In the present day world, nations...appear to have become the dominant and most powerful of all ... supra-individual influences on people's feelings of meaning and value ... They are coming to recognize more and more clearly the functions of nations or national groups as the guarantors, guardians, embodiments or symbols of a great part of that which they perceive as of lasting value in their individual existence ... .[9]

A national culture can be interpreted as a discourse which itself is composed of a set of competing discourses bound to the actions of specific social groups. Dominant groups can therefore manufacture identities through the production of meanings about 'the nation' to which we, the public, can relate. Such meanings are harboured in the 'narrative of the nation', which, immersed in mythology, is continuously communicated through the stories, memories and images located in national history, literature and popular culture. The symbolic historical ritual of this narrative is consequently loaded with connotations which constitute the 'shared experiences' (the recollection of both triumphant and disastrous common occurrences) of a people which, by reference to an 'imagined community', imparts meaning on to the nation. Yet, this representation can also become part of a person's habitus and become 'real' rather than just invented.[10]

In summary, a nation should be seen as a cultural as well as a political entity and may be categorized as a symbolic collection of cultural institutions, symbols and representations that generate an imagined community with a specific sense of loyalty and empathy. National identities are therefore ambivalently positioned between the past and the present.[11] As a result, there are simultaneous drives to return to past glories, on a wave of wilful nostalgia, whilst wanting to progress deeper into modernity. Elias writing on this dual nature of national identity in 1976, contended that:

> A striking example in our time is that of the we-image and we-ideal of once-powerful nations whose superiority in relation to others has declined … . The radiance of their collective life as a nation has gone; their power superiority in relation to their groups … is irretrievably lost. Yet the dream of their special charisma is kept alive in a variety of ways – through the teaching of history, the old buildings, masterpieces of the nation in the time of its glory, or through new achievements which seemingly confirm the greatness of the past. For a time, the fantasy shield of their imagined charisma as a leading established group may give a declining nation the strength to carry on … But the discrepancy between the actual and the imagined position of one's group among others can also entail a mistaken assessment of one's resources and, as a consequence, suggest a group strategy in pursuit of a fantasy image of one's own greatness that may lead to self-destruction … The dreams of nations … are dangerous.[12]

This is a particularly interesting historical 'moment' to be studying 'British' national culture and identity, for Britain is currently languishing amidst a 'crisis of identity'. This has been coloured by four inter-related developments. Firstly, Britain is still haunted by the incubus of its imperial past (when Britain was truly 'Great'). Secondly, processes of inward and outward migration have transformed Britain into a multicultural society (primarily through the mass immigration of former colonial subjects). Thirdly, the so-called 'Celtic fringe' (that is, Ireland, Scotland and Wales) is reasserting nationalist claims that are advocating the dissolution of Britain. And, finally, the gradual integration of Britain into a single European Community carries fears surrounding a loss of sovereignty.

This sense of dislocation in contemporary Britain can also be seen to have been accentuated by the effects of globalization. Globalization processes have three main implications for national cultures and identities. Either, they are *weakened* (as a result of increasing global integration); or national and 'local' identities are *strengthened* (in resistance to globalization); or identities are *pluralized* to create new hybrid identifications in place of declining national identities. Issues of national identity are thus implicitly located within the wider 'globalization debate'.[13] Maguire has already employed these ideas to make sense of the connection between cricket and the 'Keating Affair' and the nostalgic response in the sports world to globalization processes.[14]

It has been widely acknowledged that sport and national identity have been closely associated throughout history. Sporting competition arguably provides *the* primary expression of imagined communities; the nation becoming more 'real' in the domain of sport. Particular sports have often come to symbolise the nation – for example, the 'quintessential Englishness' of cricket is frequently referred to. Likewise, in Wales, rugby union is viewed as a central linchpin of what it means to be Welsh.

National and Sporting Identity in the British Isles

National identity is often erroneously associated with the notion of an ethnically 'pure' populace. However, most modern nation-states are cultural hybrids. For example, the history of Britain includes Celtic, Roman, Saxon and Norman invasions – each of which brought with it attempts to impose a more unified cultural hegemony. Today, the predominant, Anglo-centric, view of Britain (the product of an effective hegemony of English culture) tends to obscure the identities of Wales, Scotland and Ireland into an amorphous 'Celtic fringe' and inflate the 'English' identity to British dimensions. Despite this, and the differences (in terms of language, common law, education and religion) between the 'Home Nations', there is some evidence for a 'British' identity.[15]

The British Isles, however, is far from being a homogenous sports region and has instead a complex sporting identity. For example, at the Olympic Games athletes from the British Isles either compete for Great Britain or Ireland; on the soccer pitch there are teams representing England, Scotland,

Wales, Northern Ireland and the Republic of Ireland. In rugby union, it is significant that the Irish (essentially a divided nation) compete as a united nation-state against the English, Scottish and Welsh. As a consequence of this the 'southern Irish' also become eligible to represent Great Britain (of which they are not politically part) if selected to play in what is more usually referred to as the 'British Lions' touring team. It is appropriate to note, however, that this team should be known as the 'Great British and Irish Lions'.[16]

The significance of sport for national identity has not been overlooked by a former Prime Minister of the United Kingdom. Writing in the foreword to *Sport: Raising The Game* John Major observed that:

> Sport is a central part of Britain's national heritage. We invented the majority of the world's great sports. And most of those we did not invent, we codified and helped to popularise throughout the world. It could be argued that nineteenth century Britain was the cradle of a leisure revolution every bit as significant as the agricultural and industrial revolutions we launched in the century before. Sport is a binding force between generations and across borders. But, by a miraculous paradox, it is at the same time one of the defining characteristics of nationhood and of local pride. We should cherish it for both those reasons.[17]

This paradox was neatly displayed in terms of rugby union in a speech made to his players by Carwyn James, coach of the 1971 British Lions, before their departure for New Zealand:

> First and foremost, it is imperative that you be your own man. I want you to be not as you are perceived in your office, but as in your own home. I don't want you Irish to pretend to be English, or English to be Celts, or Scotsmen to be anything less than Scots. Yet Scots must make bosom buddies of Englishmen, Irish of Welshmen, everybody of everybody – yet at the same time the Irish must remain ideologists off the field and, on it fighters like Kilkenny cats; the English must keep their upper lips stiff and just be superior, the Scots be dour as well as radical, and the Welsh continue to be as bloody-minded as their history demands.[18]

His speech encapsulates the contradictions at play regarding identity politics in the British Isles. He is asking for four very different, and unique, national cultures to remain true to their respective stereotypical heritages whilst simultaneously all integrating for the common good as a 'United' sporting Kingdom.

Sport is clearly an arena where personal identities can be both examined and established. Since the development of sports into important national phenomena in the late Victorian era (1870–1914), they have been closely bound to the invention of traditions that connect past and present national identifications. Sport has therefore become an important conduit for a sense of collective resentment and popular consciousness and has been used by different groups (be they established, emergent or outsider) to maintain or challenge identities.

Within the British Isles, the 'Celtic fringe' has employed sport in various ways as a means of asserting their own identities. In the late nineteenth century, Irish cultural nationalists, eager to reclaim their cultural identity and forge a new Irish nation, rejected 'British' sports and established their own Gaelic games under the auspices of the Gaelic Athletic Association (formed in 1884).[19] In contrast, the Welsh and the Scottish have used traditional 'British' sports to challenge the political and economic dominance of England by trying to beat them at their own game(s). For example, in rugby union the Calcutta Cup is played annually between Scotland and the 'auld enemy'. Indeed, rugby union also provides one of the main sources of 'I/we' identity politics by which the English identify the Welsh, and the Welsh identify themselves. This link between rugby union and national identity is neatly summed up by a comment made by a former Scottish international, Gordon Brown, in the prelude to a World Cup match between Scotland and England: 'The people see this game as more than a rugby match. This is about life and politics in Scotland, the poll tax and Whitehall rule. Even the players say, while they like to beat anyone, even Japan, and love to beat the Welsh or Irish, they live to beat the English.'[20]

In addition, it was no coincidence that the Scottish Rugby Union adopted 'The Flower of Scotland' (in place of 'God Save the Queen') as their national anthem in 1990. This move not only provides an illustration of Celtic revival but, with lyrics such as '… but we can still rise now and be the nation again …', also serves to reinforce a strong sense of Scottish nationhood. The impact made by this adopted anthem was illustrated in the autobiography of Bill McLaren, the BBC's distinctively Scottish voice of rugby, who documented the build-up to the 1990 Calcutta Cup match between Scotland and England at Murrayfield thus:

> … and then came the moment that Scots will never forget – the sight of Scotland's fifteen joining with the fifty-three thousand-strong crowd in the most inspiring rendering of 'Flower of Scotland' that one ever could imagine. It was quite overwhelming … [and] I have to admit to a feeling of high emotion and intense national pride … It seemed as if the whole of Scotland was united in anthem behind the national side … [and] it certainly stirred the blood of every Scot.[21]

The work of Jarvie and Walker provides us with a less emotional and more detached assessment of the impact of sport on Scottish national identity.[22] They investigate whether the role of sport in the development of national habitus is either ephemeral (lasting only for the duration of the encounter), or of a more deeply-rooted nature. Whether sport functions in a transient or more long-lasting manner remains an open question. Nevertheless, there is some evidence for a degree of cross-transference between sport and other aspects of national culture. For example, the celebration, and general rise in awareness, of Scottish nationhood has been fuelled by recent Hollywood films – most notably *Braveheart* (which follows the story of the famous Scottish warrior-patriot, William Wallace). Indeed, the imagery of this film (which is centred around the Scots defeating the English army in the late thirteenth and early fourteenth century) has recently been used as a rallying cry to motivate both the Scottish rugby team before the 1996 Calcutta Cup match and the soccer team prior to playing England in Euro 96.

Another example occurred in a highly-publicized incident in the dressing room prior to the 1991 Rugby Union World Cup Quarter-Final against France when the English team were instructed to listen to a recording of Sir Laurence Olivier's recitation of Shakespeare's Henry V's Agincourt speech in order to motivate themselves suitably for the occasion. The English team were being asked to play, quite literally, 'For God, England, Harry and St George!' This clearly evoked past military glories with the players being asked to maintain the invented tradition, and seemingly divine rite, of defeating the French at war. These connections, so graphically made between the rugby pitch and the battlefield, illustrate just how important sport, and in this case rugby union, can be as an arena for national pride and patriotic sentiment.

This significance was reinforced by a Scottish rugby player's words before the semi-final against England in the same competition:

> It was not, said one smiling Scottish player yesterday, who thought it better not to be named, so much to do with rugby but nationhood. 'Our soccer team have not done much lately' he said. 'So I dare say we have been chosen in this match to right the ills of Thatcherism, the poll tax and Westminster government. You might say the people see us playing for the rugby-loving Celt Kinnock against the cricket-loving, po-faced English government.'[23]

Clearly, rugby union in the British Isles represents a unique arena for the construction, and contestation, of national identities. The sport provides a cultural paradox: juxtaposing the Anglo-Saxon English against the Celtic nations in the annual Five Nations Championship, whilst also uniting them as British 'Lions' every four years. Rugby union thus provides an illustration of the complex tension-balances at play between both 'British' national cultures and local-global sport processes.

The Globalization Debate

As highlighted previously, issues surrounding the concept of national identity are intimately connected with the 'globalization debate'. Hall states that: '... "globalization" refers to those processes, operating on a global scale, which cut across national boundaries, integrating and connecting communities and organizations in new space–time combinations, making the world in reality and in experience more interconnected.'[24] It is clear that globalization processes are uneven, very long-term in character, transcend the traditional boundaries of nation-states and intensify global interconnectedness. The modern era has witnessed an intensification of globalization and it has thus become increasingly difficult to comprehend events at the local or national level without reference to these processes.

Globalization is often seen to imply world-wide cultural integration and the weakening of the nation-state. However, globalization can be seen to consist of a number of counter-tendencies all in simultaneous operation. These include: homogeneity (commonality) versus heterogeneity (separation), integration versus disintegration, and unity versus diversity. So, whilst globalization *has* undoubtedly been associated with the long-term deterioration of the nation-state (by undermining its coherence, autonomy and authority), it has also worked to reawaken 'local' identities, fragment societies and stimulate the search for new identities. It is more usually the case for local, regional and national communities to react to globalization processes by wilfully clinging tighter to the mythology, nostalgia and tradition which underpin their identity. This type of reawakening can be seen writ large in Spain where provincial ethnic groups have long sought to re-establish themselves, not least through the medium of sport, as 'national' territories. Within Spanish football there is an intense historical, and deep-rooted, rivalry between those clubs representing 'separatist' communities such as Barcelona (Catalonia) and Athletic Bilbao (the Basque Provinces), and those (such as Real Madrid) seen to be more representative of the unified Spanish state.[25]

As the world has become more interconnected then so the cultures of the world have come to coexist in a more interdependent fashion. Numerous multi-causal, long-term and open-ended (or 'blind') processes have intertwined and have become part of a complex intermeshing of networks of interdependence. These networks are coloured by a series of fluctuating power balances between classes, genders and ethnicities. Such global interdependencies create a complex, dynamic and unplanned global condition where cultures are competing in a complex contest between 'sameness' and 'difference'. The unintended nature of this process corresponds, to some degree, with the idea of 'disjunctures' that Appadurai notes occur between global flows.[26] The mutual conflict between sameness and difference can be expressed in terms of the twin figurational concepts of *diminishing contrasts and increasing varieties*. Maguire eludes that:

> Globalization is best understood as a balance and blend between diminishing contrasts and increasing varieties, a commingling of cultures and attempts by more established groups to control and regulate access to global flows. Global sport development can be understood in the same terms: that is, in the late twentieth century we are witnessing the globalization of sports and of the increasing diversity of sports cultures.[27]

On first impressions sport seems to reinforce the international diminishing of contrasts with numerous global events which produce a 'coming together' of the world. Few could fail to see the significance of events such as the Olympic Games or the various World Cup competitions. However, the close affiliation sport maintains with national cultures and identities also means that sport (which even in these global events is fundamentally 'national' in nature) undermines, and will continue to undermine, any regional political integration. For example, at a European level, the Scots still 'live' to beat the English and the emotions expressed after the Danish soccer team's victory over Germany in the European Championship were mirrored by those after the 'No' result in Denmark's referendum on the Maastricht Agreement.

There are, of course, some counter-tendencies in operation which are working towards the supra-nationalization of sport in order to diffuse the 'problem' of nationalism. The gradual emergence of a European sporting identity provides an example of this new 'layer' to global sport. European teams now compete, most notably in golf's Ryder and Solheim Cup competitions, against the United States. A European team also entered the Athletics World Cup (not to be confused with either the World Championships or the Olympics), a competition based on geographical regions.

In contrast, there is also evidence of counter-cultural trends developing at a regional, or ethnic, level as a result of the resurgence of various traditional 'folk' games. These movements, often regarded as relics of the past, illustrate the tensions which are developing between 'sameness' and 'difference' in the current sporting milieu. The revival, and growing recognition, of such pastimes (often positioned within cultural festivals) help in the process of reaffirming ethnic identity. Examples of such movements include the Inuit Games (popularly known as 'The Eskimo Olympics') from Alaska, the Maccabiah Games (the Olympic Games of the Jewish people), Friesland dyke jumping, the folk games of Gotland, and, in the British context, the Gaelic games of Ireland and the Highland Games of Scotland. So, in this current phase of globalization, there are a series of 'double-bind', or contradictory, processes in operation so that at various points in space and time national identities may be strengthened, weakened or increased in variety, whilst differences between cultures may lessen.

The development of sport, as previously mentioned, can be implicitly linked to globalization processes. Since the mid-nineteenth century organized sport has undergone expansion on a truly global scale. The establishment of international sports organizations (such as FIFA), international and global competitions (such as the Olympic Games), international rules and the global migration of athletic talent all illustrate the globalization of sport. Likewise, just as globalization processes in general have accelerated in recent decades, so has the globalization of sport with an increasing number of sports (such as rugby union) inaugurating their own specific World Cup competitions.

As nationalism gained momentum (alongside sport) during, what Robertson terms, globalization's 'take-off' phase (the 1870s to the mid-1920s), certain traditions began to be employed as symbols of national identity.[28] This model of globalization was developed and first applied to sport by Maguire.[29] All these symbols, such as the national anthem and national flag, were summarily integrated into sport. This interplay between nationalism and sport was not surprising for, as Hobsbawm stated: 'the imagined community of millions seems more real as a team of eleven named people'.[30]

During times of intensified globalization (that is, the post-war era), which can 'blur' national cultures and identities, sports may act as important 'anchors of meaning' for the people of a nation. The association of sporting occasions with a specific place or season provide counterpoints to change and also a sense of stability. In addition, a sporting victory can induce a degree of status and security by providing a brief, but powerful, 'feel-good factor' for the nation. The ability of sporting encounters to uplift the nation, even in its darkest hour, has not been ignored by politicians who can 'use' triumphs on the sports field to manipulate national culture and identity. This type of 'identity politics' can, for example, limit the damage of political disasters by diverting the public's attention to sporting successes (and such diversions are made even easier if the national leader is a follower of sport and is frequently seen at the more important international sporting events held in his country). That said, there is a flip-side to the use of sport by politics. It may not be so easy for the same politicians to escape any association with sporting disasters which may (and are likely to) befall national teams at some stage. The media are quick to compare such disasters with political ineptitude and politicians are likely to find themselves the butt of satirical headlines and cartoons.[31]

This double bind of triumph and disaster has recently been exposed in the nostalgic response by English society (and the media in particular) to the economic, political, social and sporting disasters that have afflicted the nation. The main dimensions of nostalgic discourse include: a departure from the 'homefulness' of some golden era; a sense of historical decline; a sense of less individual freedom; and a sense of less personal wholeness and certainty. With reference to British society, these elements can be illustrated in terms of the following: the longing to return to some halcyon age when 'Britannia' ruled the waves; the loss of Empire; the emergence of multiculturalism; and European integration. Many of these elements have been evident in the rhetoric of John Major's speeches who, during his recent 'Back to Basics' campaign, frequently recounted a specific 'past' and the essential traits of 'Englishness'.[32]

Over the past decade a revamped, more intense 'Englishness' (modelled on the image of the Little Englander) has manifested itself in the United Kingdom. This forms a strong defensive response to European integration, the pluralization of national culture and the re-assertiveness of the 'Celtic fringe'. This reaction was exemplified during the Falklands conflict where the Empire was seen to militarily strike back.[33] Evidence of this more aggressive Englishness can be found in the context of sport in the introduction of the 'Tebbit Test' and the increasingly jingoistic celebrations surrounding any sporting success. In a new era when the English were being beaten by their perceived cultural inferiors at their 'own' sports, one of society's few havens of hope lay in a form of patriotic nostalgia. These developments, combined with the link between rugby union and identity politics, are neatly encapsulated in the cartoon on the following page.

England's 45–29 semi-final defeat by New Zealand in the 1995 Rugby Union World Cup prompted this cartoon which illustrates England attempting to reassert herself (militarily and politically) over a Commonwealth cousin who has beaten the Mother Country at her own game. Memories of the Falklands War are evoked as the ministers are gathered in the war room positioning the *British* armed forces ready to launch an attack on New Zealand. It implies that going to war will not only avenge the defeat on the rugby pitch but will also help promote collective national sentiment and political popularity. On closer inspection of the cartoon, the importance of the result of this match is further highlighted as it appears on the front page of the newspaper being held by the figure representing Douglas Hurd.

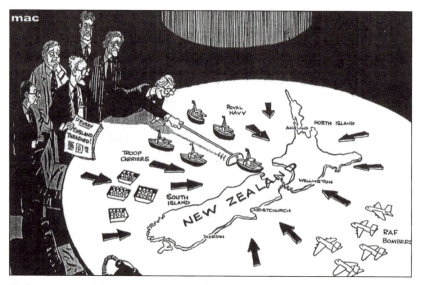

'Before we go ahead, Prime Minister, are you absolutely sure declaring war on New Zealand will make us popular again?'

Source: *Daily Mail* (19 June 1995).

Themes in the Media Representation of British Rugby Union

This section focuses on the textual analysis of reports relating to rugby union and national identity located in *The Times* between 1945 and 1975. Two particularly interesting areas of investigation that materialised during this analysis were: the development of rugby union as an increasingly strong indicator of national culture, politics and identity; and the use of national stereotypes, symbols, invented traditions and military imagery in the media representation of rugby union.

In general terms, it is clear that during this period, more frequent and extensive references were increasingly made to both rugby union and sport in general. Throughout the 1940s and 1950s reports on international fixtures were typically restricted to a column approximately six inches in length. By the end of the period whole pages were being devoted to rugby union. In addition, linkages between sport and national identity began to develop (most commonly through the consistent use of stereotypes relating both to the nation and to the national teams' playing styles) both in and out of the sports pages of the newspaper. Since the 1960s, an increasing number of 'preview' articles began to appear within the sports section and this increase was mirrored by increasingly more 'nationalist' commentary surrounding rugby union (in particular related to Ireland, Scotland and Wales). This increasing amount of preview coverage allowed both the sport to be reported in greater detail, and for more links to be fostered between rugby and national identity. For example, in the period 1945–55 of the 81 articles listed in *The Times Index* which dealt with issues of national identity, 64 per cent were found to be related to rugby. This proportion increased to 85 per cent (of 71 articles) in the period 1955–65 and was in excess of 87 per cent (of 70 articles) in the period 1965–75.[34]

Some issues, largely depicted as so-called (post)modern afflictions, were also in evidence in the early post-Second World War period. One feature of this period, for instance, was the recurring perception of crisis and a dislocation of identity. Winston Churchill made reference to the British 'crisis of identity' in the late 1940s and also demonstrated how easily England and Great Britain can become 'one'. At a luncheon speech, he said: 'How stands poor old Britain – I nearly said poor old England? How is she going to get out of her troubles and resume her place at the summit of the world not as master but as faithful servant or guide …'[35] In addition, the link between Britain's 'crisis of identity' and globalization (and specifically Europeanization) processes was addressed by none other than Sir Oswald Mosley, when he observed that: 'In Britain it was the duty of everyone to...rise above the bitterness of the old national divisions. The nations of yesterday must make way for the nation of Europe.'[36] These general sentiments have also been found to underpin discussions related specifically to sport and, for example the lack of British success in the London Olympics of 1948. The perceived crisis in modern British sport and the 'moral panic' associated with it has clearly been debated for many years. The current discussions and feelings of sporting inferiority, reawoken by a similar lack of 'gold medal success' in the 1996 Atlanta Olympics, are therefore nothing new.

Attention here, however, is given to issues relating specifically to rugby union. One of the principal invented traditions in British rugby union is the notion of the 'Triple Crown'. Although there is no trophy for winning a Triple Crown, the accolade is bestowed when one of the Home Nations defeats the other three in any one season. This was first achieved in 1883 by England and since then it has become a very 'real' element of the annual Five Nations Championship. This 'invention', evoking images of the monarchy and a 'United' Kingdom, was reinforced in print when it was reported as being 'one of those mythical, unofficial honours peculiar to rugby union … in Great Britain' and as being 'purely imaginative but immensely coveted'.[37]

In the following sections we identify three broad themes that have emerged in relation to rugby union and national identity. These are:

questions of cultural struggle and identity politics; national and sporting stereotypes; and military metaphors and the vocabulary of war.

(i) Questions of Cultural Struggle and Identity Politics

As previously mentioned, in some specific instances politicians use sporting successes for their own political purposes. In contrast, sporting disasters can expose them to media ridicule and caricature. The blending of political and sporting disasters was very evident in a cartoon (on following page) published in *The Times* during the 1995 Rugby World Cup where there coincided a heavy defeat of the England team with internal strife in the Tory Cabinet. The cartoon neatly alludes to a previous match in the tournament (the Quarter-Final versus Australia) in which one player in particular (the English fly-half, Rob Andrew, wearing Number 10) achieved notoriety by winning the game with a last-minute drop-kick. However, this success was followed by a comprehensive defeat by New Zealand in the Semi-Final, and this coincided with the questioning of John Major's stewardship of Number 10 Downing Street which then came into sharper focus. In this cartoon, Major is cast in the role of the defeated (and now belittled and ineffectual) Rob Andrew.

In the 30-year period studied, the rise of Welsh nationalism, as a response to an increasingly influential England, best demonstrated the style of the more general Celtic resurgence which was beginning to gather momentum.[38] Indeed the debate surrounding the Welsh language over this period represents a study, in microcosm, of how the Celtic and Gaelic peoples have perceived themselves as being overrun by English and Anglo-Saxon culture: '... powerful forces were trying to reduce Wales to the status of a region ... It was a time of terrible crisis in the history of our language and our nation ... On every side we have seen merciless enemies threatening our heritage ... We are a sick nation ...'[39] This debate on cultural imperialism should not be seen in isolation. Anglo-Celtic tensions are also expressed writ large on the rugby field. Perhaps the most powerful example of this is the pre-match speech delivered by Phil Bennett, the captain of the Welsh rugby team, in 1977: 'These English you're just going out to meet have taken our coal, our water, our steel: they buy our houses and live in them a fortnight a year. Gareth, they're taking your very life, your fishing, boy, by buying up all the fishing rights on our beautiful rivers. Down the centuries these English have exploited and pillaged us; and we're playing them this afternoon boys.'[40] This historic tension and rivalry between England and Wales can also be demonstrated by the 'traditional booing of the English National Anthem' which had become an accepted practice at matches between the two countries and the report that stressed that '... England are *the* enemies of Wales at this game ...'.[41]

Source: The Times (20 June 1995).

Although there were few direct connections made between rugby and politics for the majority of this period, the intertwining between rugby union and politics in Ireland was exemplified in a significant article entitled 'De Valera Comes Out for Rugby'.[42] This juxtaposed the double-bind of sport and politics, and showed that the nation's Premier (or 'Taoiseach') valued rugby union above 'traditional' Gaelic sports. It was reported that:

> Mr de Valera, Prime Minister of Eire, took sides for the first time on the controversial issue of Gaelic football versus Rugby football when he told a surprised audience last night: 'There is no football to compare with Rugby. If all sporting young Irishmen played Rugby we would have a team which would beat not only England and Wales but also France and the whole of them together ... I have not seen a Rugby game since 1913, because I do not want it being raised as a political matter and having rows kicked up about it, but I will not deny that I listen in to Rugby matches.'[43]

Peter West, Rugby Correspondent to *The Times* in 1972, further confirmed the importance of rugby to the Irish nation when he made reference to the nationalist and religious tensions in evidence there. He wrote that: 'Nothing, it is said, so unites the Irish among themselves or with the English as a game of rugby, and the hope must be that for a brief period at Twickenham this afternoon the troublous times across the water can be forgotten.'[44] These examples illustrate that rugby union, amongst other sports, has affected identity politics in the British Isles since the Second World War. It has provided the Celtic and Gaelic peoples with regular opportunities to challenge the cultural hegemony of the English. Politicians have also been keen to associate themselves with success on the rugby pitch with, most notably, the Taoiseach of Eire, identifying the potential to unite the Irish nation through rugby union.

(ii) National and Sporting Stereotypes

In addition to these trends, the exploration and collation of media stereotypes relating to playing styles and national character can also shed important light on the relationship between rugby union and national identity. A summary of some of the most frequently used national stereotypes for each of the four 'Home Nations' is illustrated in Figure 3.[45] These national stereotypes were also carried over into the reporting of British Lions matches, especially when used to define an individual player's style (for example, '... that magical Welsh fly-half ...'). However, what is unclear at this stage in the research is the degree to which distinctly 'British' playing styles were identified by the media and to what degree an English identity was transposed on to a 'British' sporting team.

From the results charted in Figure 3 it is evident that the English tended to be portrayed far differently from the three other 'Celtic' teams of the British Isles. English national stereotyping revolved around 'Anglo-Saxon' qualities of courage, such as being 'stout-hearted'[46] and 'traditional' notions of chivalry and gentlemanly conduct. Throughout the thirty year period, England were characterized as a strong defensive team with a 'never-say-die [Dunkirk] spirit'.[47]

The stereotyping of the 'Celtic' teams appeared to endorse different and more 'tribal' qualities. Whereas English national teams were typically viewed in mechanistic and orderly terms, the Irish, Scottish and Welsh were seen as more 'passionate', 'tigerish' but also 'erratic'. However, differences were reported between the three national styles of the Celtic teams. The Irish, with their 'native flair', were typically seen as the wildest and most tigerish of the Celts. For example, a reference was made comparing the Irish to Kipling's 'Fuzzy Wuzzy', in which it was noted that, for both '... 'e's all 'ot sand an' ginger when alive an 'e's generally shammin' when he's dead'.[48] The Scots were perceived as more dour and less imaginative than the Irish. The Welsh, in contrast, were consistently praised for 'maintaining a stout fighting spirit in adversity'.[49] and being the most skilful and naturally gifted (especially their 'magical' fly-halves). This mystical nature of Welsh

FIGURE 3
NATIONAL STEREOTYPES AS USED IN THE REPORTING OF INTERNATIONAL
RUGBY UNION MATCHES IN THE TIMES (1945–75)

Criteria	England	Ireland	Scotland	Wales
National Stereotypes	'English' courage Anglo-Saxon old-fashioned fine spirit gentlemanly chivalrous	emerald commotion Hibernian native flair lucky	fanatical remorseless dauntless fiery gallant	unquenchable spirit sorcerers indefatigable magical
Emotional Character	stout-hearted orderly determined strong resistant intelligent tough dependable honest purposeful steadiness competent	adventurous zealous belligerent tigerish plucky exuberant opportunistic quick-witted crafty	stamina eager determined shrewd strong lively thorough	daring truculence adroit wild creative inventive adaptive poetic quick-witted shrewd
Playing Styles	workman-like mechanical well-drilled computerized uncomplicated efficient	collective enthusiasm furious swift clumsy relentless enterprising spasmodic disruptive explosive	worried like terriers furious erratic speed dash dour virtuosity unimaginative	ingenious versatility individual flair swift spectral dynamic enterprising adventurous intimidating rhythmic artistry
Metaphors of War	aggressive	war-like tribesmen marauding violent green devils blazing ardour	fighting spirit rampaging courageous fierce	fighters ferocious violent

fly-halves was illustrated in a report which made particular reference to the
'... spectral glide ...' of Barry John.[50] His qualities were further extolled, in
the same article, in the following manner: 'As he floats hither and thither
through opposition, with little hip undulations, it is so smooth that you
forget that in fact he is deftly side-stepping. John's try on Saturday showed
a sweep of artistry that recalled the perfect range, from highest coloratura to
deep contratto, of ... a Mascagni aria.'[51] Whilst there were few occasions
when references to any of these stereotypes were extensively dealt with this
should not be seen to detract from their power or significance. In some
instances a single word can provide a specific example of a more general
process regarding national character. Consequently, this reportage of
stereotypes should be seen as a 'way into' the larger discourse of national
identity and identity politics at play within the British Isles. Within this
preliminary investigation into the divide between mediated Anglo-Saxon
and Celtic rugby characteristics, one can begin to conceptualize a wider
societal demarcation in the British Isles between an 'English' hegemonic
core and a marginalized Celtic periphery.

(iii) Military Metaphors and the Vocabulary of War

The use of military metaphors and the vocabulary of war in the reporting of
rugby internationals also increased in both frequency and variety during this
period. A typical example, referring to the annual England-France match,
stated '... there were more Frenchmen at Twickenham on Saturday than
William brought over with him in 1066, but this time it was the English who
won the battle'.[52]

Here reference is made, and the match likened to, the last time England
was invaded and its inhabitants defeated at the Battle of Hastings. This
combination of war-like imagery and tradition is also illustrated in the
following report which makes reference to the defeating of the English in
battle, 'in soundly drubbing the invading Sassenachs ... [Scotland] regained
the Calcutta Cup'.[53] Military references used to depict the playing styles of
the Celtic nations frequently made reference to that people's perceived tribal
and military heritage. For example, the following report was written about
the Irish after a match against Wales: '... [the] Irish forwards charged about
like dedicated, warlike eastern tribesmen ... [in] ferocious emerald waves
of whirling arms and legs ... [and] frantic fandangos in the loose ...'.[54] The
war-like character of the Irish was also recounted in similarly graphic
language six years later: 'Perhaps inspired by "The Minstrel Boy" [played]
on the pipes during the interval, Ireland girded on their fathers' swords and
went to war'.[55] This language clearly evokes a sense of primitive tribalism
and emphasizes the link between a 'war-like' people participating in a sport
which is characterized by a large degree of physical contact. In another

article this imagery was effectively combined with a musical metaphor to evoke Welsh rugby crowds' passion (and that of the nation) for song: '... with Wales mounting a mighty assault ..., there welled up from 60,000 voices, in spontaneous harmony and uninterruptedly, without punctuation even by applause, the matchless strains of 'Land Of My Fathers', swelling in crescendo with each minute.'[56] This report neatly captures how two of the defining elements of Welsh national culture, choral and rugby skills, come together in unison on match day. This double dose of 'Welshness' takes on added significance as it occurs in an arena which openly celebrates the distinctive Welsh emblem (the dragon), flag and anthem.

The coverage of rugby union in *The Times* clearly uses the language of war as a signifier for the sport. This language is used to reinforce the distinctions between the more tribal 'Celtic' nations and the 'Anglo-Saxon' English. Implicit connections are also made with other traditional aspects of popular culture so that rugby is seen to exist in combination with, for example, choral singing in Wales. Throughout this section we have tried to demonstrate a study, in microcosm, of the media's reporting of the link between rugby union and national identity in the British Isles since 1945. We have looked in particular at issues related to cultural struggle and identity politics, stereotyping, and the use of the language of war. In the following section, we bring together this substantive evidence and discuss more general trends which have been identified.

Concluding Remarks

The newspaper reports from *The Times* suggest, in cameo, several interesting themes and trends (many of which have been discussed in the previous section). Sport and rugby union have clearly become more central to issues of national identity during the period in question. Not only were more references being made to national identity in sports reports but, by the 1970s, there was more mention of sport outside of the sports pages in conjunction with issues of national identity. Rugby union was starting to become an important part of identity politics at this time and it is arguable that it has become a powerful indicator of internal 'British' tensions. There has been a general increase in national symbolism within the sport and the importance afforded to it by the media. This was demonstrated in the creation of the Rugby Union World Cup (inaugurated in 1987) which marked the development of the sport into a global game.

As yet it is not possible to determine whether the relationship between rugby union and national identity was either a media 'response' or a media 'function' (adapted from the notions of media representation and reflection identified by Hall) in this period.[57] In other words, is the increase in the reporting of issues related to national identity in a rugby context a valid reflection of wider societal feelings, or are the media asserting these wider tensions onto rugby union? Tentative conclusions would suggest that up to the latter stages of the period under investigation, the relationship was more a media response than a media function. However, in today's media, the relationship has undoubtedly shifted along the continuum towards becoming more a media function – this is especially the case amongst some of the infamous British tabloid newspapers with their sensationalist headlines. This increased awareness and use of nationalist sentiment in the media clearly merits further investigation.

Recent developments within the sport also pose interesting questions relating to the centrality of rugby union within the 'national' culture(s) of the British Isles and to questions of national identity. Since the beginning of the 1995/96 domestic season we have witnessed the de-amateurization and formal professionalization of the sport. This clearly has major implications for the place of the once staunchly amateur sport of rugby within the national habitus of the Home Nations. Could it be that the increasing commodification of the game will see players showing more pride in their earnings and their club, and less in their country? This tension can be illustrated in the ongoing power struggle between the English Professional Rugby Union Clubs and the RFU for control of rugby in England.[58] Can professional rugby union nestle as comfortably in the national habitus as the traditionally amateur variant of the game?

In the 1996/97 season we have also witnessed two new movements gathering momentum in British rugby union. Firstly, there has been an increasingly frequent swapping of rugby codes by league and union players. Due to rugby league's rescheduling as a mainly summer sport, it has become possible for some of the sport's better players to participate in both codes. The list of recent 'cross-code' players includes Martin Offiah (London Broncos and Bedford), Henry Paul (Wigan and Bath), and Gary Connolly (Wigan and Harlequins).[59] Secondly, with increased financial backing, there has been a dramatic increase in the recruitment of foreign migrant labour to English club rugby. This new cosmopolitanism is best demonstrated at Saracens whose officials, with the £2.5 million invested by Nigel Wray, have signed Michael Lynagh (from Australia), Philippe Sella (France) and Francois Pienaar (South Africa).[60]

In addition, Europeanization processes are also threatening the existence of both the Five Nations Championships (by inviting other European national teams such as the Italians and Romanians to join) and British Lions tours (by the introduction of a European club competition which, in conjunction with more overseas tours by national sides, would leave no more time for Lions tours).[61] An already packed rugby calendar is becoming progressively saturated with more fixtures being scheduled for outside the traditional 'season'. These additional matches are all competing for the attentions of rugby union players who, now as professionals, are being asked to play all year round. These processes indicate that rugby union is a game in flux and whatever happens in the next few years will undoubtedly have profound implications for the centrality of the sport within the national cultures of England, Scotland, Ireland and Wales.

NOTES

1. The 'Home' Unions refer to the governing bodies (or Rugby Unions) of England, Ireland, Scotland and Wales.
2. The conceptual framework for this paper is based largely on Maguire's previous work on globalization (sportization, wilful nostalgia and links with the media/sport production complex), national identity (identity politics), the re-working of Eliasian concepts such as 'diminishing contrasts and increasing varieties' and the use of personal pronouns in textual analysis. For a more detailed discussion of these concepts see Joseph Maguire, 'Globalisation, Sport Development, and the Media/Sport Production Complex', *Sport Science Review*, Vol.2, No.1 (1993), pp.29–47; Joseph Maguire, 'Globalisation, Sport and National Identities: "The Empire Strikes Back"?', *Loisir et Société*, Vol.16, No.2 (1993), pp.293–322; Joseph Maguire, 'Sport, Identity Politics, and Globalisation: Diminishing Contrasts and Increasing Varieties', *Sociology of Sport Journal*, Vol.11, No.4 (1994), pp.398–427; Joseph Maguire, 'Sport, National Identities and Globalisation', in J. Bale (ed.), *Community, Landscape and Identity: Horizons in a Geography of Sports* (Keele, 1994).
3. N. Elias and J.L. Scotson, *The Established and the Outsiders: A Sociological Enquiry into Community Problems* (London, 1994), p.xxxvii.
4. See also J. Maguire, 'Globalisation, Sport Development, and the Media/Sport Production Complex', *Sport Science Review*, Vol.2, No.1 (1993), pp.29–47; Maguire, 'Globalisation, Sport ...', loc. cit.; Maguire, 'Sport, Identity Politics ...', loc. cit.; Maguire, 'Sport, National Identities ...', loc. cit., pp.71–93; Maguire, 'Blade Runners: Canadian Migrants, Ice Hockey, and the Global Sports Process', *Journal of Sport and Social Issues*, Vol.20, No.3 (1996), pp.335–60; J. Maguire and J.C. Tuck, 'Pride and Patriotism: Rugby Union and National Identity in a United Sporting Kingdom', unpublished paper presented at the International Sociology of Sport Association Conference 'Sport: Social Problems and Social Movements', Rome, 1995.
5. S. Mennell, 'The Formation of We-Images: A Process Theory', in C. Calhoun (ed.), *Social Theory and the Politics of Identity* (Oxford, 1994), pp.175–97.
6. The concept of identity and its relationship with the nation has also been extensively investigated by other authors such as W. Bloom, *Personal Identity, National Identity and International Relations* (Cambridge, 1990); A.D. Smith, *National Identity* (Harmondsworth, 1991); and S. Hall, D. Held and A. McGrew (eds.), *Modernity and Its Futures* (Cambridge, 1992).
7. Maguire, 'Globalisation, Sport ...'.
8. A. Klein, 'Borderline Treason: Nationalisms and Baseball on the Texas-Mexican Border', *Journal of Sport and Social Issues*, Vol.20, No.3 (1996), pp.296–313; A. Bairner, 'Sportive Nationalism and Nationalist Politics: A Comparative Analysis of Scotland, the Republic of Ireland and Sweden', *Journal of Sport and Social Issues*, Vol.20, No.3 (1996), pp.314–35; E. Hobsbawm and T. Ranger (eds.), *The Invention of Tradition* (Cambridge, 1983).
9. N. Elias, *The Germans* (Cambridge, 1996), p.352.
10. The notion of the nation as an 'imagined community' was first employed by Benedict Anderson. See his *Imagined Communities* (London, 1983). 'Habitus' is used here in the

Eliasian sense of the term and refers to the deeply embodied emotions which are socially learned and become so sedimented in the sub-conscious that they become 'second nature' to the individual.

11. Tom Nairn, in his *The Break-Up of Britain: Crisis and Neo-Nationalism* (London, 1977), writes extensively on the 'crisis of identity' in Britain and links the desire to return to the past with the 'Janus-face' of nationalism.

12. Elias and Scotson, *The Established and the Outsiders*, p.xliii.

13. The 'globalization debate' involves two broad schools of thought, those who favour a single causal dynamic (such as Wallerstein, Sklair and Rosenau) to explain the phenomenon and those who purport to a multi-causal logic (such as Gilpin, Giddens and Robertson). These 'schools' are both catalogued in Hall *et al., Modernity and Its Futures*. Figurational sociology takes its place in the 'multi-causal' school.

14. Maguire, "Globalisation, Sport ..."'; Maguire, 'Sport, Identity Politics ...'.

15. It should be remembered that the 'British Isles' is composed of England, Scotland, Ireland and Wales whereas 'the United Kingdom' includes England, Scotland, Wales and Northern Ireland and 'Great Britain' pertains to England, Scotland and Wales. 'British' identity is therefore a complex, and somewhat confusing construct.

16. The British Lions are a rugby union team who tour the southern hemisphere every four years during the summer months and are composed of the best players from all four Home Unions. Their proper name is the British and Irish Lions but this is usually abridged to give the impression of a side which represents Great Britain (that is, not the Republic of Ireland). The existence (and increasing media profile) of a British rugby union team raises questions regarding the degree to which a British identity exists within the sport. This particular theme remains an avenue for further research.

17. Foreword to Department of National Heritage, *Sport: Raising the Game* (London, 1995), p.2.

18. Cited in *The Guardian*, 15 May 1993, p.18.

19. The Gaelic Athletic Association (GAA) is arguably the most important organization in the figuration of sport and Irish identity. Its history has been documented by, amongst others, J. Sugden and A. Bairner, *Sport, Sectarianism and Society in a Divided Ireland* (Leicester, 1993).

20. *The Guardian*, 26 Oct. 1991, p.20.

21. Bill McLaren, *Talking of* Rugby (London,1992), p.210.

22. G. Jarvie and G. Walker (eds.), *Scottish Sport in the Making of the Nation: Ninety Minute Patriots?* (London, 1994).

23. *The Guardian*, 26 Oct. 1991, p.20. See also Maguire, 'Globalisation, Sport ...', pp.293–322.

24. Hall *et al., Modernity and Its Futures*, p.299.

25. J. MacClancy, 'Nationalism at Play: The Basques of Vizcaya and Athletic Bilbao', in J. MacClancy (ed.), *Sport, Identity and Ethnicity* (Oxford, 1996).

26. A. Appadurai, 'Disjuncture and Difference in the Global Cultural Economy', *Theory, Culture and Society*, Vol.7 (1990), pp.207–36.

27. Maguire, 'Globalisation, Sport ...', p.310.

28. R. Robertson, *Globalisation: Social Theory and Global Culture* (London, 1992).

29. Maguire, 'Sport, Identity Politics ... '.

30. Hobsbawm and Ranger, *The Invention of Tradition*, p.143

31. Maguire, 'Sport, Identity Politics ...'.

32. See Maguire, 'Sport, Identity Politics ...'.

33. Maguire, 'Globalisation, Sport ...'.

34. *The Times* was analysed by using *The Times Index* to search for keywords, or 'signifiers', which related to rugby union and issues of national identity. These signifiers were developed, over time, from extensive reviews of literature on the subject in combination with a short pilot study. Whilst the use of such an index did not guarantee that every reference to national identity was found, it did provide us with the most comprehensive 'search tool' available for the newspaper.

35. *The Times*, 28 May 1948, p.4

36. *The Times*, 26 Sept. 1950, p.2.

37. *The Times*, 12 March 1948, p.6; *The Times*, 18 March 1957, p.3.
38. The enigmatic nature of Scottish national identity is investigated by T.C. Smout, 'Perspectives on the Scottsh Identity', *Scottish Affairs*, Vol.6 (1993), pp.101–13.
39. *The Times*, 8 Aug. 1972, p.14. See also Nairn, *The Break-Up of Britain*; L. Colley, *Britons: Forging the Nation 1707–1837* (New Haven, CT, 1992).
40. Cited in *The Guardian*, 2 Feb. 1993, p.18.
41. *The Times*, 24 Oct. 1972, p.17; *The Times*, 22 Jan. 1962, p.4, italics in original.
42. *The Times*, 30 April 1957, p.5.
43. Ibid.
44. *The Times*, 12 Feb. 1972, p.6.
45. The stereotypes listed in Figure 3 represent the most frequently recounted perceptions of the correspondents in *The Times*. These characteristics all appeared at least four times during the course of the period under study. From over 280 international matches involving the Home Nations played in this period, 175 match reports yielded relevant information, and an additional 38 reports made reference to issues related to national identity. Although the proportion of references to stereotypes may not be high, we would argue that their presence in these reports is of some significance.
46. *The Times*, 22 March 1965, p.4.
47. *The Times*, 11 Feb. 1957, p.12.
48. *The Times*, 13 March 1961, p.18.
49. *The Times*, 4 Feb. 1946, p.2.
50. *The Times*, 8 Feb. 1971, p.7.
51. *The Times*, 8 Feb. 1971, p.7.
52. *The Times*, 24 Feb. 1969, p.6.
53. *The Times*, 23 March 1964, p.4.
54. *The Times*, 9 March 1964, p.4
55. *The Times*, 16 March 1970, p.9.
56. *The Times*, 19 Jan. 1959, p.12.
57. S.Hall, 'The Rediscovery of "Ideology": Return of the Repressed in Media Studies', in M. Gurevitch *et al.* (eds.), *Culture, Society and the Media* (London, 1990).
58. The conflict between the English Professional Rugby Union Clubs (headed by Peter Wheeler of Leicester) and the Rugby Football Union (who are represented in this regard by their executive chairman, Cliff Brittle) is a by-product of an amateur game trying to convert to a professional sport. The EPRUC represents the top twenty-four English rugby union clubs and is calling for its players to boycott the RFU by taking 'industrial action' and refusing to play representative rugby for England. An uneasy peace deal was reached prior to England's first Five Nations match in 1997, allowing a full-strength representative side to play Scotland in the Calcutta Cup. The clubs have willingly embraced the new era of professional rugby and are making it work, but the RFU seems reluctant to shed its control (and amateur ideology) too hastily. However, this unrest is likely to continue until the power struggle between the two organizations is finally resolved. Currently, the organization of English rugby seems precariously balanced between a fragile stability and anarchy.
59. The return of rugby league players to the union fold has undoubtedly boosted the strength of the Welsh national side. Traditionally the most vulnerable nation to 'poaching' by the league code, Wales fielded some notable 'returnees' in the squad for their first Five Nations match in 1997, against Scotland. They included: Alan Bateman (formerly of Warrington), Scott Gibbs (St. Helens), Scott Quinnell (Wigan), and Jonathan Davies (Warrington).
60. There has also been a significant movement of players from within the British Isles to England where more commercial opportunities exist. International players such as Doddie Weir and Gary Armstrong (both Scotland) have moved south of the border to Newcastle. The 'exiles' teams such as London Irish have also received a healthy influx from their 'home' nations. Other notable transfers to the English Courage National League include: Joel Stransky (from South Africa) to Leicester, Federico Mendez (Argentina) to Bath, Laurent Cabannes and Thierry Lacroix (France) to Harlequins, and Shem Tatupu (Western Samoa) to Northampton. This movement is also likely to lead to an increase in the number of 'dual

nationals' (that is, players eligible to play for more than one country) which will also have an impact on a national team's identity.

61. These Europeanization processes are, perhaps, most evident in the development and growth of The Heineken European Cup (inaugurated in 1995/96). The culmination of the 1996/97 competition was a final between Leicester and Brive played at Cardiff Arms Park before a near-capacity crowd. The success of this pan-European club competition is likely to continue and will create even more fixtures for the region's top players.

Sport and the Contestation of Cultural and Ethnic Identities in Scottish Society

JOSEPH M. BRADLEY

Introduction

This study considers the role and place of Glasgow's Celtic Football Club in the context of forging social identity for the largest immigrant group in Scotland. Originating from Ireland, this is a minority group whose origins, symbols and religion are often considered to be oppositional by significant sections of the larger dominant, more indigenous community. Sport itself may have no intrinsic value structure, but it is a ready and flexible vehicle through which ideological associations can be reinforced,[1] and has become a highly visible medium of Irish identity in Scottish society.

Although football in Scotland has been elevated beyond its sporting, athletic and artistic qualities, and is an important vehicle for a number of social, cultural and political identities, this is not unique. In a number of countries, football often has a broader ethnic and political resonance. In Brazil, the success of the national side has until recently been used by undemocratic regimes to defer potential protest. When Zaire withdrew from the qualifying matches for the 1978 World Cup, it was the team's 'unpatriotic behaviour' which was forwarded as the reason.[2] In England, football at international level has become a conduit for deeper social and political concerns over the state of the national identity and as an outlet for racism. This has origins in the legacy of British imperialism: political and economic subjugation was supplemented by cultural and ideological forces, of which sport and recreation formed central features.[3]

Spain has provided one of the most significant examples of this feature of football. The country's twentieth century dictator, General Franco, utilized the successes of the famous Real Madrid club of the late 1950s and the early 1960s, as well as victories of the Spanish national team. These assisted his cause of creating a centralized Spain with its focus in Madrid in addition to gaining a measure of European acceptance.[4] Although these tactics may have had some effect on Spain's pariah status in Europe as a whole at the time, Franco's attempts at cultural and linguistic centralism were resented bitterly in the Catalan and Basque regions of the country and this rancour was to find an expression in soccer.[5]

Many regional symbols were banned by the Franco regime as its brand of
Spanishness was imposed upon society. Regional languages and cultures
came under attack and it became an offence to fly a regional flag. Such
widespread repression meant that a number of otherwise neutral avenues
developed a para-political and extra-cultural dimension. A football ground,
often with vast crowds, invariably became a safer environment for the
expression of otherwise repressed views and indeed, this is what happened in
the Catalonia and Basque regions where Barcelona and the Basque Athletico
Bilbao football clubs became the focus for regional identities. One observer
recounted how a woman told him: 'I detest football, but Barca is more than
football. In the bad days, when we had nothing else, Barca meant Catalonia.
People used to go to the stadium just to speak Catalan.'⁶ Although Spain has
undergone considerable change in the years since Franco died many clubs
retain strong ethnic and regional identities. The example of Spanish football
shows how sport has a capacity to go beyond the mere aesthetic and
entertaining and become socially and politically significant.

     This study focuses on football in Scotland and reflects on the capacity of
sport in that society to acquire a similar meaning. It centres particularly on
Celtic Football Club and a significant section of the Irish diaspora in
Scotland maintaining an Irish identity in what has often been perceived as a
hostile environment. The first sections briefly reflect on aspects of the early
history of Celtic as well as make reference to some of the Irish diaspora's
political aspirations and cultural affinities in Scotland. Secondly, the
analysis details a number of events casting Celtic's Irishness in a strong
light: this, added to the club's Catholic identity, is the cause of perceived
hostility towards it. This research will subsequently refer to several
examples of perceived hostility which Irish Catholics have traditionally
experienced in Scotland. Fourth, this work will survey the part which the
historical 'troubles' in Ireland have played within Scottish society. The
penultimate section of this work will consider some elements of the
discourse over Celtic's Irishness, Catholic socio-cultural identity and the
problems connected with Irish identity in Scotland. The conclusion of the
study will look at the changing nature of anti-Catholicism and anti-Irishness
in Scotland and also assess Celtic's place in the Catholic community with
which it has long been associated.

The Irish Diaspora in Scotland: Politics and Cultural Symbolism

At the time of the founding of Celtic Football Club in 1887/88, the vast
majority of Catholics in the country were from Ireland and the words
Catholic and Irish were interchangeable in the west of Scotland. All the
club's founders were expatriate Irishmen or of Irish stock and the new club's

support was drawn largely from the swelling Irish community in the Glasgow area. Celtic's tradition of donating money to charity frequently included some to Irish causes such as the Evicted Tenant's Fund, then an important aspect of Irish nationalist politics. Off the field, the national question was of crucial importance to Celtic's founders as it was to many in the immigrant community. Like the wider immigrant community, club officials, players and supporters alike, were often involved in politics: supporting Irish Home Rule, campaigning for the release of Irish political prisoners, opposing what they viewed as British imperialism in the Boer War and South Africa and supporting the contentious petition for Catholic schools to be maintained within the State system.

Although the struggle for independence for Ireland became more complicated during the 1920s (particularly in relation to the Irish Civil War), affecting the hitherto strong Irish political nature of the immigrant community (as did the increasing salience of labour politics), the tradition of 'the cause' of Ireland was often maintained. This was particularly evidenced within the environs of Celtic. The Catholic Irish community built and sustained Celtic and there was an interlocking of spirit between the club and the community. There are few post-1920s references to involvement in Irish politics on the parts of Celtic directors or players, but the wider Celtic supporters have remained politically minded in respect to Ireland. The eruption of 'the Troubles' in Northern Ireland almost half a century later, and the alignment of many supporters with the nationalist cause, reflect the part Irish nationalism continues to play in being a Celtic supporter.

In any case, there was little question of Celtic's Irishness as such. One of the club's most famous players and managers, Jimmy McGrory, made this clear in his description of a Celtic celebratory dinner in 1936: 'the toasts were to St Patrick and Our Homeland, whilst the night was rounded off with the singing of the Irish National Anthem'.[7] On tour of the USA in 1931, the hosts of the club requested that Celtic play under the flag of the Irish Republic and be introduced to the sound of the Irish National Anthem, such was its association with Ireland.[8]

Patriotic symbolism was evident in the 1960s when the club launched its own newspaper, *The Celtic View*. Prominent adverts were included for 'Irish Rebel Records' including 'The Merry Ploughboy' and 'James Connolly'.[9] Commemorative concerts for Irish patriots 'Sean South' and 'Kevin Barry' were also advertised, as was a Glasgow concert to celebrate the 50th anniversary of the 1916 Easter Uprising, and which included the appearance of readers' favourite Celtic stars.[10] In the 1990s such adverts remain popular with the Celtic supporters. The politically minded singing group known as the Wolfe Tones, as well as a number of others, have frequently advertised in the Club newspaper as they are popular among the Celtic supporters.[11]

Emphasizing the significance of Irish identity to Celtic's followers, a survey conducted in 1990 revealed that Celtic supporters (and Catholics generally) have a lesser affinity with many Scottish symbols than have other significant sections of the population in Scotland (including other football clubs' fans, the Orange Institution and members of the Church of Scotland). In fact, a majority of Celtic supporters chose Irish symbols over Scottish ones while almost no other fans chose these.[12]

It is in the context of Celtic participation in Scottish football that much of the offspring of the Irish in Scotland's Irish identity is expressed. Perhaps the greatest manifestation of Celtic fans' lack of association with Scottish symbols is seen in a popular perception of their paucity of support for the Scottish international football team.[13] Although identifying with the Scottish national team is seen by the wider football community (including the media) as being typical, this is not the view of Celtic fans. The 1990 survey demonstrates that all other categories of Scottish football fan are significantly more likely to attend Scotland matches than Celtic fans. This indicates the faint ties between this significant symbol of modern Scottish identity,[14] and the 'Irish club', which has its home in Scottish football. In fact, the fans of all clubs other than Celtic are similar in terms of their attachment to the national team.[15] Contrasting with Scottish Clubs' fans support for the Scottish national team, the 1990 survey also shows that Celtic fans are distinctive in their support for the Republic of Ireland. It appears that for a majority of Celtic fans exhibiting this support is an adjunct of the Celtic culture, indeed, a manifestation of Irish cultural attachment.

Early Signs of Antagonism Towards Celtic

Since the Reformation, a strong anti-Catholic culture has existed in Scotland and infuses numerous aspects of social and political life. This complex culture has involved many different strands and dimensions over both time and place, and the arrival of Irish Catholic immigrants to Scotland during the nineteenth century added a racial aspect to traditional antagonism.[16] As it developed in the late nineteenth and twentieth centuries, the modern football environment proved one of the most visible arenas for expressing antagonism and hostility towards Catholic and Irish manifestations in Scotland. Although Irish football clubs existed in other parts of Scotland (for example, in Dundee, Edinburgh and Lanarkshire), antagonism towards such obvious manifestations of 'Catholicism' and Irishness alienated these clubs and many were forced out of existence.[17] However, its sound management, a fervent support and on the field success helped sustain Celtic in a hostile environment.[18] In particular, its location

Apes and Aryans. *Scottish Referee*, 3 February 1905

Apes and Aryans

Celtic supporters

amongst a significant and supportive Irish community was a crucial factor in its establishment and survival.

Despite rising to become the most significant Irish team in Scotland, Celtic's presence and subsequent success also caused problems. For example, in 1896 Celtic and Hibernian (an Edinburgh side which had also emerged from the Irish community there) were top of the Scottish league: this prompted the newspaper, *Scottish Sport*, to note the dominance in Scotland of two Irish teams and ask where was the Scottish team that could challenge them.[19] Such comment was a refined example of the antagonism faced by Irish clubs in Scotland, but the challenge by *Scottish Sport* explicitly reflects the ethnic nature of the Scottish game from its earliest years.

However, most football clubs grew out of pre-existing social relationships: many had political, national and religious dimensions to them.[20] Sporting clubs require a base for both establishment and support and these things have made a crucial contribution to the very existence of sport and competition across the globe. Therefore, Celtic's ethnic and religious origins are less unique than is often thought the case.[21]

The most noteworthy counter to the success of Celtic was Glasgow Rangers. Like many Scottish clubs, from its earliest days Rangers had a significant Protestant and increasingly anti-Catholic and anti-Irish character.[22] Although Rangers had existed for around 15 years before Celtic its early years had not been marked by any significant degree of success. None the less, steady advance in both trophies and finances meant that Rangers came gradually to provide an answer to the question asked by *Scottish Sport*. For many Scots, the task of defending native prestige eventually fell to Glasgow Rangers.

Thus, the intolerance displayed towards Irish Catholics in Scotland was partly reflected in the development of football. While a complex interweaving of sport, culture, tradition, nationalism, religion and politics was closely linked to the establishment and evolution of many clubs in Scotland, it was particularly so in the case of Rangers and Celtic. Celtic's Irish identity has been a significant problem for many people in Scotland. Just as Hibernian's Irishness in the late nineteenth century was viewed as problematic by the Scottish football authorities on its application to join the Scottish League, the pressure upon Celtic to remove its 'offending' Irish symbols and associations has long been a feature of Scottish society. This notion has a bearing on Irish symbolism in Scotland.

In 1952 the traditional flying of the Irish national flag at Celtic Park came to threaten the place of Celtic in Scottish football. Celtic's official club historian, in its centenary year, describes how 'an attempt was made to force Celtic out of business if they would not agree to remove the Irish flag from their home ground'.[23] This controversy arose after spectator trouble in the Celtic versus Rangers match in January of that year. After recommendations by the Magistrates' Committee of Glasgow Corporation in relation to future crowd disturbances, the Scottish Football Association (SFA) eventually decided that among other things, both clubs should avoid the display of any flag or emblem which had no association with this country or the game. The reality was that Celtic was the only club that flew a flag which could be construed as being nothing to do with Scotland. There were also shamrocks on the Celtic corner flags and a reserve strip incorporating a large shamrock design. Robert Kelly, the Chairman of Celtic, saw this as an attack upon the nature of the club as well as upon the Irishness of Catholics in Scotland. In a speech to a lay Catholic organisation, Kelly stated: 'We have no need to be ashamed of our fathers, nor have we any cause to be ashamed that those founders [of Celtic] came from that country that has provided protagonists for liberty wherever they have settled.'[24]

Celtic were ordered to take down the flag or be suspended from football in Scotland. The SFA adopted these recommendations by a vote of 26 to 7, showing the strength of feeling against Celtic. With the support of the Celtic followers, Kelly refrained from complying with the order, determined to protect the identity of the club: the Irish flag would remain or Celtic would indeed stop playing. At one point Kelly considered introducing Gaelic games to Celtic Park if the SFA instruction was carried out. However, the SFA lacked recourse to legitimate means of enforcing its demand. Most clubs eventually waned in their attack on Celtic recognising that the income generated by them was a major factor in Scottish Football's vibrancy. The furore eventually died down and Celtic continued to fly the Irish flag.

Although historically an Irish club, Celtic's involvement in Scottish football allowed for the participation of the Catholic community in a popular facet of the larger society: the club, like the immigrant community from which it had emerged, thus acquired a Scottish dimension. Football and Celtic were avenues for interaction and integration with the host community, despite the ethnic competitiveness of the game itself. None the less, the example of the flag reflected that manifestations of Irishness within Scotland remained largely unacceptable.

Opposition expressed towards Celtic's Irish symbolism, particularly the flying of the Irish flag, seemed to indicate that all vestiges of Irishness had to be removed if acceptance was to be possible. For many of the immigrant community who followed the events surrounding the flag issue, this seemed to be emphasised by this particular example in the way that no reference was made during the disputation in relation to Rangers policy of refusing to sign Roman Catholic players. Indeed, for some sections of the Catholic community, lack of reference to this matter indicated an endorsement or acceptance of the policy and was linked to similar practices on the part of the wider society . In recent decades, the presence of the Irish flag at Celtic Park as well as Irish identity amongst Celtic's supporters, have continued to invite antagonistic comment.[25]

When Rangers fans became notorious for rioting at stadia in England and abroad in the late 1960s and 1970s, and the discussion of football hooliganism took on a sectarian dimension, the Scottish press frequently balanced discourse of Rangers 'no Catholics' policy with mention of Celtic's symbols. Comment also extended to criticism of Catholic schools. In the wake of Rangers' supporters rioting in Birmingham in 1976, *The Daily Record,* recognising that too strong a criticism might antagonise its mainly Protestant readership, and ignoring the fact that events had taken place in England, tempered its editorial criticism of rioting fans by stating that Celtic should be: ' … willing to be recognised as a sporting bastion of Catholicism. They must bear a share of the guilt.'[26]

In 1991 Scotland's most popular Sunday newspaper, *The Sunday Mail,* reflected a cultural and political orthodoxy in Scotland when it focused on Celtic's Irish image, reporting the popular group The Pogues as being guests of the club. The Pogues' IRA connection was considered to have been established because they had written a song protesting about the wrongful conviction of the 'Birmingham Six', who had been imprisoned (on evidence which was eventually discounted) for a lethal explosion in that city in the early 1970s. This song was subsequently banned 'under the Government anti-terror regulations in 1988'.[27] In 1994 the *Sunday Mail's* chief sports columnist (also a major influence in Scottish Television and Scottish radio's football coverage) criticised Celtic fans for singing and the club for playing the Irish ballad, 'The Fields of Athenry', at home matches.[28] Whether in a racial, ethnic or religious context, or whether displays of Irishness are confined by their antagonists to a discourse or sphere of 'sectarianism' (a condition which can encompass all three of these), manifestations of Irish identity in Scotland are largely viewed as offensive and unwelcome.

The anti-Catholic and anti-Irish social and political pressures of the late nineteenth and early twentieth centuries which assisted in the discontinuation of a number of Irish football clubs or, which eventually forced them to change their identities, have remained a feature of Scottish life.[29] Such pressures have alienated the Irish and their offspring by making it appear as though they have largely been responsible for sectarianism and religious bigotry in Scotland. As during the flag issue, part of the dominant or orthodox view has perceived Irish and Catholic manifestations as at the root of the religious or 'sectarian' problem in Scottish football and in society generally. In effect this view augmented the already prejudicial attitudes rejecting Catholics and Irish Catholic immigrants, primarily because they were Catholic and Irish. The flag issue in the 1950s, and continued reference to it in many sections of Scottish society, has become a symbol of the unacceptability of the Irishness of the immigrant population (now overwhelmingly Scottish born) in Scotland. Such manifestations of hostility towards Irish and Catholic identities have also had a wider resonance in Scottish society.

Wider Reactions to the Diaspora in Scotland

Anti-Irish and anti-Catholic feeling in Scotland has rarely been uniform. For many individuals, organisations and communities, it is a complex and differentiated phenomenon. Also, for other Scots, it has no part to play in their lives.[30] None the less, the history of ethno-religious cleavage in Scotland has meant that opposition and prejudice towards the immigrant community has been widespread, and its wider resonance in Scottish society has not been restricted to the Irishness of Celtic or the club's followers.

Cooney asserts that as late as 1938, the Church and Nation Committee of the Church of Scotland emphasized ' ... the elementary right of a nation to control and select its immigrants'.[31] The debate which had resulted in such a way of thinking was conducted solely with Irish Catholics in mind. In fact, Brown states that from around the time of the Education Act (Scotland) 1918, until the outbreak of the Second World War, there was an 'official' Presbyterian campaign against the Irish Catholic community in Scotland. This campaign was both institutional and popular, and is viewed by Brown as an attempt at 'marginalising, and even eliminating an ethnic minority whose presence was regarded as an evil, polluting the purity of Scottish race and culture'.[32]

The pre-Second World War period seems to have been fertile for such activities as well as a time when they were acceptable to, and supported by, the wider society. Such sentiments found expression in popular literature, for example in the works of Andrew Dewar Gibb (later to become Regius Professor of Scots Law at Glasgow University) and of journalist George Malcolm Thomson.[33] Political activists, like Alexander Ratcliffe and John McCormick, gained success at the ballot by declaring similar anti-Irish and anti-Catholic opinions. Other significant political figures at the time reflected these widespread feelings regarding the Irish in Scotland. For example, Conservative member of Parliament, Lord Scone, believed that:

> culturally the Irish population ... has not been assimilated into the Scottish population. It is not my purpose to discuss now whether the Irish culture is good or bad, but merely to state the definite fact that there is in the west of Scotland a completely separate race of alien

origin practically homogeneous whose presence there is bitterly resented by tens of thousands of the Scottish working-class.[34]

Such attitudes recorded in the recent past also have contemporary manifestations. In 1989 ex-British Cabinet minister Norman Tebbit demonstrated a comparable perspective when he suggested a novel type of cricket test (or loyalty test). Asian immigrants' integration could be tested by asking which cricket team they supported: England or Pakistan/India. He went on to suggest: ' ... that those who continue to cheer for India and Pakistan, are wanting in Britishness ... that the only satisfactory way to be an Asian in Britain was to cease being Asian'.[35]

The test, in its form as a 'football test', has also been applied regularly by the Scottish/British press in the 1980s and 1990s as it became common for British born second and third generation Irish to represent and support the Republic of Ireland in international football. Critical comment, mainly regarding the immigrant identity of many members of the team, occurred in parts of the British media during this period, in particular during the 1988 European Championships and the 1990 and 1994 World Cups.[36] Some of the logic underpinning such an argument was exposed by a respected British journalist: 'the assertion that we are one people, has always been a lie used to justify the unjust dominance of one group (whites, Protestants or Anglo-Saxons, for example) over the society as a whole'.[37]

Such cases, which in themselves might be viewed as insignificant and normally unrelated, could in fact be repeated many times and reflect a widely-held broad ideological and attitudinal position. For example, the unacceptability of Irish-Catholics to the Orange community in Scotland is one of the most perceptible contemporary manifestations of this attitude:

> Study the [Irish-Catholic] names of some of the 'Labour' candidates elected. ... What do Glasgow's Protestant clergymen think of this situation? What do the genuine patriots, in the SNP's rank-and-file, think about it? ... There isn't a Scoto-Eirishman in Scotland, a Lally, a Murphy, or a Gaffney, who is not Eirish under his skin. Scratch them and their Eirish bit comes out ... .[38]

Similar sentiments have frequently been expressed by some of the Reformed Churches in Scotland. In 1986, the Moderator of the Free Church of Scotland addressed its annual Assembly. His speech included criticism of the Catholic and Irish nature of those of immigrant extraction:

> In 1755 there were no Roman Catholics in Glasgow, our largest city today. In 1786 there were about seventy and by 1830, they numbered 30,000, with 14,000 in Edinburgh. ... Today the Roman Catholic

system is virtually triumphant in Scotland. Being allowed by its constitution to lie and cheat as long as its own ends are realised, its close organisation and its intelligence set-up has enabled it to infiltrate the whole educational framework of the land.[39]

Since the years shortly before the founding of Celtic, the 'educational framework' referred to by the Scottish Church leader, that is, the issue of Catholic schools in Scotland, has been controversial. The controversy also provides an interesting focus for studying sectarian discourse and discontent on the part of Protestant Churches, overtly anti-Catholic organisations and political parties. In the 1930s, the Scottish Protestant League and Protestant Action gained a significant degree of electoral support in Glasgow and Edinburgh respectively. Both parties included the dissolution of Catholic schools amongst their central policies, whilst John Cormack, the leader of Protestant Action, also called for the expulsion of Catholics.[40] In the 1990s, the Free Church of Scotland, the Free Presbyterian Church of Scotland, other smaller Protestant Churches as well as the more secular Loyal Orange Institution of Scotland are all strongly opposed to the presence of Catholic schools. In recent years their existence has also invited the criticism of a secular lobby.

The most popular Scottish broadsheet, *The Herald*, regularly prints letters on the subject:

> The only contribution the [Catholic school] system makes to the Scottish Nation, and to the West of Scotland in particular, is to provide us with a breeding ground of superstition and mistrust. The sooner the children come together, the sooner they will stop growing up to perpetuate their parents hatred.[41]

> The answer is simple. The Roman Catholic Church should be given two options: their schools remain within the state system and appointments are made by the education authority; or Roman Catholic schools opt out of the system and are funded by the Church. ... The situation as it stands is unacceptable.[42]

The school debate shows that there are wider features of opposition to Catholic (as well as historically Irish) expressions in Scotland, which are a focus for prejudice and intolerance. In addition, antagonism towards Catholic schools is an example of the stronger dominant groups attempting to direct and form crucial aspects of the identity of the less strongly indigenous community.[43] As a further demonstration of this prejudice and intolerance, the history of Celtic can be viewed as being a central feature of the experience of the Irish Catholic immigrant community in Scotland.

In a secular society which *inter alia* involves popular conceptions of 'liberalism', and given the social and political progress made by the offspring of the Irish in Scotland, most of the overt statements and activities of half a century ago are unlikely to gain the currency they once had. Today, society in Scotland is more complex: for some sections of the population, ethnic and religious identity is less significant than in the past. However, publications and assertions of some Protestant Churches, organisations and individuals, clearly remain anti-Irish and anti-Catholic.[44] In contemporary society more subtle and re-cycled forms of antagonism remain a feature of modern society which continues to have an impact upon Irish identity in Scotland.

One recent example of antagonism towards Irishness in Scotland emerged from a writer to *The Herald* newspaper in 1990, replying to a Celtic supporter's attack on Rangers' allegedly sectarian playing staff policy. He wrote:

> I suggest that, when the flag of a foreign and frequently hostile state, whose constitution impudently claims sovereignty over part of the United Kingdom, and whose land and people the present pope has declared to be 'Mary's Dowry', no longer flies from the mast-head of 'Paradise', there may be, I say only may be, less 'bigoting' in the stands of Ibrox.[45]

The foreign state is the Republic of Ireland, Mary is the Virgin Mary and Paradise is the colloquial Celtic language for Celtic Park. Ibrox is the home of Glasgow Rangers Football Club. In such views, religion, politics and football are compounded.

Conflict in Ireland and Scottish society

Part of the legacy of the historical involvement of Scots in the colonisation of the north of Ireland (in addition to their significant role in building the British Empire) has traditionally seen the identification of many Scots with the Ulster Unionist cause. This has been particularly manifest in relation to the Orange Institution and within the context of Rangers Football Club. Until recently, this affinity was also partly expressed in a significant working class support for the Conservative Party in Scotland.[46] Strong feelings in Scotland for Ulster Unionists as well as an historic opposition toward manifestations of Irishness, has meant that reference by members of the Irish diaspora in Scotland to an independent and united Ireland has been largely viewed as antagonistic to other more dominant views.

Of course, Celtic fans have long made known their Irish allegiances. Historically, Irish 'patriotic' songs as well as related emblems have played a significant role among the Celtic support. However, Celtic fans as well as

Catholics' association with favouring a united Ireland is at odds with many people in Scotland, and decidedly in opposition to those groups and organizations which are distinctively Protestant.[47] This has meant that with the re-emergence of the 'Troubles' in Northern Ireland, Celtic's associations with Ireland and its supporters' links with Irish nationalism has attracted further criticism and condemnation.

In addition, since media discussions have frequently shaped discourse on the Northern Ireland troubles around questions of nationalist violence, support for Irish nationalism in Scotland is often viewed solely in this context. People who are seen to support an Irish 'nationalist' agenda, have correspondingly become marginalized within Scottish/British societies. There is a popular assumption that support for Irish nationalism or criticism of Britain's role in Ireland implies support for, or ambiguity towards, violent atrocities on the part of militant Irish nationalists. Although a united and independent Ireland is the preferred option for the vast majority of Catholics in Scotland,[48] there are few occasions when this sentiment is made overt – though it can find popular expression in the context of Celtic.

In the past, the pressures which forced some Irish clubs out of business and others to change their identities, have shown that 'troubles' in Ireland only add a further dimension to anti-Irishness and anti-Catholicism in Scotland. A context of heightened troubles in Ireland is not a prerequisite for hostility towards Irishness in Scotland. Nevertheless, pressures exerted both explicitly and implicitly by the dominant Scottish and Protestant cultures condition many aspects of Catholic and Irish identity by negative references. Popular antagonism towards the nationalist dimension of the Celtic identity is frequently expressed. In October 1989, *The Sun* newspaper broke the news of a meeting attended by the editor of Celtic's club newspaper, *The Celtic View,* together with a number of football fanzine editors and parties. The meeting became notorious for the pro-IRA (Irish Republican Army) statements made by the editor. *The Sun* demanded that Celtic terminate the editor's employment.[49] Celtic complied, stressing that the editor's views did not represent those of Celtic.[50]

Celtic were entitled to dispose of the services of an employee, but a significant aspect of the affair was its sensationalist treatment by *The Sun,* which has often been characterised by anti-Irish comment and confusion of things Irish with IRA violence.[51] Moreover, the former *Celtic View* editor believes that the editor of the Rangers Fanzine *'Follow Follow'* attempted to induce a number of newspapers to buy the story which *The Sun* subsequently published. The Rangers fanzine itself reflects an ideological convention of viewing everything Irish and Catholic as synonymous and insidious. It also demonstrates what Finn has referred to as Protestant conspiracy theories which cast the Catholic Church and her faithful daughter in the shape of Ireland and its people as trying to destroy Protestantism and to take power using deception as its tactic.[52] It is also in this context that the view is forwarded that everything Irish and Catholic converges and their varying features are simply different facets of the same threatening force. As Hickman and Curtis have argued,[53] the very concept of Irishness, in this context, is besmirched with a de-contextualized and demonic taint of militant Republican violence. To this extent, *The Sun*'s front page headlines over the affair are not unusual with regard to things Irish as perceived popularly in Scottish and British society.[54]

Historically in Scotland, most hostility towards the Irish has revolved around their religious and national character. However, for many people and groups demonstrating this hostility, the insidiousness attributed to these features has been deepened further by perceived links with Irish nationalist aspirations. In all, Irish and Catholic immigrant identities are frequently considered pernicious and oppositional on the parts of many differing strands within Scottish/British societies and as such may be seen as deviant influences and forces within those contexts.

Questions of Irish identity among the diaspora in Scotland

The antagonism displayed towards Celtic and other Irish clubs in the late nineteenth and twentieth centuries has been an aspect of the immigrant experience which has reflected upon the Irishness of the Catholic immigrant population in Scotland. One effect is that since the inter-war period, partly in response to hostility towards Irish manifestations in Scotland, the Irishness of Celtic and of the community it has historically represented, has become contested within that community itself. As a result, they have emerged as a community which frequently interrogates its own identity.[55] The fluctuating but ultimately indeterminate nature of this identity was summed up succinctly by a member of staff at Celtic Park when he said of himself, 'I'm Scottish, though I've an Irish name. I'm more non-English. I am born in Scotland, but the blood that runs through me is Irish. If my background was black, I wouldn't be a half-caste. I'd be black'.[56]

Over the past few decades Celtic football literature has contributed to this discourse. The Celtic fanzine *Not The View* makes small reference to Celtic's Irish origins and stresses its intention to 'studiously avoid' the emotive subject of Ireland, itself a reflection of the difficulty over things Irish in Scotland.[57] However, an alternative Celtic fanzine, *Tiocfaidh Ar La*, is dominated by both the Irishness of the club and, as the name indicates, by the Irish nationalist tradition of large numbers of the fans. Since the 1960s the *Celtic View* has also reflected some features of the debate.[58]

Confusion, dispute and contestation over the modern 'ethnic' identity of most Catholics in Scotland is also reflected elsewhere. The editorial staff of a number of Catholic newspapers periodically criticize Catholics who express Irishness, especially if this is perceived to be at the expense of a Scottish identity. After one such newspaper attack upon the Irish in Scotland,[59] a number of readers responded:

> It is hardly the function of a Catholic paper nor indeed of the Church to tell people where their loyalties should lie. Too many people in the Church in Scotland are ashamed of, and want to hide our Irish ancestry, this is why we never hear them decrying those of Italian or Polish descent who are not all that bothered about a Scottish birth either.[60]

Questions relating to Celtic fans' attachment to the Scottish international side were also echoed in two Celtic pre-match programmes during 1991:

> It was a little sad some Celtic supporters, Scots born and bred, seemed completely non-plussed by Scotland's achievement [in reaching the European Championship Finals] and that a number of these people would have been happier to see the Republic of Ireland reach Sweden.[61]

A different sentiment was expressed in a later programme:

> If a Celtic fan wishes to support Scotland, Ireland or both then good luck to him/her … but the highs and lows of the Scottish side hold little interest for many of us. If we wish the Irish success then we're quite entitled to do so.[62]

In the context of perceptions of prejudice and antipathy shown to Irish immigrants in Scotland, expressions of Irishness and Catholicism have often been problematic for that community. This is partly reflected in the discourse on Irish and Catholic identity within the community itself. None the less, for many Catholics of Irish extraction, football provides an environment in which to make known otherwise repressed or unarticulated political attitudes, cultural affinities, national allegiances and prejudices. The prestige afforded by victories in the football arena cannot be underestimated in terms of their value for many in that community. It could be argued that the improvement in the social and political position of the Catholic community in Scotland from the 1960s[63] was partly assisted by a new self confidence emanating from the Scottish and European success of the Celtic club during this period, when the club was a dominant force in football.

A Changing Discourse

For many members of the consciously Irish Catholic community,[64] Celtic is the greatest single 'ethno-cultural focus' because it provides the social setting and set of symbolic processes and representations through which the community's sense of its own identity and difference from the indigenous community is sustained. In effect, in the late nineteenth century, the emergence of Celtic allowed Catholics to participate in what were otherwise sometimes exclusive aspects of the wider society. Although it retained its identity as Irish and Catholic, by signing players of non-Irish and non-Catholic background Celtic showed that the immigrant community were willing to integrate. None the less, some anti-Catholicism developed within Scottish football in response to the social, cultural and political phenomenon Celtic became. A Celtic match may involve the 'ceremonial reaffirmation of memories of past [and present] hostilities and unfinished business [and] is a powerful strategy of identity building'.[65]

Finn shows how contemporary accounts of Irish football clubs in Scotland have assisted in distorting assessments of ethno-religious conflict and prejudice in Scottish society.[66] Alongside a long tradition of Scottish anti-Catholicism the negative reaction of native Scots to the influx of the Irish,[67] significant involvement of Protestant Scots in the colonisation of Ulster and the strong Unionism that has historically been present in Scotland,[68] have all contributed to a culture of rejection, whereby many Scottish Protestants either renounce or continue to be disturbed by the presence, practices or attitudes of the Catholic Irish in Scotland. This account of some of the problems encountered by the most successful Irish club in Scotland (indeed, Celtic are the only club to have survived as a perceptibly Irish club) shows that this prejudice retains a significant role in Scottish football as well as for other areas of Scottish life.

As with other social characteristics anti-Catholicism and anti-Irishness have changed in Scotland. Indeed, the Catholic community has also undergone change. Secularization has affected religious identities. Anti-Catholicism is not a united force in Scotland, and its manifestations, both in terms of significance and impact, are multi-varied. Better understanding between many Protestants and Catholics as well as ecumenism have also assisted the breakdown of barriers between the denominations. Religion has a varyingly different influence in parts of Scotland as compared with recent decades. None the less, religious identity and the prejudice arising from the clash of relevant cultural attributes continues to have a significant impact on Scottish life.

Indeed, the significance of religious-cultural questions can be viewed in the overwhelming uncertainty among many Catholics in their relationship to Ireland. Although many Catholics maintain strong links with their country of origin, the historical hostility and alienation they have faced along with present recycled versions of earlier demonstrations of racism have invariably given rise to uncertainty. This recycled racism is less obvious than in the past but often has a similar intention: that is, that Celtic and its Irish Catholic support remove their offensive Irish and Catholic manifestations.

Therefore, anti-Catholicism in Scotland is by no means monolithic or ubiquitous, and its contemporary form appears to be undergoing some change. In the last century and in the early decades of the twentieth, much anti-Irishness in Britain was cast in genetic terms. A cartoon published in a Scottish football newspaper early in this century depicted two Old Firm players in a bar, playing pool. The cartoon portrayed the Celtic player as 'typically' Irish, dumb with grotesque and brutish facial features. The Rangers player was handsome and with intelligent looking eyes. The cartoon was captioned 'Apes and Aryans'.[69] Although there are fewer examples of this kind of racism today, in recent decades the content of the previous stereotype has been adapted. Emphasis on genetic factors has declined: arguments are more evasive and less simplistic. None the less, and crucially, the form and content constantly identify the minority as both the 'problem' and the originators of the 'problem'. As in the case of anti-black prejudice in the USA, its present emphasis is on socio-cultural factors rather than on genetic ones – with corresponding alterations in racist discourse.[70]

In a related sense in Scotland, ethno-religious disputes are often viewed as matters of sectarianism, and many of the social and political attributes of Catholic and Irish identity are judged through a discourse of sectarian concepts and language.[71] As a result, not only is Celtic Football Club and its support regularly seen as sectarian, but also, Catholic schools, Irish symbols in Scotland, support for a united Ireland and occasionally, the historically strong links between Catholics and the Labour Party are viewed in a similar light. The consequence of this is that sectarianism in Scotland is frequently located among Irish Catholic immigrants, their perceived contributions to change in the socio-political constitution of the country, as well as their often lack of affinity for important elements of Scottish and British nationhood and the way their institutions, beliefs and practices are perceived as impeding Scottish progress.[72] In a football sense, this is evident in the criticism levelled at the many Celtic supporters who do not give allegiance to the Scottish team, criticism which has long been a feature of Scottish sports writing.[73]

Conclusion

It would be misleading to believe that there is a straightforward and simple dichotomy of identity among people in contemporary Scotland. Like any other society Scotland has a number of regional, class and racial features which affect wider issues of identity in different ways. In terms of the cultural, social and political dimensions of Scottish/British Protestantism and Irish Catholicism, people can have one dimensional affinities, they can inhabit a multi-layered set of identities or they can lie at any point in between. In addition, no point is fixed and is subject to a number of influences. None the less, religion has been the most significant contributor to social and sometimes, political identity in Scotland, since the Reformation, and a significant, pervasive, though fluctuating, ethno-religious cleavage remains between many people, groups and communities in Scottish society. For Gallagher, 'Presbyterianism was not just a state religion but, for more than three centuries, defined the Scots to one another and to the rest of the world'.[74] Muirhead opines that for much of this period, 'in Scotland anti-Romanism had become a religion and a way of life'.[75] With regard to Scottish society today, Gallagher and Walker stress:

> the variety of social, cultural and political phenomena which have a peculiarly Protestant dimension. Protestantism has certainly never been monolithic in Scotland, notwithstanding the daunting rigidity of Calvinist doctrine.[76]

The importance of Catholicism to Irish people has been just as significant:

> Irish Catholicism has been more than the official pronounce-ments of the hierarchy: it is a set of values, a culture, a historical tradition, a view on the world, a disposition of mind and heart, a loyalty, an emotional psychology – and a nationalism.[77]

Of course, not all Catholics in Scotland are of Irish origin: some thousands of Catholics have migrated from Italy as well as Poland and Lithuania during the course of this century. There is also the small number of Scots who remained Catholic after the Reformation. Obscuring these differences, inter-marriage, secularization and the growth of mass and popular cultures also influence socio-cultural identity. Nevertheless, it remains the case that the vast majority of Catholics in Scotland originate from Ireland and a strong bond exists between many of those Catholics and Celtic Football Club: an institution conceived and constructed from within, and sustained by, the immigrant community.[78]

The problems associated with Catholic and Irish identity in Scotland reflects the historical Scottish/British antagonism towards these identities. It is an antagonism which has its roots in the anti-Catholic aspects of Scottish Protestantism and in the contentious involvement of Scots in the conquest and colonisation of Ireland. Although circumstances and time have altered past relationships, society in Scotland lives with the legacies of these important historical factors: they are factors with a contemporary relevance. The marginalization of Irish identity has been a long historical process tied up with Protestant Scottish/British domination of not only the island of Ireland but of its people and its diaspora. Historically, this is evidenced in a quotation from Sir William Parsons about the Irish in 1625. For Parsons, only the depreciation and destruction of Ireland's cultural traits and identity could result in the Irish being absorbed into the Crown's realm: 'We must change their course of government, apparel, manner of holding land, their language and habit of life.'[79]

Contention within the Catholic community regarding its identities also demonstrates the effects on the self-perceptions of the immigrant community of constant negation and marginalization within Scottish society. Being of the Catholic Irish immigrant community and retaining an Irish identity are largely incompatible with the dominant cultures. For Finn, the consequences are racism as well as religious and social prejudice.[80]

In Scotland, hostility towards Irishness and Catholicism often attain their most obvious manifestations in football. As football is an important vehicle through which ideological associations are made in Scotland, and as the most important medium for secular Catholic and Irish cultural expression and identity, Celtic and its support are frequently the primary focus for this hostility. Celtic's history shows that many from the Irish immigrant community express their Irishness through this institution, seeing it as representing Ireland. This has advantages for them in providing a public space for expressing their identity, but this very fact also means that it acts as a magnet for antagonism and rejection of the same. It is also this which makes Celtic such a unique and well supported club. None the less, this study also reflects that these manifestations are but extensions of other opposition which Irish Catholics have encountered in Scotland. This opposition is not an undifferentiated phenomenon, but often its clearest or most obvious manifestations centre on Celtic and its supporters. Therefore, ethno-religious cleavage in Scotland is expressed outside as well as inside the football environment: football is but an extension of other social and political perceptions, myths and realities.

The majority of those who follow Celtic, either passively or actively, are the Irish who view their origins as important, and who are least prepared to subvert their identity amidst the perceived hostility. Thus, the intensity of being Irish is both raised by, and expressed through, Celtic Football Club. Celtic is therefore of major importance to vast numbers of Catholics in Scotland: the club functions as a socializing agent into a unique form of Irish cultural activity. In Scotland, although Irish cultural forms, expressions and confidence increased amongst the diaspora during the 1980s and 1990s, the fact that by 1998 Celtic had the greatest number of season ticket purchasers amongst football clubs in Britain, as well as one of the largest in Europe, reflects the continuing importance which this institution retains for many of the offspring of the Irish immigrants who initially built and sustained Celtic in 1887/88.[81] For many Catholics in Scotland, Celtic – not unlike Barcelona Football Club and Catalonian identity in Spain – has, over the years, become something of a metaphor for the whole Irish and Catholic immigrant tradition.[82] In Scotland, football is bound up with the process of individual socialization and community construction. The history of Irish–British relations has meant that for the Irish in Scotland, as well as for those of an anti-Catholic and anti-Irish disposition, Celtic Football Club has emerged as a definition of Irishness itself.

NOTES

1. J. Hoberman, in J. Sugden and A. Bairner, *Sport, Sectarianism and Society in a Divided Ireland* (Leicester, 1993), p.10.
2. S. Kuper, *Football Against the Enemy* (London, 1994), p.102.
3. See D. Hill, *Out of His Skin: The John Barnes Phenomenon* (London, 1989).
4. D. Shaw, 'The Politics of Futbol', *History Today*, Vol.35 (Aug. 1985), pp.38–42.
5. See K. Medhurst, *The Basques and Catalans*, The Minority Rights Group Report, No.9 (London, 1987).
6. L. Allison, *The Politics of Sport* (Manchester, 1986), pp.2–3.
7. J. McGrory and G. McNee, *A Lifetime in Paradise*, published by authors (Glasgow, 1975).
8. B. Murray, *The Old Firm: Sectarianism, Sport and Society in Scotland* (Edinburgh, 1984), p.66.
9. *Celtic View*, 9 March 1966, p.4; 20 July 1966, p.4; 19 April 1967, p.1.
10. Ibid., 6 April 1966, p.3.
11. Ibid., 13 Dec. 1995, pp.12–13.
12 See J.M. Bradley, *Ethnic and Religious Identity in Modern Scotland: Culture, Politics and Football* (Aldershot, 1995).
13. Ibid.
14. For the symbolic role of the Scottish international football side in Scottish politics and culture, see also, B. Moorhouse, 'Scotland versus England: Football and Popular Culture' *International Journal of Sport*, Part 4 (1987), pp.189–202 and 'Repressed Nationalism And Professional Football: Scotland Versus England', in J. Mangan and R. Small (eds.), *Sport, Culture, Society* (London, 1986), pp.52–9. Also J. Brand, *The National Movement in Scotland* (London, 1978).
15. See Bradley, *Ethnic and Religious Identity.*
16. See E. McFarland, *Protestants First: Orangeism in 19th century Scotland* (Edinburgh, 1990), T. Gallagher, *Glasgow: The Uneasy Peace* (Manchester, 1987) and T.M. Devine (ed.), *Irish Immigrants and Scottish Society in the Nineteenth and Twentieth Centuries: Proceedings of the Scottish Historical Studies Seminar, University of Strathclyde, 1989/90* (Edinburgh, 1991).
17. G.P.T. Finn, 'Racism, Religion and Social Prejudice: Irish Catholic Clubs, Soccer and Scottish Society – I The Historical Roots of Prejudice', *The International Journal of the History of Sport*, Vol.8, No.1 (1991), pp.72–95; also, 'Racism, Soccer and Scottish Society – II Social Identities and Conspiracy Theories', *The International Journal of the History of Sport*, Vol.8, No.3 (1991), pp.370–97.
18. T. Campbell and P. Woods, *The Glory and the Dream: The History of Celtic F.C. 1887–1986* (Edinburgh, 1986).

19. Murray, *The Old Firm*, p.31.
20. G.P.T. Finn, 'Faith, Hope and Bigotry: Case Studies of Anti-Catholic Prejudice in Scottish Soccer and Society', in *Scottish Sport in the Making of the Nation: Ninety-Minute Patriots* (Leicester, 1994). Also see 'Sporting Symbols, Sporting Identities: Soccer and Intergroup Conflict in Scotland and Northern Ireland', in I.S. Wood (ed.), *Scotland and Ulster*, (Edinburgh, 1994), pp.33–5.
21. Murray, *The Old Firm*; also see B. Murray, *Glasgow's Giants: 100 years of the Old Firm* (Edinburgh, 1988).
22. Finn, *Scottish Sport in the Making of the Nation.*
23. B. Wilson, *Celtic: A Century with Honour* (Glasgow, 1988), p.94.
24. Ibid., pp.97–8.
25. For example, see Gerry McNee, chief sports columnist of *The Sunday Mail*, 2 Oct. 1994, p.75. During current research among the Scottish international football support a recurrent focus for dissatisfaction amongst some of the fans has been the presence of the Irish flag at Celtic Park (as well as the Irishness of Celtic's support).
26. *Daily Record*, editorial, 13 Oct. 1976, p.2. Such was also the case in the late 1950s when *Glasgow's Evening Citizen* almost crashed financially after the publication of an article critical of the Orange Institution: 'A readership boycott ensued which caused such panic that Donald MacDonald, then a journalist on the paper, recalls that nothing was written about the Order in the Glasgow press for many years to come.' See Gallagher, *Glasgow: The Uneasy Peace*, p.256.
27. *Sunday Mail*, 17 March 1991, p.5.
28. See the *Sunday Mail* article by Gerry McNee, 23 Oct. 1994, p.71. This sentiment has been repeated by McNee on both radio and television at least until 1996, a time also characterized by his personal campaign to have Celtic remove the Irish flag from above their stadium and his belief that Celtic supporters should not display the same (Radio Clyde, 13 Jan. 1996). By the end of 1995 the Celtic Football Club's supporters had apparently influenced the uptake of the Fields of Athenry on the part of the followers of the Republic of Ireland's football team.
29. See J.R. Mackay, *The Hibees, The Story of Hibernian Football Club* (Edinburgh, 1986); G. Docherty and P. Thomson, *100 Years of Hibs 1875/1975* (Edinburgh, 1975); M. Watson, *Rags to Riches: The Official History of Dundee United* (printed in Dundee, 1985). Also see Finn, 'Racism, Religion and Social Prejudice', for concise accounts of the changing nature of these once Irish clubs.
30. See Bradley, *Ethnic and Religious Identity.* Also see T.M. Devine (ed.), *St Mary's Hamilton: A Social History, 1846–1996* (Edinburgh, 1995).
31. J. Cooney, *Scotland and the Papacy* (Edinburgh, 1982), p.19.
32. S.J. Brown, 'Outside the Covenant: The Scottish Presbyterian Churches and Irish Immigration, 1922–1938', *The Innes Review*, Vol.XL11, No.1 (Spring 1991), pp.19–45.
33. Gallagher, *Glasgow: The Uneasy Peace*, pp.168–72.
34. *Hansard*, 261, 22 Nov. 1932, p.245.
35. Michael Ignatieff, *The Observer*, 16 Sept. 1990, p.17.
36. Such comment was particularly evident during the 1988 European Championships and the 1990 and 1994 World Cups. For examples see *The Sun*, 27 June 1990, p.6; *The Evening Times*, 10 June 1994, pp.58–9; *Daily Record*, 16 June 1994, p.35, also, articles in *The Irish Post*, 12 Dec. 1992, p.33 and 27 March 1993, p.35.
37. Adam Lively, *The Observer*, 22 July 1990, p.18.
38. *Orange Torch*, June 1984.
39. July/Aug. 1986. Moderators address to the Church Assembly. From Church records.
40. Gallagher, *Glasgow: The Uneasy Peace*, p.162.
41. *Glasgow Herald* (also 'The Herald'), 14 Dec. 1990, p.14.
42. Ibid, 5 Nov. 1990, p.10.
43. It should also be noted that although there are no anti-Protestant organisations in Scotland, nor has there been any apparent Catholic plans to invoke or propagate such sentiments, sectarian and bigoted Catholics also exist.
44. See Bradley, *Ethnic and Religious Identity.*

45. Dr B.C. Campbell, letter to the *Glasgow Herald*, 6 May 1989, p.6.
46. S. Kendrick, 'Scotland, Social Change and Politics', in D. McCrone, D. Kendrick and P. Straw (eds.), *The Making of Scotland: Nation, Culture and Social Change* (Edinburgh, 1989).
47. See Bradley, *Ethnic and Religious Identity*. In Britain as a whole, most surveys indicate the population favouring a united Ireland. J. Curtice and T. Gallagher, in R. Jowell, S. Witherspoon, L. Brook (eds.), *British Social Attitudes: The 7th Report*, Social and Community Planning Research (Aldershot, 1990); also see System 3 Poll in *The Herald*, 9 Feb. 1995, p.6. See also J. Mitchell, 'Religion and Politics in Scotland', unpublished paper presented to Seminar on Religion and Scottish Politics, University of Edinburgh, 1992. In addition, J. Curtice and D. Seawright, 'The Decline of the Scottish Conservative and Unionist Party 1950–1992: Religion, Ideology or Economics?', *Journal of Contemporary British History*, Vol.9. No.2 (1995), pp.319–42.
48. See Bradley, *Ethnic and Religious Identity*.
49. *The Sun*, 30 Oct. 1989, pp.1 and 7, and 31 Oct. 1989, p.5.
50. *Daily Record,* 31 Oct. 1989, p.17.
51. *The Sun*, 27 June 1990, p.6.
52. See Finn and collection of papers on sectarianism, racism and conspiracy theories at Strathclyde University, Jordanhill Campus. Also, see feature writer, John McLeod, *The Herald*, 20 Oct. 1994, p.21.
53. M. Hickman, 'A Study of the Incorporation of the Irish in Britain with Special Reference to Catholic State Education: Involving a Comparison of the Attitudes of Pupils and Teachers in Selected Catholic Schools in London and Liverpool', Ph.D. thesis, University of London, 1990. Also *Religion, Class and Identity: The State, the Catholic Church and the Education of the Irish in Britain* (Aldershot, 1995). See L. Curtis, *Ireland: The Propaganda War* (London, 1984), and *Nothing but the Same Old Story: The Roots of Anti-Irish Racism* (published by Information on Ireland, 5th edition, 1988).
54. See Donall MacAmhlaigh, *Ireland's Own*, 5 July 1985, for reference to John Junor's (editor of the *Daily Express*) remark that he would rather go looking for worms in a dunghill than visit Ireland as 'but one example of a quite unrepentant anti-Irishness of so much of the Tory press'. Also article by Michael Foley, 'Skin Deep Impression of Emigration' in the *Irish Reporter*, Issue 1, First Quarter, 1991, pp.14–15. Also see Curtis's studies of anti-Irish racism in Britain.
55. In considering Catholics as a 'community' in Scotland, this relates to the vast majority of them sharing a common background, schools, religion (churched and unchurched) and often a common perception of many features of their identity. In an era of Americanization, globalization, and with the pervasiveness of popular television and sport, they also share features with the non-immigrant or more indigenous population. See Bradley, *Ethnic and Religious Identity*.
56. Interview with member of staff at Celtic Park.
57. *Not The View* (a Celtic fanzine), Nov. 1990, No.24.
58. *The Celtic View*, 3 Aug, 1966, No.52, p.3; 31 Aug. 1966, No.56, p.3; 21 Sept. 1966, No.59, p.3. 2 Nov. 1987, No.979, p.2.
59. *Scottish Catholic Observer* (SCO) 19 Oct. 1990, p.4.
60. *SCO*, 16 Nov. 1990, p.7.
61. Celtic match programme versus Dunfermline, 30 Nov. 1991. Article written by *Celtic View* editor, Andrew Smith.
62. Celtic match programme versus St Mirren, 14 Dec. 1991. Article written by freelance reporter, Joe McHugh.
63. See Gallagher, *Glasgow: The Uneasy Peace*, pp.251–86.
64. There are, of course, a number of conceptual problems when it comes to viewing the Irish in Scotland. For example, the significant number of marriages across communities invariably affects this concept, as does the fact that many also consider themselves as 'Scots'. However, for others, particularly in the towns and areas of the west of Scotland, where there are meaningful numbers (almost all of whom are of the Catholic faith) who owe their descent to Irish-born parents, grandparents and great grandparents, 'Irishness' is a clearly distinguishable identity

65. S. Rokkan and D. Urwin, *Economy, Territory and Identity: Politics of West European Peripheries* (London, 1983), p.89.
66. See Murray, *The Old Firm* and *Glasgow's Giants.*
67. J.E. Handley, *The Irish in Scotland* (Glasgow) (this book incorporates both *The Irish in Scotland 1798–1845* and *The Irish in Modern Scotland 1943 & 1947* (Cork, 1964).
68. See J. Mitchell, 'Religion and Politics in Scotland'. Also J. Curtice and D. Seawright, 'The Decline of the Scottish Conservative and Unionist Party 1950–1992', pp.319–42.
69. *The Scottish Referee*, 3 Feb. 1905. Similar more recent comment denigrating the Irish has originated from some writers in Glasgow and west of Scotland newspapers. See also the *Irish Post*, 27 Feb. 1993 for two such reports.
70. See Finn, 'Religion and Social Prejudice', p.73.
71. See Bradley, *Ethnic and Religious Identity*, pp.176–97.
72. See M. Ritchie and M. Dyer, *The Herald*, 25 Sept. 1991, p.8 and 26 Sept. 1991, p.8: 'It would be even more helpful to the separatist cause if the Catholic community could lose its religious and political faith, allowing a reinvented national community [and identity] to transcend historic divisions'. Another writer on the Irish in Scotland and the religious divisions therein also supported this idea in an interview with the author.
73. A further example of this discourse is found in several articles by *The Herald's* then main sports journalist, James Traynor, in which he argues for a 'united' support for the Scottish team. The appeal is essentially aimed towards Rangers fans British Ulster-Loyalist culture and to Celtic fans Irish identity. In part however, it is an appeal which exemplifies a lack of understanding of religious and ethnic identity as well as the possibility of a multicultural and pluralist society in Scotland, whilst it also resembles the arguments of such as Norman Tebbit. Irish identity and anti-Catholicism are construed as opposites and therefore both are condemned in the guise of 'neutrality' and 'unity'. Despite its high claim (and one which is a popular one), Traynor fails to recognize cultural and ethnic diversity and seeks to marginalise a large proportion of the Irish community by invalidating their identity. In addition, for Rangers fans, their British identity sits comfortably above or alongside that of a Scottish one. A similar view was expressed by the same writer in a later column (22 Aug. 1994, Sports Section, p.9) which argued that Rangers in Europe in 1994 should be supported by everyone in Scotland. Everyone had to set aside their 'trivial little loyalties' while 'only the most bigoted' would not allow themselves to support Rangers.
74. Devine, *Irish Immigrants and Scottish Society*, pp.19–43.
75. Rev I.A. Muirhead, Catholic Emancipation in Scotland: the debate and the aftermath, *The Innes Review*, Vol.24, No.2 (Autumn 1973), pp.103–20.
76. G. Walker and T. Gallagher (eds.), *Sermons and Battle Hymns; Protestant Popular Culture in Modern Scotland* (Edinburgh, 1990), p.5.
77. P.O. Farrell, *Ireland's English Question* (New York, 1972).
78. A 1990 survey showed 93 per cent of Celtic supporters as Catholic and four per cent of the Protestant faith. Three per cent claimed no religion. See Bradley, *Ethnic and Religious Identity*, p.61.
79. *Irish Post*, 8 Dec. 1990.
80. By 1998 Celtic had 50,000 season ticket holders. For growing confidence amongst the Irish diaspora in Scotland during the 1980s and 1990s see forthcoming research as well as Joseph M. Bradley, *Sport, Culture, Politics and Scottish Society: Irish Immigrants and the Gaelic Athletic Association* (Edinburgh, 1998).
81. Jay Raynor, *The Independent on Sunday*, 28 June 1992, p.28.

Racial Minorities in a Marginalized Sport: Race, Discrimination and Integration in British Rugby League Football

TONY COLLINS

Introduction

On the face of it, few British sports, if any, have a record of racial integration on the playing field which can compare to that of rugby league. Black players first played professional rugby league before the First World War, appeared at international level in the 1930s and from the 1960s were such a common sight on rugby league pitches that it almost ceased to be a matter for comment. Certainly in comparison to soccer, the contrast is striking. Whereas George Bennett became the first black player to appear in international rugby league in 1935, it was fully 44 years before Viv Anderson became the first black soccer player to play for England. Similarly, although Clive Sullivan first captained the British rugby league side in 1972, it was not until 1993 that Paul Ince became the first black player to captain the England soccer team. And still no top flight British soccer club has appointed a black British person to the role of manager/head coach, almost half a century after Roy Francis, and many others in his wake, achieved the feat in league.[1]

Ellery Hanley's achievement of becoming the national coach of the Great Britain rugby league side in 1994 is even less likely to be emulated in any of the other football codes. Rugby union in England and Wales fares no better than soccer. Aside from the isolated example of James Peters in 1906, no black player appeared in an England rugby union national side until Chris Oti in 1988. Similarly, despite numerous black players appearing in the Welsh national rugby league team, no black player was selected to play for the Welsh rugby union side until the 1980s. National captaincy or appointment in a senior coaching role in either country is, at the moment, simply beyond the bounds of imagination.

This contribution seeks to explore a history which is both hidden and deeply contradictory. Hidden, in that few writers on the history of black people in British sport are aware of the achievements of black players in rugby league. For example, Ernest Cashmore's otherwise comprehensive *Black Sportsmen*, published in 1982, contains no reference to rugby league whatsoever.[2] Contradictory, in so much as despite the prominence of black players, British rugby league shares with other sports the tendency for black players to be racially segregated, or 'stacked', in particular positions, generally of a non-decision-making nature. While black players are numerous, black supporters are extremely rare. And the sport's failure to build any support at all among northern England's Asian community is ample testimony to the limits of its racial integration.

It will be my thesis that the circumstances of rugby league's formation caused it to develop an ideology ostensibly based on meritocracy and opportunity for all. This allowed it to welcome black players into the highest levels of the sport at a time when most other sports shut their doors to them. Nevertheless, the racial integration found in league was shaped and constrained by business exigency and the underlying racist assumptions of British society. On a broader level, the extent and limits of rugby league's racial equality poses a question mark over the ability of any sport to transcend racism in a racist society.

Race, Empire and the 1895 Rugby Split

Rugby in the nineteenth century, including rugby league's precursors in the English rugby union, was shaped by its self-defined role in building the imperial character. In the eyes of the Rugby Football Union (RFU), the amateur ethos was about much more than the denial of monetary remuneration: it was about building character for the greater game of running an empire. The game's middle class leadership believed rugby to be a sport which would train young men to serve their country at home and abroad – as the ardent rugby union correspondent of the *Yorkshire Post* said in 1886, rugby's aim was 'to educate in those important elements which have done so much to make the Anglo-Saxon race the best soldiers, sailors and colonists in the world'.[3] As the roll-call of English rugby union players killed in the slaughter of the First World War testifies, this was a belief which was far more than mere drawing-room rhetoric. But, conversely, those working-class players and spectators who did not accept the ethos of the RFU, either because they demanded payment for playing or because they jeered and heckled referees and opposing teams, were viewed in the same light as those subject to British imperial rule overseas: 'I could not expect worse from the heathens of darkest Africa', claimed J.H. Jones after his refereeing had been hooted and catcalled during a match at Hull.[4]

This intersecting of imperial ideology, class conflict and race came to the fore most explicitly in this period during the predominantly Maori 1888 New Zealand Native tour of the British Isles.[5] Initially the tour was welcomed in a spirit of colonial reconciliation by the RFU – a generation earlier, the Maori people had fought a bitter and bloody war against the imposition of British rule, only being subdued by a British force of proportionately unprecedented size.[6] The English rugby authorities no doubt hoped that, like the 1868 Aboriginal cricket tour to England, the Native tour would combine both sporting and non-sporting entertainment. But the New Zealanders soon demonstrated that ability on the rugby field was not the genetic inheritance of English public schoolboys. Well-organized, powerful and highly skilled, the predominantly Maori tourists embarrassed a number of leading British sides, winning 49 of their 74 matches.

Such success was not appreciated by their hosts, whose indulgence did not stretch to having rugby's hierarchy of playing ability threatened. Joe Warbrick, the organiser of the tour, later summed up the attitude of the RFU: 'As long as [the tourists] were losing they were jolly good fellows in the eyes of the crowd. But as soon as they commenced to win they were hooted and the papers were full of the weakness of the home side and the rough play of the visitors.'[7] In the latter stages of the tour, a number of leading Southern sides even turned down the opportunity to play the tourists. The most notorious incident of English antipathy occurred when, during the international with England, the New Zealanders conformed to the supposedly gentlemanly ethics of the RFU. When they stopped play to form a circle around England's A.E. Stoddart while he changed his torn shorts, England's Frank Evershed picked up the ball and scored a try. The referee, RFU secretary Rowland Hill, refused to countenance New Zealand protests that they were only doing the decent thing and allowed the try to stand. As the tourists departed, *The Field,* the sporting magazine of London society, disdainfully referred to 'our dusky brothers' and expressed the hope that Maori players would be excluded from any future New Zealand touring sides.[8]

But in the north of England, the future heartland of rugby league, where players and spectators were overwhelmingly working class, attitudes differed. While not free of the racism expressed by *The Field,* northern crowds flocked to watch the tourists, appreciating their brand of rugby and identifying with the fact that, like the tourists, they too had suffered at the hands of the social exclusivity of the RFU and its ideological code of amateurism, which sought to curb payments to working-class players and restrain the partisanship of northern working class spectators. More importantly, in the north the game was viewed as a spectacle, as a form of entertainment. The growing commercialization of the game, which was eventually to dissolve the amateur links which bound rugby union together, meant that the tourists were welcomed for the competition they provided and for the element of the exotic, both of which brought in the crowds. Such was their popularity in the north that many clubs, flushed with the success of their initial matches with the tourists, arranged a second game. Unsurprisingly, given the symbiotic relationship between sport and the press, the sports journalists of the north were also among the biggest supporters of the tour, becoming, in the words of the tourists' manager Thomas Eyton, 'almost members of the Maori Brotherhood'.[9]

Given the ambiguous attitude of the RFU towards the 1888 tour, there is little wonder that no further touring sides visited the British Isles until the 1905 New Zealand tour, which was, unlike its 1888 predecessor, most decidedly planned and undertaken in the spirit of colonial *pakeha* vigour. But in the intervening period English rugby had been torn apart by the RFU's insistence on pristine amateurism, which had resulted in 1895 in the driving out of the leading northern clubs and their formation of the Northern Rugby Football Union (NU).[10] The very elements which had made the 1888 tourists popular in the north – a shared sense of exclusion and a view of the sport as a commercial spectacle – now occupied the central position in the NU's ideological world view. In particular, this sense of exclusion was reinforced both by the RFU's purge from its ranks of anyone who had any form of contact with the NU and by its portrayal of the NU as being beyond the pale of British sporting respectability. A typical characterisation came from the former RFU president Arthur Budd, who described the new organization as a 'most admirable drainpipe. A man who would cook accounts would steal your watch, and is capable of any kind of inequity. We are well rid of such persons.'[11]

Such contempt was reciprocated by a large section of the supporters of the NU game (although not entirely by its leadership, many of whom were never comfortable with the split from the RFU and harboured hopes of a compromise), most remarkably by a correspondent to the *Yorkshire Post* who identified the rebel rugby organization with the spirit of Huckleberry Finn, the hero of the classic anti-slavery novel: 'I say with Mark Twain's bold, bad boy, that we glory in the sentence of outlawry pronounced on us, as freeing us from the tyrannical bondage of the English union, and we breathe pure air in being freed from the stifling atmosphere of deceit in which we previously existed.'[12] Thus from its very inception, the NU began to define itself as a sport of the unjustly excluded.

By the time the first New Zealand rugby league tour took place in 1907, such attitudes had crystallized and hardened, causing the NU to evolve into a distinct sport with its own unique rules and culture. Although race appears to have played no role in the selection of the touring side – indeed there was little press comment about the racial origins of the players, although some of them were of Maori descent – the tour brought back memories of the events of 1888 to NU clubs and crowds, not least because two of the tourists, W.T. and J.R. Wynyard, were nephews of the three Wynyard brothers on the original tour.[13] Indeed, most reporters saw the 1907 tourists as the heirs of the 1888 side and eagerly regaled readers with stories of their particular club's previous meetings with the New Zealanders. Vilified in their own country and scorned as a 'phantom side' by supporters of the RFU, the success of the 1907 tourists helped to cement rugby league's self-image as an open, democratic sport.

This ideological stance was underpinned by commercial opportunism. Some of the 1907 players, and many of the following year's Australian tourists, were approached to play for English clubs. Exclusion from the national sporting arena and the appeal of overseas players meant that the NU had little compunction about recruiting from outside of the mainstream. Australian winger Albert Rosenfeld, New Zealand centre-three-quarter Lance Todd and former All-Black forward Charlie Seeling became household names in the rugby-playing areas of the north of England, emphasizing for the leaders of the NU the fact that overseas players brought a glamour and verve to the game which provided success on the pitch and increased attendances off it.

The idea that 'an extra "turn" on the bill might add to the club's coffers', in the words of the *Yorkshire Post's* rugby correspondent, was undoubtedly one of the reasons which lay behind the Hunslet club's signing in 1912 of the game's first black player, Lucius Banks.[14] Banks, an American soldier, was spotted playing American football by a former member of Hunslet's management committee living in New York. The club, then challenging for the league championship, bought Banks out of the US Army and brought him over to England, where he made his debut in his new sport on 27 January 1912, scoring a try in a match against York.[15] Although his presence significantly swelled the attendance at his first game, the welcome was not unanimous. 'Hunslet's Coloured Coon' was the headline in the local evening paper, while the generally anti-Northern Union *Yorkshire Post* complained that his selection was unfair to local players and patronizingly suggested that if the club wanted to sign 'coloured' players they should go to South Africa, where 'they are reputed to be capable goal kickers with bare feet'.[16] Despite this racist opposition, Banks and the club persevered with their attempt to translate his abilities in one football code to another – playing on the wing he scored four tries in his first three games but the strength of Hunslet's back division limited his opportunities. An attempt to develop his skills in the playmaking position of stand-off half, the nearest equivalent then to his reported gridiron position of quarterback, was unsuccessful and he faded from the scene in 1913.

In the same year that Banks' rugby league career was closing, Barrow signed the first black Englishman to play the game, James 'Jimmy' Peters, a dockworker from Plymouth of West Indian background. Unlike Banks,

Peters had a rugby pedigree, having played as a stand-off half for the England rugby union side five times between 1906 and 1908. Despite his acknowledged ability, his inclusion in the national rugby union side was highly controversial, one journalist commenting that 'his selection is by no means popular on racial grounds'.[17] In contrast, none of the Barrow newspapers which announced his signing for the rugby league side even mentioned the colour of his skin. In his early thirties when he switched to league, Peters was unable to transfer his rugby union skills and he spent most of his time playing in Barrow's reserve side before moving to St Helens the following year, where his career was ended by the onset of the First World War.

Black Players to the Fore

The combination of commercial exigency and a willingness to recruit on the basis of merit rather than social status meant that by the 1930s, British rugby league had developed a uniquely cosmopolitan flavour, as its traditional base of white northern working class players was supplemented not only by white players from Australia, New Zealand and South Africa but also by black players. At a time when black boxers were barred from fighting for British championships – despite being prominent in British boxing for well over a century – and other black sportsmen rarely achieved prominence of any sort, still less play at international level, black players began to make their presence felt at the highest levels of rugby league.[18] Most notable was Wigan stand-off half George Bennett, who signed for the club in 1930 and quickly established a reputation as a skilled playmaker, eventually making 232 appearances for the club and recording over a century of tries. In 1935 he made the first of his three appearances for Wales in their inaugural international match against France. Even more successful internationally was Oldham loose-forward Alec Givvons, who missed only two of Wales's eight matches between 1936 and the outbreak of the Second World War. Of particular note is the fact that both played in central, decision-making positions on the field and appear not to have suffered from stereotypical assumptions about black players being suited only for positions based on speed or strength. Nevertheless, this did not stop Bennett being nicknamed 'Darkie' by the press.

   But the most prominent black rugby league player to play in the 1930s only began to make an impact in the following decade. Roy Francis signed for Wigan as a seventeen year-old in 1936. A winger or stand-off half, he played just twelve matches in the first team before being transferred to Barrow. With Barrow, as a guest player for Dewsbury during the war, and in war-time rugby union games, Francis became noted both for his elusiveness and his leadership on the field: he was not only 'a man capable of snatching the vital try at a critical stage, he is also talented at keeping up the morale of his team generally ... it is he who, with a choice remark or slight action, can rapidly dispel the tension of a critical moment'.[19] After making his debut for Wales in March 1946 it was widely expected that he would be named in that year's British side to tour Australia and New Zealand, yet, seemingly inexplicably, he was omitted. It later became an open secret that he was left out of the tour party by the rugby league authorities so as not to offend the Australian government's 'White Australia' policy.

Francis eventually played for the Great Britain side in 1947, two years before he moved to Hull, where he became probably the first ever black person to coach a professional sports team in Britain. Brilliant as he was as a player, his achievements as a rugby league coach were even more outstanding. He turned a mediocre Hull side into championship winners – but more than that, he brought to the game motivational techniques, fitness regimes and tactical innovations which were generally unknown to the sport until Australian coaches such as Terry Fearnley and Jack Gibson began studying American football in the late 1960s. Moving to become coach of Leeds in 1963, he enjoyed further success and built a side still remembered for its skilful attacking play involving every player in the team. In 1968 he was appointed head coach of the North Sydney club in Australia. At a time when Australian rugby league was taking the first steps in a playing and coaching revolution which would take the sport to unprecedented levels, Francis seemed the ideal man to usher in a new age. Instead, he faced a wall of hostility. While many put it down to his being a 'Pom', Australian slang for British, it was animated by racism – *Rugby League Week* even compared him to Othello and Malcolm X, the courageous American fighter for black liberation, in order to imply that his race made him an unreliable troublemaker.[20] Deeply disillusioned, he returned to England to coach Leeds and later Bradford.

The success of Roy Francis in the 1940s heralded the beginnings of a significant presence of black players in professional rugby league in England. In 1951, Cec Thompson, a second-row forward with the Hunslet club who had been born in Leeds, became the first black Englishman to be selected for Great Britain when he played against New Zealand. In 1955 he was made captain of Workington Town, where he had transferred in 1953, and in 1960 he was appointed as coach of the Barrow club. More famously, in 1953 Wigan signed winger Billy Boston, a man who was to become a local legend. Boston was such a phenomenon that he was selected for the British tour of Australia a matter of months after making his rugby league debut, becoming the youngest-ever tourist and, while on tour, establishing a new record for tries on a tour. He became one of Wigan's greatest players, and his total of 571 career tries, the second highest ever recorded, won him a founder's place in the British Rugby League Hall of Fame. But despite his status, he too was to suffer from racist humiliation – the British league authorities deliberately left him out of the sides which played exhibition games in South Africa following Australasian tours in 1957 and 1962, and in the latter year he was detained by New Zealand immigration officials when entering that country with the British touring party.

In 1954, winger Johnny Freeman, who went to the same school in Cardiff as Boston, signed for Halifax and eventually became holder of the club record for tries in a career, appearing for Wales in 1963. Colin Dixon, a centre three-quarter, followed the same route from South Wales to Halifax in the early 1960s, becoming club captain at the age of 23 and making 14 international appearances in a career which spanned three decades. On retirement as a player, he too become a coach. Of even greater prominence was Clive Sullivan, who was signed by the Hull club in 1961. A winger with a trademark of drifting infield to take advantage of play, he became the first black captain of a major British sports team in 1972 when he was appointed Great Britain captain, eventually leading the British side to victory in that year's World Cup Final. He eventually made 22 international appearances, scored career centuries of tries for both of Hull's professional league sides and ended his career as coach to the Doncaster club.

This roll-call of black players achieving at the highest levels of rugby league continued through the 1980s and 1990s. Des Drummond, Henderson Gill, Roy Powell, Martin Offiah, Phil Ford, Sonny Nickle, Alan Hunte, Carl Gibson and Jason Robinson all appeared for Great Britain, but no player, of whatever race, dominated British rugby league in this period like Ellery Hanley. Born in Leeds, Hanley rose to prominence as a stand-off half in the early 1980s, when he became the first player since Billy Boston to score sixty tries in a season. Transferring to the Wigan club in 1985, he switched to the loose-forward position and as captain of the side helped steer it to become league's world club champions. In 1987 he was appointed Great Britain captain, a position he held until his retirement from international football in 1992, and in 1995 he became British coach, the first black person to coach a major British national sports side.

Integration and Discrimination

Why is it that rugby league has such a record of apparent integration on the playing field? As we have seen, from its inception the game found itself excluded from the mainstream of British sport – both the RFU and the Amateur Athletics Association banned its players from participating in their events and even the Football Association at one point buckled before RFU pressure and banned a NU player from soccer – and its self-perception as a democratic sport open to all allowed it to welcome players who would be excluded from other sports or whose opportunities would be severely restricted. This emphasis on ability and merit meant that racial barriers did not carry the same weight in the game as they did in other, more socially conservative, sports. As we saw earlier in the use of the quotation from *Huckleberry Finn*, there were also elements in rugby league who were quite conscious, and in some cases proud, of their aberrant position in relation to middle class sporting norms. Thus it was far easier for a predominantly white sport with such an ideological stance to accept black players in positions of authority.

Moreover, the commercial necessities of the sport obliged it to seek crowd-pleasing players from wherever it could find them. Unlike soccer, its main rival in the north of England, rugby league did not have the national presence to ensure consistently high levels of spectator interest and constantly sought to bolster itself through the importation of overseas players, cup competitions and international tours. Its quest to enhance itself as a spectacle therefore obliged it to ignore many of the social norms governing other sports. Thus it embraced open professionalism in a way which even soccer did not, was not above poaching players from other football codes, especially rugby union, and did not feel itself bound by the racial restrictions which then dominated British sport. If a player was good enough to attract more paying spectators through the turnstiles, rugby league officials were unlikely to worry about the colour of his skin. Similarly, when appointing coaches, the key criterion was the ability to mould a winning side, regardless of race or other social factors, because a victorious team would bring commercial success.

On a broader level, the fact that rugby league existed in an almost entirely separate sphere from that occupied by the middle and upper classes meant that it was not wholly part of national public life. In this, it was a cultural expression of what Tom Nairn has described as the working classes' consciousness of being 'something of an exile inside the society which [they] supported'.[21] The game's marginalised position in society was reinforced by the attitudes of its opponents, particularly those in rugby union, who portrayed it as mercenary and morally inferior to other sports. Its exclusion from the public and grammar schools, the universities and the armed forces meant that it was identified exclusively with the industrial working classes of northern England and lacked the social status of other sports, even soccer. To a limited extent, it therefore shared with those who suffered from racial oppression a sense of exclusion from society. This intersection of race and class status was captured by Cec Thompson, the international rugby league player of the 1950s, when he remembered the problems he faced as a young man: 'It was bad enough being black ... How much lower down the social scale could one go than be seen as a black, uneducated rugby league player ... .?'[22]

These ideological, commercial and social factors therefore created a recognition that rugby league offered something of a relatively open and meritocratic alternative to those sports more tightly bound to the prevailing racism in British society. Such a belief may well have helped to persuade Lucius Banks – who knew that however great his talents, the racism of American sport meant his prospects were meagre – to sign for Hunslet. It certainly animated Wally McArthur, the Australian aboriginal sprinter, who signed to play for Rochdale Hornets in 1953 after he had been left out of the 1952 Australian Olympic athletics squad because of the colour of his skin. Similarly, a small but significant number of black South African rugby union players escaped the iron heel of apartheid by moving to play with English rugby league sides in the 1960s and 1970s, none more successfully than Green Vigo, a linchpin of the Wigan side of the seventies. Although it did not come to fruition, possibly the most spectacular example of this sense that rugby league did not march in step with other sports was Wakefield Trinity's attempt to sign Thommie Smith, the American 200 metres gold medalist at the 1968 Olympics whose black power salute on the victory rostrum led to him and John Carlos being vindictively banned from international athletics.

But it is the case of black Welsh players which provides the hardest evidence in support of the idea that rugby league's aberrant position in society made it attractive to players from racial minorities. Many of them, such as Billy Boston, Johnny Freeman and Colin Dixon, came from the docklands area of Cardiff, home to one of Britain's oldest and largest black communities, and their families had experienced racism at its most stark. In 1919 the community was attacked for two days by rioting white racist mobs.[23] Using the provisions of the Aliens Order of 1920 and the Special Restriction (Coloured Alien Seamen) Order of 1925, the Cardiff police classified all black men as aliens, regardless of place of birth or legal status. In 1935 black seaman were effectively purged from all jobs on the Cardiff docks, forcing the black community into even greater poverty.

In addition to the overt racism experienced off the field, black rugby union players were disadvantaged by the symbiotic link between the sport and Welsh national identity. As expressed through rugby union, Welsh nationalism was closely tied to British imperial identity: indeed, Welsh rugby was 'profoundly pro-British'.[24] Rather than being separatist or oppositional, it was predicated on proving that the Welsh nation was the best representative of the British imperial ideal – which meant that a white skin was a prerequisite for success. Faced with open hostility in their daily lives and institutionalized racism in their sport, there can be little wonder that young black rugby union players eagerly accepted the offer of contracts from rugby league clubs in the north of England. The fact that they would be banned for life by the Welsh rugby union authorities for violating the amateur ethic and signing for a rugby league club was far less of a threat to the futures of these players than to those who were white. While the open professionalism of rugby league meant that players could make more money than under the covert payments system operating in Welsh rugby union, it is clear that by the 1950s and 1960s the presence of black players at the highest levels of league acted as a positive incentive for other black players to switch sports – one of the key factors in persuading Clive Sullivan to sign for Hull was the success of fellow black Welshman Billy Boston.[25] And few black players went back to Wales after their league careers were over, most staying in the towns where their talents had earned respect and made them a living. Indeed, Boston and Sullivan became heroes in their adopted homes of Wigan and Hull, developing the same iconic relationship with these towns as that which C.L.R. James described West Indian cricketer Learie Constantine having with the Lancashire town of Nelson.[26]

But the relative openness of rugby league was not simply confined to its geographic position in the north of England, nor was it the case that it simply chronologically anticipated the greater acceptance of black players by other sports in the latter part of the twentieth century. This can be seen by the fact that its ideological stance was carried with it wherever the game was established. This was particularly true in New Zealand, where the sport became closely identified with the Maori and Polynesian communities. Here the domination of rugby union and its central position in the national identity of *pakeha*, or white, New Zealand heightened rugby league's sense of exclusion and marginalisation. Especially in Auckland, rugby league has been traditionally the sport of working class Maori and Polynesian immigrants. The identification of league with the non-white communities of New Zealand has grown stronger over the past two decades, especially with the decline of the mining and associated industries of the west coast where the sport was strong among the area's white working class. It is now common for the New Zealand national team to be composed entirely of Maori and Polynesian players. Indeed, the most recent confirmation of the symbiotic relationship between league's ideological stance and its commercial exigencies can be seen in the creation of the Auckland Warriors side. Formed to take part in the expanded Australian premiership competition in 1995, the club was an avowedly commercial proposition, geared to take advantage of the massive upsurge in the popularity of league in the early 1990s. Despite, or perhaps because of, this, the club adopted Maori imagery and symbolism in its marketing strategy. Its name was a deliberate appeal to Maori culture, as was the club logo, and the club's game day entertainment and supporters' activities are almost exclusively drawn from Maori and Polynesian cultural activities. Nevertheless, the contradiction between the club's image and the fact that its key decision-makers off the field are almost all white has led to regular criticism of the functioning of the club from Maori and Polynesian supporters and players.[27]

In Australia, rugby league's position differed from the English and New Zealand games in that it was the dominant sport in the eastern states of New South Wales and Queensland. Moreover, its close relationship with the Australian Labor Party, a supporter of the long-standing 'White Australia' policy, meant that league was neither subject to the same exclusion from society nor as immediately identifiable with racial minorities who suffered from institutionalized discrimination. Nevertheless, the ostensibly democratic ideological underpinnings of the league game remained a powerful force. Perceived by both itself and wider society as being 'the working man's (sic) game', and drawing its playing strength and supporters overwhelmingly from the working classes, it has, claims Colin Tatz, the historian of aboriginal sport, 'been more generous to aborigines [than other Australian sports]: it has provided easier access, readier acceptance, better facilities, and more encouragement … '.[28]

Although this may be an overstatement, it is undeniable that a number of black and aboriginal players made their mark on Australian rugby league as early as the inter-war years. The earliest pioneers were George Green, a hooker, who played for Sydney's Eastern Suburbs side in 1908 and went on to play for and coach North Sydney in the 1920s, and Paul Tranquille, a New South Wales sprint champion, who also played for Norths at the same time. Recent research has suggested that Green and Tranquille were respectively of Afro-Caribbean and Mauritian descent, rather than aboriginal.[29] Aboriginal players made appearances for state representative sides in the 1920s and 1930s. Probably the most notable aboriginal player of this period was Lin Johnson, who played twice for New South Wales and kicked the winning goal for Canterbury-Bankstown in the 1942 Sydney Grand Final. His brother Dick also played in the 1939 and 1947 Grand Finals. By the 1970s, following the liberalisation of some aspects of Australia's official racism towards the aboriginal population, Australian rugby league had achieved an apparently high level of racial integration on the playing field. Beginning with Lionel Morgan in 1960, aboriginal players regularly played for the Australian national side, with Arthur Beetson achieving the rare distinction of both captaining and coaching his country, and Mal Meninga, of Solomon Islands descent, making an unprecedented four Australian tours of Britain, twice as captain.[30]

Nevertheless, there remains a great degree of racial segregation in the lower levels of rugby league, where all-aboriginal teams were, and remain, common in local competitions. Such teams have become an expression of racial pride and a means of competing with white people on equal terms, opportunities for which were largely precluded from the daily lives of aboriginal people. Such has been the identification of aboriginal people with the sport that there have been a number of calls to form a professional all-aboriginal team to play in the national Australian rugby league competition. Thus the same open, meritocratic ideology has allowed league to became the sport of choice of another marginalized, racially oppressed group.

The Limits of Ideology

Faced with such evidence, it is undeniable that, in many ways, rugby league has a unique record of racial integration when compared to other sports. But does that also mean, as others have claimed, that the sport 'remains admirably committed to a radical policy on race and colour' and that 'it has sought to blend together, over the last sixty years, indigenous and immigrant cultures in new and experimental forms'?[31]

This is a claim too far. Rugby league's ideological stance of openness and democracy has definite limits. While it may be excluded from the mainstream of British sport, it is still very much part of British society. On the field of play, where the sport appears to be far more integrated than other sports, there is incontrovertible evidence that, while black league players may have greater opportunities to rise to prominence in the game, they are restricted by racial prejudice in the positions they occupy on the field. The phenomenon of 'stacking', or positional segregation, has been well documented in studies of American professional baseball and football, and, to a lesser extent, in English soccer and Australian rugby league.[32] All of these studies found that black players largely occupied non-central, non-decision making positions – for example, few black players played in the quarterback role in American football or in the critical midfield positions in soccer. In particular, these studies noted that black players were confined to positions which required speed and strength, and conformed to racially stereotyped notions about black people being 'natural athletes' and 'fast runners'.

As Table 1 indicates, similar conclusions can be drawn about British rugby league. In the years 1984 to 1994 the Great Britain rugby league side, made up of the best English, Welsh and occasionally Scottish players, played sixty-five games, in which thirteen black players made an aggregate total of 152 appearances. In only one game during that time was there no black player in the side. Despite this representation, over 68 per cent of the appearances made by black players were in the wing or centre positions, traditionally those roles in which speed is the most important factor. Even more tellingly, not a single black player appeared for the national side in the two critical playmaking positions of scrum-half and hooker. Of the other positions, all of the stand-off half and loose forward appearances were made by one man, Ellery Hanley, and, of the other 12 black players, only Phil Ford at full-back, Roy Powell at prop and Sonny Nickle at second-row forward appeared in any position other than winger or centre. Similar findings were reported at club level by Long *et al.*, who discovered in their study of racism in professional club rugby league that of 38 black players in English divisions one and two, 24 were wingers, fully 63 per cent of the total. This also conforms to the pattern found in Australian rugby league, where Hallinan found that almost 60 per cent of aboriginal players played in the positions of winger or centre.[33]

TABLE 1

APPEARANCES BY BLACK PLAYERS IN THE
GREAT BRITAIN RUGBY LEAGUE TEAM 1984–1994

Position	Appearances	Percentage of Total
Full back	2	1.3%
Wing three-quarter	83	54.6%
Centre three-quarter	21	13.9%
Stand-off half	6	3.9%
Scrum half	0	0.0
Prop forward	4	2.6%
Hooker	0	0.0
Second-row forward	21	13.9%
Loose forward	15	9.8%
Totals	152	100.0%

Source: *Rothman's Rugby League Yearbook 1995–96* (London, 1995).

Indeed, such positional segregation has historically been the norm for the sport. By and large, the vast majority of black players who have become famous in league have been wingers, despite the ability of many of them to play in other positions. Similar stereotyping can also be seen in the fact that, of black players coming to prominence in the forward positions, most of them have played as second-row forwards, traditionally seen as a role requiring great speed and strength. That such stereotypical views run deep within the sport were highlighted by the remarks of Barry Maranta, owner of the London Broncos rugby league side, when he announced in 1995 that his club was going to target its player recruitment drive on local black youths: 'They can't play soccer because of their size, but ... they're Wendell Sailors [Brisbane Broncos' star black winger/second-row forward]. They can sit on the wing and bust through tackles'.[34] As this statement demonstrates, rugby league does not share English soccer's widespread racist belief that black players lack physical courage or, to use the vernacular, that they 'do not have the bottle'. This is probably due to the sheer physicality of the rugby league game as compared to soccer, making it impossible to accuse any player of physical cowardice. Nevertheless, the sport's emphasis on the speed and strength of black players fits perfectly with racist images of black men as entertainers or labourers.[35]

Off the field, there is little evidence to suggest that the sport poses a conscious challenge to prevailing attitudes on race. As we saw in the cases of Roy Francis and Billy Boston, the rugby league authorities have been only too willing to bow before racist pressure and leave black players out of touring sides when their presence would have been embarrassing to host governments. Throughout the 1950s, there were constant accusations from senior figures in the game, such as leading journalist Eddie Waring and former Great Britain captain Gus Risman, that racism on the part of the selectors was responsible for keeping Cec Thompson out of the British side.[36] More recently, in 1988 Des Drummond was left out of the British touring party to Australia and New Zealand after defending himself from a supporter who rushed on to the field shouting racist abuse during a match. Racial abuse of players by crowds has been commonplace, although not on the widespread and horrific scale of English soccer. Even in the 1950s, Billy Boston, a seemingly universally popular player, was subject to such taunting, as Eddie Waring noted: 'there were many matches in England when Boston had to stand up to crowd comments about his play and colour – and more than once he went towards the crowd'.[37] Long *et al.*'s study of racism in rugby league in the mid-1990s noted that racial abuse of black players by supporters was 'a small but significant problem'.[38]

The crowds at rugby league matches have remained overwhelmingly white. Significantly, Long *et al.* discovered that, on the date of their survey, there were more black people, 38, playing professional rugby league than were watching it, who totalled just 24. Despite the success of black players in the sport, there appears to be little incentive for black people to become supporters. Rugby league's continuing lack of status means that it is not perceived as a method of social integration, unlike in Australia where the sport has been seen as a route to integration by immigrant communities. More to the point, league is perceived by black and Asian communities as being an exclusively white sport – for example, when noted black British author Caryl Philips made a radio programme about race and sport in the

1980s, he made no mention of rugby league, despite the achievements of black players in it and the fact that he was raised in Leeds, home to three professional rugby league clubs.[39] This perception reflects the reality both of the racial composition of league crowds but also the lack of relationship of the sport with its local minority communities. It is notable that those players who became heroes of the towns in which they played, such as Boston in Wigan or Sullivan in Hull, were not native to rugby league's heartland, suggesting that it is easier for the sport to accept as heroes those black players who appear to be unconnected to the racial divisions of their locality. Even Ellery Hanley, arguably a far greater player than either Boston or Sullivan and certainly a higher achiever, never gained a similar level of universal admiration or affection, despite being born and bred in Leeds.

These factors are most graphically highlighted by rugby league's relationship, or lack of it, with its local Asian community. In the early 1960s many Asians emigrated from the Indian sub-continent to take jobs in the textiles mills of the north of England, traditionally a key industrial base of rugby league support. By the 1970s, large numbers of rugby league clubs found themselves in towns and cities with significant Asian populations; some, such as Halifax and Keighley, found that the working class housing areas surrounding their stadia had become the centres of local Asian communities. However, the sport has done little to attract Asian players or spectators to the game. In contrast to the success of players with an Afro-Caribbean background, to date only two Asian players, the brothers Ikram and Tony Butt, have played professional rugby league – Ikram Butt playing for the English rugby league side in 1995 – and only two others, Safraz Patel and Gurjinderpal Pahal, have received representative honours in amateur rugby league, both as youth internationals. Just as racist stereotypes have helped to segregate black players in peripheral positions in league, stereotypes about Asian people not being physically strong enough for the game, despite the popularity of wrestling and Kabaddi in Asian communities, are used to explain the lack of Asian participation in the game. The close proximity of many rugby league clubs to Asian communities only serves to emphasise – by way of contrast – the huge gulf between the sport's ideological rhetoric and the reality of the limited degree of integration it offers.[40]

Conclusion

Rugby league is therefore a deeply contradictory phenomenon. A long history of achievement by black players and coaches coexists with deep-rooted racial stereotyping and estrangement from local minority communities. How can these seemingly mutually contradictory factors inhabit the same sport?

The key to understanding rugby league's relationship to racial minorities lies in the importance of commercial exigency to the game. It was the clash between the amateur ideology of the rugby union authorities and the commercial necessities of the game in the North of England which led to the 1895 split and the creation of rugby league. The combination of exclusion from the imperial British sporting mainstream and the need to provide a spectacle to attract paying spectators allowed league to develop an ideology more meritocratic and open than other mass spectator sports. In a very real sense therefore, rugby league provided players of all races a chance to take advantage of the 'equality of the balance sheet'.

But this equality was open only to those who could help the sport fulfil its commercial needs. Thus the vast majority of black players in league before the 1970s came from outside the traditional rugby league-playing regions and had already established sufficiently high reputations to increase spectator interest in the clubs for which they signed. The sport therefore saw no need to combat racial stereotyping in the game or racist assumptions among its almost entirely white following – what it desired was players who would help its clubs become successful, regardless of race but also regardless of any need to oppose racism. This also explains why the sport has done little or nothing to encourage the participation of local black and Asian communities in the sport: the effort required to stimulate interest in these communities is not viewed as being cost effective, not to mention an unwillingness to do so because of the prevalence of racist attitudes to non-white communities within the game. The fact that its star black players were usually from outside its localities also allowed the game to step aside from confronting the problems of racism in its own regions.

The ambiguous history of rugby league must also throw doubt on the widespread belief that sport can somehow be a force in helping to overcome racism in society. As we have seen, even a sport with league's ideological predisposition to identification with those facing discrimination is largely incapable of confronting deeper aspects of racial stereotyping and institutionalised discrimination. Moreover, it may well be the case that league's apparently successful record of on-field integration serves as a self-congratulatory barrier to it confronting its inability to break out of its traditional white working class constituency and build support among its local black and Asian communities. In short, rugby league demonstrates that having a significant number of black players in prominent positions does not mean that a sport is either free of racism or represents a clear alternative to sports more overtly committed to racist policies.

Nevertheless, as a sport which was marginalized in its relation to British national identity and society, rugby league offered an opportunity to excel in sport to those who also felt themselves marginalised by society and had been denied such opportunities by other sports. But, driven by commercial necessity, the game was also a product of that society and reflected, albeit in different forms, its racism – the chains which shackled black people in other sports had not been broken by rugby league, merely loosened.

NOTES

1. In 1996 Chelsea appointed black Dutchman Ruud Gullit as manager, although, like Michael Jordan, such was the superstar's reputation that he appeared to transcend the issue of race. For the abundant number of qualified black British candidates, the doors to managership remain locked.
2. Ernest Cashmore, *Black Sportsmen* (London, 1982).
3. *Yorkshire Post*, 29 Nov. 1886, p.8.
4. *Yorkshire Post*, 21 Feb. 1893, p.8.
5. The original intention of the organisers was that the team should be an exclusively Maori side. However, the addition of five *pakeha* players to the tour resulted in the team being called the New Zealand Native Football Representatives. For full details of the tour see Greg Ryan, *Forerunners of the All Blacks* (Canterbury, NZ, 1993).
6. For a comprehensive account of the New Zealand Wars see James Belich, *The New Zealand Wars and the Victorian Interpretation of Racial Conflict* (Auckland, 1986). At the height of the war, the British had 18,000 troops in place to oppose a total Maori population of just 60,000.
7. Quoted in Ryan, *Forerunners of the All Blacks*, p.94.
8. *The Field*, 30 March 1889, p.7.
9. Quoted in Ryan, *Forerunners of the All Blacks*, p.91. The popularity of the New Zealand side with northern English crowds is also attested to by Greg Ryan in his '"Handsome Physiognomy and Blameless Physique": Indigenous Colonial Sporting Tours and British Racial Consciousness, 1868 and 1888', *The International Journal of the History of Sport*, Vol.14, No.2 (Aug. 1997), pp.78–9.
10. The NU changed its name to the Rugby Football League in 1922.
11. Arthur Budd, 'The Past Season', in *Athletic News Football Annual 1897* (Manchester, 1897), p.194.
12. 'A Member of a Northern Union Club', writing to the *Yorkshire Post*, 21 Sept. 1895, p.10. Unfortunately for the historian, pseudonymous letters to newspapers were the norm at this time.
13. W.T. Wynyard was also to become the founding treasurer of the New Zealand Rugby League, and another brother, G.A., was also a founding member of the NZRL executive committee. Thus New Zealand rugby league preserved a level of continuity with the 1888 tour which does not seem to have been felt by the New Zealand rugby union authorities.
14. *Yorkshire Post*, 29 Jan. 1912, p.3.
15. In the process, Banks also became the first American to play rugby league and probably only the fourth black American to play professional football of any code. Only three black American footballers had played professionally up to 1912. See Mike Rathet and Don R. Smith, 'We're Here to Play Football', in Richard Whittingham (ed.), *The Fireside Book of Pro Football* (New York, 1989), pp.229–36.
16. *Yorkshire Evening Post*, 26 Jan. 1912, p.3; *Yorkshire Post*, 29 Jan. 1912, p.3.
17. *Yorkshire Post*, 17 March 1906, p.11. For details of Peters' signing for Barrow rugby league club, see *Barrow News*, 11 Oct. and 29 Nov. 1913 and the *North West Daily Mail*, 6 Oct. 1913.
18. For black boxers, see Peter Fryer, *Staying Power: The History of Black People in Britain* (London, 1984). Only one black athlete represented Britain at the Olympics during this period, sprinter Jack London in 1928. Although evidence is at best sparse, it appears that very few black players appeared for professional soccer sides in England before the Second World War: three of the most notable being Arthur Wharton, a former sprinter who played as

goalkeeper for Preston North End in the 1880s; Walter Tull, who signed for Tottenham Hotspur in 1909; and Jack Leslie, who made over 350 appearances for Plymouth Argyle in the 1920s. See Caryl Phillips, 'Can Sport Break Down Racial Prejudice?' *The Listener*, 24 May 1984, pp.9–10.

19. 'Airlie Robin' quoted in Robert Gate, *Gone North: Welshmen in Rugby League*, Vol.1 (Ripponden, 1986), p.50.

20. For an account of the racism experienced by Francis at Norths, see Andrew Moore, *The Mighty Bears! A Social History of North Sydney* (Sydney, 1996), pp.214–26.

21. Tom Nairn, 'The English Working Class', in Robin Blackburn (ed.), *Ideology in Social Science* (London, 1972), p.198.

22. Cec Thompson, *Born On The Wrong Side* (London, 1995), p.27.

23. See Neil Evans, 'The South Wales Race Riots of 1919', *Llafur*, Vol.3, No.1 (Spring 1980); Ron Ramdin, *The Making of the Black Working Class in Britain* (Aldershot, 1987) and Peter Fryer, *Staying Power.*

24. David Smith, 'People's Theatre: A Century of Welsh Rugby', *History Today*, March 1981, p.37. Despite the emphasis of many historians on the inter-twining of Welsh national identity and rugby union, no work has been done on the relationship of the Wales' black population to the national game. Interestingly, Welsh soccer has often been portrayed, like rugby league, as being antithetical to Welsh national culture and it too has a better record of racial integration, at least at a national level. In 1931 Eddie Paris became the first black player to play for the Welsh national soccer side. I am grateful to Phil Vasili for this information.

25. See Sullivan's biography by Joe Latus, *Hard Road to the Top* (Hull, 1973), p.35.

26. For C.L.R. James on Constantine and Nelson, see *Beyond A Boundary* (London, 1963), p.127. After his death in 1985, the local council in Hull renamed the main arterial road into the city 'Clive Sullivan Way'.

27. For a recent example, see 'Monie Digs In', in *Rugby League Week* (Sydney), 26 Feb. 1997, p.7.

28. Colin Tatz, *Aborigines in Sport* (Adelaide, 1987), p.80.

29. Much of the detail here is taken from Colin Tatz, *Obstacle Race: Aborigines in Sport* (Sydney, 1995). Andrew Moore has researched the backgrounds of Green and Tranquille in *The Mighty Bears!*, Ch.2.

30. Colin Tatz, *Aborigines in Sport*, p.83.

31. Phil Melling, 'Definitions for the Definers, not the Defined', *The Sports Historian*, No.16 (May 1996), p.29.

32. J.W. Loy and J.W. McElvogue, 'Racial Segregation in American Sport', *International Review for the Sociology of Sport*, Vol.5, No.25 (1970). J.A. Maguire, '"Race" and Position Assignment in English Soccer: A Preliminary Analysis of Ethnicity and Sport in Britain', *Sociology of Sport Journal*, Vol.5, No.3 (1988). C.J. Hallinan, 'Aborigines and Positional Segregation in Australian Rugby League', *International Review for the Sociology of Sport*, Vol.26, No.2 (1991), pp.69–79.

33. J. Long, N. Tongue, K. Spracklen and B. Carrington, 'What's the Difference? A Study of the Nature and Extent of Racism in Rugby League' (Leeds Metropolitan University, 1995). For Australia, see Hallinan, 'Aborigines and Positional Segregation … ', pp.74–5.

34. Barry Maranta, quoted in *Rugby League Express*, 28 April 1995, p.5.

35. For more on racism in English soccer, see Dave Hill, *Out of His Skin: The John Barnes Phenomenon* (London, 1989).

36. See Cec Thompson, *Born on the Wrong Side*, pp.29 and 34.

37. Eddie Waring, *The Great Ones* (London, 1969), p.95.

38. Long *et al.*, 'What's The Difference?', p.3.

39. Caryl Phillips, *The Listener*, loc. cit.

40. Little work has been done on the relationship of Britain's Asian population to sport. One exception to this is Pnina Werbner, 'Our Blood is Green: Cricket, Identity and Social Empowerment Among British Pakistanis', in J. MacClancy (ed.), *Sport, Identity and Ethnicity* (Oxford, 1996), pp.87–111.

'When the World Soccer Cup is Played on Roller Skates': The Atttempt to Make Gaelic Games International: The Meath–Australia Matches of 1967–68

MIKE CRONIN

Introduction

In the late summer of 1967 the players of County Meath won the All-Ireland Gaelic football final and lifted the Sam Maguire trophy. Usually the All-Ireland final victory was the end of the season for football players, the applause had been taken and there was nothing to do but return home and begin planning for next year's campaign. In 1967, however, an innovative contest awaited the players of Meath. Playing on the similarities between the Gaelic and Australian football codes it was arranged that Meath, as representatives of Ireland, were to play an Australian side drawn from the ranks of Australian rules players in a Gaelic football match at Croke Park in the autumn of 1967, and in the spring of 1968 they would travel down under to play further matches against certain provincial teams as well as a national side. In the late 1960s, an era of increasing globalization and rapid international travel links, such sporting contests hardly seem surprising. International test matches in cricket and rugby were well established and the different European competitions for soccer clubs were highly popular.

What is different about the Meath–Australia matches is that they were an attempt to internationalise sporting traditions which, previously, had nothing but a domestic outlet. In developing Gaelic games and Australian rules during the nineteenth century, the Irish and Australians had rebelled against the overriding dominance of the British Empire by ignoring colonial games such as cricket, rugby or soccer, and had thereby stressed their national independence and cultural difference. While the development of such native sports was important in the anti-colonial mission of self-determination, in the long term it left Gaelic games and Australian rules

---

The help of Peter McDermott, who was instrumental in organizing the Meath tour to Australia, and Mick O'Brien, who was a player at the time, was central to the work which went into this contribution.

players isolated and without the important outlet of glory in international competition. Both games were and still are highly popular with the stars of the games promoted as sporting heroes. However, neither game offered sporting success on an international platform. By using the apparent similarities between the two codes the 1967 and 1968 matches were an attempt to bring about an international match which would allow the winners to pose as the world's best, rather than merely domestic county or provincial champions.

The aim of this chapter is to examine the matches between Meath and Australia (as well as the accompanying matches against Irish-Americans as representatives of the USA) in 1967–68. The matches were played in the context of the need for an international platform for games which had only a domestic appeal. It will be argued that the attempt to internationalise Gaelic games took place in order to promote national prestige and identity in a manner that solely domestic competition could not. Notions of identity are formed at many different levels, but in sport one of the most important has been the creation of nation states competing against each other in an 'us and them' contest. This allows national prestige to be played out on the sports field with all the supporters of that nation investing their identity in the fortunes of their representatives. A victory against another nation produces a sense of elation, national pride and unites the individual behind the team (or individual sportsperson) and the accompanying symbolism of the national strip, the flag and the anthem. Solely domestic competition does not allow for this as all emotional attachments are invested in communal opposition or support, for or against the town or region rather than the unifying ideal of the nation.

Although a particular sport may have a specific resonance for a particular nation (for example, baseball for Americans), may encapsulate the spirit of a specific culture (for example, sumo wrestling for the Japanese) or may, through the style which an international game is played exhibit national characteristics which are real or imagined (for example, the natural flair of Brazilian soccer players), the real test of identity is in comparison with others. Any given ethnic, minority or national group, whether as willing (for example, Lennox Lewis as a representative of Britain rather than Canada in World Boxing) or unwilling (for example, Dynamo Kiev as representatives of the former Soviet Union rather than the Ukraine) members of the nation state, become the symbols of that nation on the sports ground when international competition is entered into. It is through successful comparison with the 'other' that a celebratory notion of 'ourselves' emerges. This contribution charts how the Irish and Australians tried to evolve a measuring stick for their previously isolated football players. The attempt at internationalism was a failure as the proposed tour to Australia of the 1968 All-Ireland champions, Down, was cancelled, and despite an attempt at a composite rules test series during the mid-1980s, both Gaelic games and Australian rules remain only domestic concerns.

Historical Connections

That two games separated by thousands of miles should be viewed as natural partners for the invention of an international competition is not all that surprising. Despite the obvious differences of the modern games, the oval pitch and ball of Australian rules and its three separate point scoring posts as opposed to the round ball, rectangular pitch and rugby-style posts of Gaelic football, the two games are very much alike in the style of play. The similarities between the two codes has led to a debate as to which came first. Some argue that it was Irish labourers and servicemen who took the Gaelic code to Australia and which was eventually translated into Australian rules, while others maintain that Gaelic football was the imitator as Australian rules were codified some twenty years earlier and those ideals were brought back to Ireland by travellers of the mid-nineteenth century.[1] The similar origins and style of play of the two games made them natural partners. Such similarities were a way out of domestic isolation, a point not missed by Harry Beitzel, the Australian organiser and financier of the 1967 and 1968 tours, who later wrote: 'I had seen a game of Gaelic Football played by a world touring New York team ... [they] had come to Australia and on a Sunday morning in late September just prior to our own Victorian League Grand Final they played "a type of Gaelic Football" against Geelong ... After seeing it played I was firmly convinced our own Australian boys could adapt their talents and abilities and play the Gaelic game'.[2]

From an historical perspective, Daly has argued that 'it is the modern version of Gaelic and Australian football which gives rise to the dubious belief that the two codes are the first cousins or even father and son'.[3] While accepting Daly's argument that the origins of the two codes are difficult to trace accurately, the fact that the two games appear so similar offered each a potential outlet from domestic isolation. It was this fact that was grasped by men such as Beitzel in Australia and Peter McDermott in Meath who were so instrumental in organizing the matches.

International Sport and the Construction of Identity

The place of Gaelic games within international sport does pose continuing difficulties. In the Gaelic Athletic Association's (GAA) centenary year of 1984, the then Director General of the Association, Liam Ó Maolmhichil, assessed the shape of the GAA in the future. One question which he pondered was whether the GAA could ever become international. He wrote: 'From the point of view of the players, the representation of one's country is a great honour and the players will give every support to international competition. It will be very expensive to promote International games in the early years, however, and there will also be a danger of a loss of identity. The GAA should be strong enough, however, to withstand such a threat'.[4]

The dichotomy facing Ó Maolmhichil in 1984 was one that has plagued the GAA since its inception and one which threads through this chapter. Gaelic games were established as part of the cultural reawakening of Ireland in the late nineteenth century and have been at the forefront of nationalist identity ever since.[5] The strength and appeal of the game to Irish nationalists has been its exclusion of foreign elements by the ban on non-native games and uniformed personnel who represent the forces of occupation in Ireland.[6] The exclusiveness of Gaelic games has produced a situation where the sport is solely the preserve of one identity in the island of Ireland, Catholic/Nationalist which excludes the other, Protestant/Unionist. By maintaining the singular identity of the games and excluding those forces opposing Catholicism/Nationalism, the code has failed to spread. They have remained the preserve of the Irish domestically and, to a lesser extent, of the Irish diaspora overseas. Such exclusivity does not allow for internationalism and excludes players from representing their country. Gaelic games are an Irish sport without an Ireland to represent on a world platform. In discussing the appeal of rugby union to the Afrikaners Albert Grundligh noted:

It has to be recognised that even if nationalist cultural entrepreneurs had hoped to establish a completely new and authentic all-Afrikaner culture, such a project was not always feasible or viable. To create a pure, hermetically sealed culture is not easily accomplished; it is often more practical to adapt, reshape and mould whatever promising material is at hand. In the case of rugby, Afrikaners had already proved that they could excel at the game, and therefore it made sense to proceed in Afrikanerizing rugby.[7]

Whereas the Afrikaners had failed to produce an authentic native culture and had been forced to appropriate and adapt a sport (rugby) connected with the prestige of empire, the Irish had managed to hermetically seal themselves in the sporting arena by developing Gaelic games. The Afrikaners were able to use their Springbok team as a symbol of their identity and achieve global success, both prior to and after the apartheid sanctions, because rugby is an inclusive game in which nation states can compete in test matches and a world cup. The Irish have not developed a similar international outlet for their primary sport. Thus, although the GAA have been successful cultural entrepreneurs, they failed to play on an international platform in any sustained fashion and have thus robbed the Irish nation of morale-boosting and identity-forming national success. This is in stark contrast to the recent success of the Irish soccer team who have galvanized the nation behind them with their qualification for, and success at, the 1990 and 1994 World Cups. The importance of international competition and success was made clear by Michael Billig, who wrote:

> I read the sporting pages, turning to them more quickly than is appropriate, given the news of suffering on other pages. Regularly I answer the invitation to celebrate national sporting triumphs. If a citizen from the homeland runs quicker or jumps higher than foreigners, I feel pleasure. Why, I do not know. I want the national team to beat the teams of other countries, scoring more goals, runs or whatever. International matches seems so much more important than domestic ones: there is an extra thrill of competition, with something indefinable at stake.[8]

In the 1960s Ireland was starved of international sporting success. Its athletes competed poorly at the Olympics, its soccer teams, both club sides in Europe and the national squad, performed badly, and the rugby union squad rarely made headway in the Home Internationals. As the most popular sporting spectacle and pastime during that era Gaelic games could not offer any respite from the poor international performance of Irish sportspeople as the sport had nothing but a domestic outlet. In light of the continued failure of Gaelic games to find an international platform it is other sports that have come to represent the nation against the wider world. Although Gaelic games remain quintessentially Irish and offer an outlet for domestic expressions of nationalism, there is no accompanying 'us and them' mentality afforded by the games which is such a fundamental part of modern international sport.

Two examples illustrate perfectly the continuing problem of the isolation of Gaelic games. In 1995 a selection of Ireland's leading sports journalists came together to select their heroes of the nation's sport.[9] While 30 per cent of those sporting heroes selected were from the world of Gaelic Games, twice the number from soccer or horse racing, the notion of success for these sportsmen was couched solely in terms of domestic awards. For all the other entries in the selection there was talk of Olympic success, world titles, world cups, and representation of Ireland. With the exception of the Gaelic games' players and jockeys, all other sportspeople had represented Ireland. As such the journalist's assessment of the athletes who are able to compete internationally are based on recollections of them beating the world's best, of representing the nation, and of giving the people back home something to be proud of. For the Gaelic games' players, while there is an assessment of their skill and their excellent performances, there is no attempt to appropriate their success for the nation at large. Equally illustrative is the assessment of Michelle Smith's gold medal haul at the 1996 Atlanta Olympics – Ireland's first multiple gold medal winner. Writing in *The Guardian* David Sharrock commented:

> Ireland was beside itself with astonishment and pride at the latest twist in the tale of a small nation seemingly coming of age. Sporting success was a reflection of a new found confidence born of the knowledge that being Irish was chic. Nobel prizes, booming economies, international rock stars, Hollywood movies by the barrel-load – all had become commonplace. Now Smith's victories were the latest extension of the dream.[10]

For Sharrock it seemed that Michelle Smith had completed the inventory of what is needed to be considered a successful nation – victory at the Olympics, the biggest international platform of them all. Gaelic games cannot perform such a function as they are not attractive for the global media, are not understood by many outside of Ireland and have no international platform which allows 'us' to beat 'them'.

A sport needs international success. Without it the sport might prosper domestically in terms of spectator numbers or participants, but it cannot galvanize a nation and become representative of a successful competitive identity. International events allow 'the imagined community of millions [to] seem more real as a team of 11 named people. The individual, even the one who only cheers, becomes a symbol of his nation himself'.[11] Likewise Grant Jarvie has argued that 'sport itself provides a uniquely effective medium for inculcating national feelings; it provides a form of symbolic action which states the case for the nation itself ... sporting struggles, and international triumphs and losses, are primary expressions of imagined communities'.[12] In discussing the Meath–Australia Gaelic football matches of 1967–68 it becomes apparent that those who organized the matches were attempting to offer Gaelic games (and to a lesser extent Australian rules) a way out of domestic isolation and a pathway into international competition which would allow those games to become the (hopefully successful) representatives of the nation's prestige.

The late 1960s was a period when sportsmen and women were increasingly becoming commodities within the media and advertising worlds but those athletes taking advantages of such changes were those who were successful at an international level. There were undoubtedly examples of indigenous sports which prospered such as baseball, American football and basketball in North America but the huge domestic market for these sports and the modern nature of the US media meant that an international outlet was not necessary. In Britain the biggest change in the commodification of soccer players came with the victory at the 1966 World Cup and the success of domestic clubs in the key European competitions. Overnight Bobby Moore, Bobby Charlton and George Best became internationally known. In the current era sports such as basketball may have failed to break out of the US mainstream into other nations but the machinery of advertising and sponsorship, which is by its nature global, has made athletes such as Michael Jordan a global phenomenon. In the late 1960s the power of Nike and Reebok did not exist and the globalization of the media was only beginning. As such those sports and athletes which came to global attention were ones which were understood by large numbers of people across different nations such as soccer, cricket, rugby, athletics and so on. Games such as Gaelic football and Australian rules which did not attract interest outside of their domestic arena were not globalised and the lack of an international opposition meant that they never could be. It was for the men of Meath and Australia to artificially try and create such an outlet.

The 1967 Australian Tour of Ireland

In 1967 an Australian entrepreneur, Harry Beitzel, drew together a team of Australian rules players with the intention of playing in Ireland against the cream of Gaelic football. Beitzel was not satisfied with merely playing exhibition games in Ireland but wanted to play serious matches. As his telegram to the GAA headquarters at Croke Park demanded, 'We challenge your Irish team to full sixty minute game Gaelic – no compromises. Think we can win. Do not wish to travel 12,000 miles for exhibition match'.[13] After the initial telegram to the GAA, Dermot McKeever of Aer Lingus in Sydney approached Meath as the reigning All-Ireland Champions, to enquire if they were prepared to provide the serious opposition which was demanded by Beitzel. The prospect of a return trip to Australia was mentioned as a way of ensuring Meath's participation. After some re-scheduling of domestic matches the Meath team cleared the last Sunday in October and prepared to face the visiting Australian Galahs at Croke Park. On their arrival at Dublin airport the Australians were met by an official party which included all the high ranking officials of the GAA and the Chairman of the Meath County Board, Reverend Tully. The officialdom present at the airport and the press interest generated by the Australians demonstrated how seriously the Irish were taking the opportunity to welcome a visiting international team to play them at their own game. Although there had previously been visits by Irish-Americans to play games in Ireland, the Australians were the first genuinely 'foreign' visitors. The optimism that the visit of the Australians would change the isolated and domestic nature of Gaelic games was summed up by the GAA newspaper, *Gaelic Weekly*. Prior to the Australians arrival it stated: 'The Australian Rules footballers will arrive in Dublin on Friday next for their mammoth spectacular at Croke Park. It could mark the beginning of a new era with regular Ireland versus Australia games and Irish teams making trips Down Under'.[14]

In their first warm-up match against a Civil Service team the Australians played poorly and were beaten. Despite the allure of international competition concerns were expressed that as the Australians were playing Gaelic football not Australian rules (and despite any similarities which may have existed between the two codes), they might not be up to the task of translating their skills to another code and thereby providing decent opposition. If the game against Meath was a poor spectacle then the long term future of this innovative international match could be in doubt. The paying public needed to see a genuine contest if they were to keep coming back. Despite these concerns the match did provoke interest and many of the commentators in the lead up to the game were looking ahead to regular international competition in the future. Paddy Hickey wrote:

> There can be no doubt at all but that these Australians are serious in their bid to beat the best team in Ireland ... What motivates the Australians? There is much more to this than wanting a serious hours football. What they really want to do is establish international trips for themselves. The Australian footballers are completely isolated. No other country plays their game. Our football is the nearest relation so they have chosen us. If Sunday's game goes well the Australians have almost certainly won their international outlet. If for example they were to beat Meath we would simply have to have them back. The idea of somebody being better than ourselves at our own game is fantastic. There would have to be a return bout.[15]

As with all good sporting stories the fantastic happened. Despite being advised to take it easy as the 'Aussies were only moderate footballers'[16] the crowd of 23,149 saw the Australians defeat the champions of Ireland 3–16 (25) to 1–10 (13). The following weekend the Australians defeated the losing All-Ireland finalists, Mayo, 2–12 (18) to 2–5 (11) in front of 20,121 spectators. They immediately flew out to New York and a day later played a New York Gaelic Stars squad but this time went down 4–8 (20) to 0–5 (5).

What then was the reaction to the Australian performances in Ireland? The *Gaelic Weekly* was clear in its assessment of the matches. It stated:

Last Sunday at Croke Park must be recognised as having been a great blessing. It was the most significant milestone in the development of Gaelic football since the Association drafted its first set of rules in 1885 ... It is now obvious that our game has suffered in isolation. The Australians have shown us how we can improve it, possibly quite a number of ways ... It is quite probable that the discussion [at a GAA Central Council meeting] will be extended to a broad consideration of the entire international future in the light of the sensational Australian visit. Already both the Australians and the GAA have expressed a view in favour of an annual three country competition, the semi final of which would take place in New York and the final in Dublin and Melbourne on alternate years.[17]

It appeared in the autumn of 1967 that the success of the Australian games against Meath and Mayo had transformed the atmosphere of the two codes and had offered both a possible international outlet. It was probably in the interests of both games that the Australians had won their two matches at Croke Park. If the Australians had been comfortably beaten the view from GAA circles would have been that while such matches were entertaining, the lack of real competition on the pitch did nothing to further the fortunes of the Gaelic code. Defeat however had a galvanizing effect on Gaelic games and its observers in a manner comparable to the English soccer team's defeat at the hands of Hungary in the 1950s. The Australian visit ended the isolationism of Gaelic games and offered a standard against which the games could be measured. The journalist Michael Barrett was less than impressed by the comparison offered, writing, 'I feel that the Australians really showed the depths which Gaelic football in Ireland has sunk'.[18] In a more promising vein Seamus O Ceallaigh wrote, 'both football codes – the Australian and Gaelic types suffered from the same ills – a lack of international competition ... this is a problem that has to be seriously faced and some sort of solution found'.[19] The proposed solutions concerning the difference in rules were many and varied, but little was advanced in either Ireland, Australia or America which was concrete.

The only definite project for the future which would continue the moves towards international competition was the invitation for Meath to tour Australia in 1968. The invitation was offered by Harry Beitzel after the Meath–Australia game at Croke Park. It was accepted by Reverend Tully as Chair of Meath GAA Board subject to approval by the GAA and the raising of necessary finance. The approval for the tour was given by the County Board of the GAA on 31 December 1967. After the acceptance of the invitation to tour Australia the full importance of Meath's task became apparent in comments made to the press. This was not merely a club tour of

Meath team to tour Australia, 1968

a foreign land undertaken for enjoyment, but a tour which could change the very nature of the sport. Senator Jack Fitzgerald stated, 'We hope that we are only the first of many counties who will make this trip. We will go to Australia fully conscious that we are representing not alone the GAA but Ireland and we will do everything in our power to do justice to both'.[20] In a similar vein, and equally aware of the long term importance of such a tour, Peter McDermott said, 'Win or lose the greatest benefit of this tour will be to the GAA in the future. It badly needs competition on an international basis. As well, there is an enormous pool of young players in Australia just waiting to be tapped. It is simply a matter of marrying the two codes. The tour is vitally important both to the GAA and the Australians'.[21]

The financing of the tour was a minor miracle and Peter McDermott and the other members of the Finance Committee deserve credit for the fact that Meath ever made it to Australia. Although Harry Beitzel had promised Meath AUS$12,000 towards the cost of the tour another £10,000 had to be raised by Meath in the space of eight weeks. Gaelic games were (and still are) strictly amateur and it was not a game which was awash with money from sponsorship or the media. As such Meath relied on goodwill and the belief of people in Meath and elsewhere that such a tour was worth paying for. Despite the seeming importance of the tour for the future of Gaelic games and international competition the Central Council of the GAA contributed only £1,000. By organizing raffles, dances and relying on personal donations a staggering £14,504 was eventually raised.[22] This allowed the touring party to be expanded and the whole of the 1967 All-Ireland Championship panel was able to fly out to Australia.

The 1968 Meath Tour of Australia

When Meath left Dublin airport at the beginning of March 1968 it was clear that they were the pioneers representing Gaelic Football's first steps into international competition. If the tour was a success then other teams could follow and domestic isolation could end, a fact not lost on the team coach, Peter McDermott: 'We realise fully our responsibilities and what our tour means to the future of the GAA and possibly other tours. We also appreciate the help – the outstanding and generous help – given to us by the people of Meath and Ireland to make the trip. But we hope to justify their confidence by playing performances and by our general behaviour that will ensure hearty welcomes for other touring parties in years to come'.[23]

At the higher institutional level, Sean O Siochain, the General Secretary of the GAA revealed his hopes for the Meath tour and what it would produce in the future. In an interview with *Gaelic Weekly* he explained how the GAA saw the tour as a precursor to the permanent ending of domestic isolation stating: 'The Central Council attaches great importance to the tour. Speaking to last Saturday's Council meeting the President stated that the Association looked to this tour being the precursor of a permanent arrangement. He also spoke of it being important to future development of Gaelic football … [in the future there should be] a formal international competition involving Ireland, the US and Australia'.[24]

The actual tour was a huge success for Meath as they won every game they played and were afforded a warm welcome by those involved in the Australian side of the tour and by Irish-Australians. On their arrival in Perth the Meath team were met by a band of pipers playing 'God Save Ireland'. At the press conference at the airport the Meath County Board chairman, Revered Tully, again restated what everyone hoped the outcome of the tour would be: 'The tour is just a forerunner of things to come. We are really just pioneers. I can see a day when there will be regular international competition'.[25]

When the Australians had travelled to Ireland in 1967 they had elected to play under Gaelic rules to make the tour more appealing to the Irish spectators. One problem for the return tour was that it would again be played under the Gaelic code. This undoubtedly posed problems in marketing the tour in Australia as it was a foreign game. There was an element of interest in the tour because of its esoteric interest – here was a game which most Australians had never seen before. To try and engender a wider appeal changes were made to the rules so that Australian rules supporters would recognise the basic shape of the game. The most central change was to allow players to pick the ball up directly from the floor, something allowed under Australian rules but forbidden under the Gaelic code. The alterations were seen as central to the future success of such tours. John Murphy, Secretary of the Western Australia Irish Clubs summed up the reasons behind the changes: 'There is great interest in this tour in Ireland because it is hoped that something concrete will come from this trip and international vsits will become annual affairs. On this occasion the Irish are prepared to make a compromise – with the rules of their Gaelic code – to try to promote international competition'.[26]

The rule change was greeted warmly by the Western Australia team coach, Tolly Farmer, who stated, 'Now that we have agreed to pick up the ball the local players should have little difficulty in playing the game because there is not much difference between this code and Australian football'.[27] Despite the agreed alterations the Western Australian team were soundly beaten 6–6 (24) to 0–3 (3) in front of a crowd of 13,000. It is clear that the changes made to the rules of Gaelic football were an attempt to make more popular a match between teams from two different footballing codes. If some kind of compromise or even composite game could be arrived at which was understood by the followers of both the Gaelic and Australian codes then spectators would pay their way into the ground, the media would cover the matches and the spectacle of an international match would become a long standing proposition. However, such compromises came at a cost, a fact not lost of Meath's Peter McDermott who, when interviewed by the *West Australian*, stated:

> There is a great deal of nationalism connected with Gaelic football and this helps to explain the tremendous support the game has at home. It is our heritage and this could be a barrier in the establishment of an international game based on a combination of our game and Australian football. I would like to see a new game of football emerge from an amalgamation of the codes … however, I envisage strong opposition to the introduction of this new code at home as well as in Australia and it probably could only be played in the near future on an international basis.[28]

In McDermott's comments lie the crux of the problem. To adjust the rules enables the creation of an international contest where players can adapt their own skills in a game which is still recognizable to both sets of supporters. However, such rule changes would not be allowed to impinge on the domestic running of the two codes as such changes would alter the nature of games with such long and popular traditions. The unchanging nature of the two domestic games, remaining as they would do, as separate codes, would mean that any future international would still rely on a compromise set of rules. It is difficult to see how this would have any credible long term future. In 1967 and 1968 the prospect of the games were an interesting sideline, but long-term supporter and media interest would surely wane as the internationals would not be true contests drawn from a common code. The strength of international soccer competitions for example, either at a club or national level, relies on the fact that supporters around the globe are watching the same game with the same rules as they watch every week at home. Because of this the supporter can invest their support in the team carrying the flag for their nation and measure one performance against the other. In this they can make demons of the opposition and cheer the success of 'us' against 'them' in a genuine competition. If however, as with the Gaelic and Australian attempt at internationalism, the game is not a commonly agreed one, either set of supporters can dismiss the importance of the game for measuring national prestige and performance by arguing that any defeat came because it was not 'our' game. While such contests remain a game which can be dismissed as belonging to the 'other' then interest, emotional investment, national pride and media support will be difficult to maintain.

Reaction to the Tour

The victories continued throughout the tour but as time progressed some of the press reaction to the Gaelic code became critical as the problems mentioned above became apparent. Obviously if the Australians were not won over by such international competition in the same way the Irish crowds had been in 1967, then the whole future of the endeavour looked in doubt. Alf Brown led the criticism in the *Melbourne Herald* after the Australian team had lost the first match. He wrote: 'Australian Rules can relax. There is no danger of it being supplanted by Gaelic football ... I am glad I saw yesterday's match but I doubt if I would watch Gaelic football again. The absence of physical clashes makes it a dull game after a time. But if the Irish like watching games between the Galahs and their own midgets, then good luck to them. Its one way our players can get a trip overseas'.[29]

In assessing the Australian press coverage of the tour on Meath's return the *Gaelic Weekly News* was plainly aware of the criticism which both Gaelic football as a spectacle and the tour as an attempt at international competition attracted.

> Heading the knockers was radio commentator Monty Menhennet who slammed Saturday's football match as 'a parlour game for old ladies'. WANFL President Ken Miller said the match had obviously been a financial success. It was worth seeing for curiosity but he was hardly likely to go again. East Freemantle centre half-forward Fred Lewis, who played in the match series: 'it was a good experience but if it is

going to become an international game something will have to be done about the tackling rule' ... Columnist Kirwan Ward in the *Daily News* saw little hope of a merger between Gaelic and Australian rules to make an international code. "When the New York Yankees switch to cricket, when the world soccer cup is played on roller skates and when a camel wins the Melbourne Cup and St Patrick's Day is celebrated on Oliver Cromwell's birthday, Australian and Gaelic Rules will merge and make the big time ... as far as football is concerned Gaelic is Gaelic, Aussie is Aussie and never the twain shall meet.[30]

Despite the muted response in the Australian media, the Irish press and those who had organised the tour were more hopeful that Meath's 1968 trip to Australia would be the start of regular international competition. The *Gaelic Weekly* led the way in looking forward:

If the tour has proved a financial success there is every hope that an international series is on its way. Besides, the Australians do not like to be beaten, and it is they who will now be all out in quest of revenge. And that is why I, for one, will not be surprised to see a really powerful Australian side show up here next October. In the meantime, surely there can be no doubt at all now as to who are the Gaelic Football champions of the world. Meath won the title in Croke Park with a decisive victory against New York ... and now after those victories over Barassi and Co. in Melbourne they must be entitled to full recognition as champions of the world. And why not? Who else have they to beat?[31]

The victory by Meath over the Australians in Melbourne allowed Irish commentators to talk of the Irish as world champions. By allowing for such success on an international platform, the victory of 'us' against 'them', the players of Meath had elevated Gaelic football from a domestic to a global game. The impetus from the tour had to be harnessed so that future internationals could be planned and such competition became the norm, not an interesting and occasional distraction. The General Secretary of the GAA, Sean O Siochain, said that the tour '... focused attention on the possibilities of a regular series of official games between Ireland, Australia, USA, and possibly Britain' and made clear that the Australians '... need a proper international outlet as much as we do'.[32]

Problems for the Future

The Irish thus considered the tour of Australia a great success and many were keen to see the links maintained. In the autumn of 1968 the Australians again decided to travel to Ireland and play the winning All-Ireland team at Croke Park. Although the Australian team was again brought together and paid for by the entrepreneur Harry Beitzel, with only a limited official backing from the Australian Rules Boards, there was a demand within Ireland that the GAA should be more open in their backing of the 1968 competition. The rumours started early of how important the game would be and what form it should take. In August 1968 a story began circulating that rather than merely playing the winning All-Ireland team, the Australians would in fact face a team selected from the best footballers across Ireland, and 'as a result the game against Australia is likely to be a real international contest'.[33] If such a step had been taken it would have been a landmark decizion. Although the 1967 Meath team could undoubtedly claim to be Ireland's best and were more than able representatives of the nation, a team made up of all the best players in Ireland from all the County squads could genuinely claim to be international representatives as this would produce a selection procedure which was used in all other international sport. The GAA would not, however, sanction such a selection and insisted that if any game were played then it had to be between the Australians and the 1968 All-Ireland champions, Down. Those promoting a more genuine sense of international competition were less than impressed. The *Gaelic Weekly* in an editorial titled 'Only Part-Catching the International Boat', asked:

> Is the Association missing out a significant opportunity in not fielding an Ireland team against the Australians and thereby creating full international competition? We live in an era which is very conscious of international games and the GAA could have benefited from it. An Ireland team to play the Australians would be a truly significant selection. There has been nothing to compare since the Tailteann Games.[34] ... The Australians have opened up a complete new vista for Gaelic Football – a vista undreamt of a year ago. It offers very sizeable opportunities for expanding the prestige and attractiveness of our game. It will be a tragedy if these opportunities are not availed of.[35]

In addition to the arguments over who would represent Ireland another damaging argument had begun which would hurt the long term future of the international games. It had been argued throughout 1967 and 1968 that any genuine international series could only survive if other nations were included. It was envisaged that Britain would eventually be able to field a team built around its Irish-born residents, but from the start the US had always been included in the plans for the Irish-Australia matches. In 1967 the Australians did indeed play at the Gaelic Grounds in New York, but Meath were unable to play there on their return from Australia due to poor weather conditions. In 1968 the New York visit again entered the plans of the touring Australians but this encountered serious difficulties. For many years relationships between the GAA and the self-appointed head of Gaelic games in New York, the entrepreneur John O'Donnell, had been poor. There were constant battles over money, the promotion of Gaelic games in the US, and the lack of control which the GAA had over the New York organization. One of the major stumbling blocks was John O'Donnell, whose major concern was that the games should eventually be profitable. In contrast, the GAA saw the promotion of the games and the ethos of the Association as being of prime importance. The disagreements came to a head in the autumn of 1968 and the New York GAA was open in outlining its grievances:

> [New York is] largely taken for granted in the Ireland-Australia programme – being simply used as a stop over to acquire an extra game. It had originally been visualised that the winners of the New York versus the All-Ireland champions would play the Australians here in what would really be a World Cup game worthy of that name. 'Whatever happens we are not going to allow ourselves to be used in this business. Either we are in on a proper basis or not at all' said John O'Donnell.[36]

After Harry Beitzel had received unsatisfactory assurances over gate receipts from New York, that part of the autumn 1968 series was abandoned. Although a blow for the series of matches, the game at Croke Park with Australia versus Down was still on. The *Gaelic Weekly News,* although trying to drum up interest in that game by forecasting an Australian victory, was aware of how damaging the cancellation of the New York match would be. It stated:

> What a pity we cannot get a real world cup competition going. I mean a New York touring team could come here simultaneously with the Australians and they would meet either the Irish champions or an Ireland team in a three team league competition. We are in an age of international competition and every avenue should be explored to build up even further the international image of our games.[37]

In addition to the disappointment of not going to the US the Australians played a game at Croke Park in front of a low crowd numbering only 14,000. They won the game but the tour was a financial disaster which cost its organiser Harry Beitzel some £12,000. Beitzel was angry at the outcome of the tour, especially in the light of Meath's successful tour to Australia six months earlier. He said, 'It seems to me that I'm the only bloody one who is really bothered about international tours and I don't see why I should keep carrying the can ... Neither the GAA in Ireland or New York were particularly concerned about developing international games on a permanent basis'.[38]

Although making the same invitation to Down as he had done the year before with Meath, the attempt at internationalism had failed. In December 1968 the GAA Central Council voted not to accept the invitation for Down to tour Australia.

The Failure of Internationalism

What conclusions can be made in relation to the Meath-Australian adventure? It is clear from talking to those who took part and reading the *Meath Chronicle* that those involved at the county level were offered and took the chance of a lifetime. It is obvious that the Meath team took great pride in beating the Australians in Melbourne and were especially delighted with their reception from the Irish-Australian community. To 'see tears in the faces of old men who never felt they would see a game of Gaelic football again'[39] allowed those who travelled from Meath to feel that they were bringing something special to the Irish diaspora in Australia. From the comments of those who were instrumental in organizing the tour it appears that they truly believed that the tours would be the start of genuine competition.[40] International competition did not stem from the events of 1967 and 1968 and both Gaelic Football and Australian Rules remain isolated with no international outlet. Both games however, have prospered domestically as they have carefully cultivated a solid popular following and have courted the support of domestic television and print media to ensure that the games have a high profile.

The long-term failure of internationalism does not necessarily lie with men like Harry Beitzel. As he said himself, he had 'a dream come true' in establishing the 1967 and 1968 matches, but that dream 'will remain slightly a nightmare unless the two official groups in Ireland and Australia get together and make our world tours a regular event'.[41] The real failure was with the custodians of Gaelic football and Australian rules. Without a willingness to release players, put money into international competition, work with possible loose cannons such as New York's John O'Donnell, and alter the nature of their domestic games so that supporters became used to a common code, internationals had no future. As Micheal O' Hehir concluded, 'any suggestion of continuing a haphazard arrangement or set of arrangements, can only mean the end of the whole idea'.[42] Genuine international competition relies on a common game. All the great international contests which are used to measure national prestige and to demonize the opposition exist in widely played and commonly understood sports – the 100 metres at the Olympics, the soccer World Cup, cricket Test Series or any round of the Formula One Motor Racing season. All these prosper and engender widespread support and attention because of their familiarity. The athlete or the team represent 'us' against 'them' on a level playing field, no-one has had to adapt or change their skills for a one-off competition. Isolation of any given sport does not result in that sport ceasing to have a mass support base and serving an important function in the construction of identity as the US experience of basketball, baseball and American football all clearly demonstrate. But a sport which exists on the international platform 'underpins and heightens nationalist consciousness without which political nationalism would have no chance of success'.[43]

Gaelic football and Australian rules are undoubtedly important in creating and sustaining a national identity and perform an important function in underpinning national cultural difference, but they can never, while they lack an international outlet, allow the national, as opposed to the local, to triumph. 1997 saw Adelaide victorious in Australian rules and Kerry take the All-Ireland football final. These victories were undoubtedly a source of great local pride and an excellent television spectacle for the supporters of the game, but the flags of victory flew in confined areas and they were the flags of city or province. Neither victory could be translated into international success and neither national flag could be waved in triumph. In this the men of Australia and Meath have no lasting legacy as both games remain the domestic definition of sporting prowess, never allowing for the identity boosting victory of the nation against the 'other'.

NOTES

1. For further details see P. Daly, 'The Gaelic Myth', in *GAA Coaching News*, April 1996, pp.20–24.
2. H. Beitzel, 'One Man's Dream', in P. McDermott (ed.), *Gaels in the Sun* (Drogheda, 1970), p.105.
3. Daly, 'Gaelic Myth', p.22.
4. L. Ó Maolmhichíl, 'The GAA of the Future', in Cumann Lúthchleas Gael, *A Century of Service, 1884–1984* (Dublin, 1984), p.96.
5. For further details see M. Cronin, 'Defenders of the Nation? The Gaelic Athletic Association and Irish Nationalist Identity', *Irish Political Studies*, Vol.11 (1996), pp.1–19.
6. See M. de Búrca, *The GAA: A History of the Gaelic Athletic Association* (Dublin, 1980) or W.F. Mandle, *The Gaelic Athletic Association and Irish Nationalist Politics, 1884–1924* (London, 1987) for details.
7. A. Grundligh, 'Playing for Power? Rugby, Afrikaner Nationalism and Masculinity in South Africa, c. 1900–c.1970', in J. Nauright and T.J.L. Chandler (eds.), *Making Men: Rugby and Masculine Identity* (London, 1996), p.186.
8. M. Billig, *Banal Nationalism* (London, 1995), p 125.
9. L. Hayes, V. Hogan, and D. Walsh, *Heroes of Irish Sporting Life* (Dun Laoghaire, 1995).
10. D. Sharrock, 'Swimmer Who Sank', *The Guardian 2,* 24 Feb. 1997, p.2.

11. E.J. Hobsbawm, *Nations and Nationalism since 1780: Programme, Myth and Reality* (Cambridge, 1990), p.143.
12. G. Jarvie, 'Sport, Nationalism and Cultural Identity', in L. Allison (ed.), *The Changing Politics of Sport* (Manchester, 1993), pp.74–5.
13. Quoted by P. Hickey in *Gaelic Weekly*, 28 Oct. 1967, p.1.
14. *Gaelic Weekly*, 21 Oct. 1967, p.1.
15. *Gaelic Weekly*, 28 Oct. 1967, p.1.
16. McDermott, *Gaels*, p.7.
17. *Gaelic Weekly*, 4 Nov. 1967, p.1.
18. *Gaelic Weekly*, 18 Nov. 1967, p.2.
19. Ibid.
20. *Gaelic Weekly*, 27 Jan. 1968, p.1.
21. *Gaelic Weekly*, 24 Feb. 1968, p.7.
22. For details of funding see McDermott, *Gaels*, pp.10, 117–22.
23. *Meath Chronicle*, 2 March 1968, p.1.
24. *Gaelic Weekly*, 2 March 1968, p.3.
25. *Melbourne Herald*, 6 March 1968, p.16.
26. *The West Australian*, 6 March 1968, p.40.
27. *Melbourne Herald*, 7 March 1968, p.16.
28. *The West Australian*, 7 March 1968, p.38.
29. *Melbourne Herald*, 12 March 1968, p.38.
30. *Gaelic Weekly News*, 13 April 1968, p.11.
31. *Gaelic Weekly*, 23 March 1968, p.10.
32. S.O. Siochain, 'Ard Runai's Impressions', in McDermott, *Gaels*, p.102.
33. *Gaelic Weekly News*, 3 Aug. 1968, p.1.
34. The Tailteann Games were staged in Dublin in 1924 and were essentially a Celtic Olympics where the different competing nations entered teams to take part in a variety of 'traditional' sports.
35. *Gaelic Weekly*, 12 Oct. 1968, p.15.
36. *Gaelic Weekly News*, 19 Oct. 1968, p.10.
37. *Gaelic Weekly News*, 26 Oct. 1968, p.2.
38. *Gaelic Weekly News*, 2 Nov. 1968, p.1.
39. From an interview with Peter McDermott and Mick O'Brien, Navan, County Meath, July 1997.
40. See McDermott, *Gaels*, for the comments of Seamus O. Riain (GAA President 1967–69), p.100, Sean O. Siochain (GAA General Secretary 1967–70), pp.101–2, Rev. P. Tully (Chairman Meath County GAA Board 1949–68), pp.103–4, Harry Beitzel (Australian organiser), pp.105–8, and Micheal O. Hehir (Head of RTE Sport), p.115.
41. H. Beitzel, 'One Man's Dream', in McDermott, *Gaels*, p.108.
42. M.O. Hehir, 'With Time Ticking Away', in McDermott, *Gaels*, p.115.
43. J.G. Kellas, *The Politics of Nationalism and Ethnicity* (London, 1991), p.21.

Braveheart Betrayed?
Cultural Cloning for Colonial Careers

J.A. MANGAN

Introduction

'Let's say goodbye to Britain' – this exasperated plea from the former staunch Scottish devolutionist, senior figure of the post-war Scottish Establishment and doyen of Scottish broadsheet journalism, Sir Alastair Dunnett, appeared in *The Independent* in September, 1996.[1] The former editor of *The Scotsman* bemoaned a nation's alleged loss of name and identity, 'The name of Scotland has ... largely disappeared ... an inexplicable thing to have happened to a country that was a nation longer than most.' The major cause of loss of identity, and associated prosperity and pride, appeared to lie 'south of the border'. 'Almost the only Scottish problem is England', and a minor cause, he implied, citing Samuel Johnson's 'prophetic' warning to a MacDonald chief, was that Scotland's sons had been tamed into insignificance by English education. A somewhat different view of more recent Scottish educational events will be presented here more along the lines of the rebuke to his polemic which appeared in a subsequent letter to *The Independent*: ' ... Sir Alastair Dunnett parades ... tedious anti-English sentiment, and worse, a casual re-writing of History'.[2]

By the middle of the eighteenth century, as Linda Colley makes clear, 'Scotland was coming to be seen by those in power as useful, loyal and *British*'.[3] This loyalty, she makes equally clear, was to be paid for 'by giving its titled and talented males increased access to London and its plums'[4] – a process still in place today. Colley goes on to describe the enthusiasm with which Scots made full use of the opportunities of Empire with the result that, again in her words, 'Whatever some Scottish nationalists choose to maintain today, it was not simply a case of Scottish ability being creamed away from its proper home for the benefit of an English empire'.[5] Of course, loss of identity has been a long-standing concern. Sir Walter Scott died in 1832 convinced that 'everything distinctively Scots was about to die' but

A shorter and somewhat different version of this contribution will be published by the Ethnographical Research Centre, National Museum of Scotland in its forthcoming multi-volume study of Scottish Culture and Society under the title, 'Missionaries to the Middle Class: English Muscular Morality for a Scottish Colony'.

equally certain 'as to the virtues of empire in enhancing Scotland's prosperity' and, according to one contemporary commentator, subscription to 'the virtues of union and empire and … anxiety about the loss of a distinctive Scottish culture, have been mirrored in all subsequent writing about Scotland and the Empire … '.[6] All this is germane to the nineteenth century and a Scottish educational revolution that took place in the second fifty years.

In the middle of the nineteenth century, of course, Britain was without an efficient state system of secondary education. It did possess a ramshackle, amorphous private system of varying degrees of competency, organisation and order. At the upper end of the system – in the few schools for the wealthy and the well-placed – the situation institutionally, educationally and morally was far from satisfactory.[7] Not to put too fine a point on it these schools, mostly in England, were largely a shambles.

In the wake of Evangelical revivalism, public criticism and shocking revelations, reform of these private schools began. It is customary to point to the Clarendon Commission of 1862 as the resuscitating life-force in the return to vigorous existence of the *soi-disant* public school system but in fact, there was another source of renewed vitality which operated in parallel, and in conjunction, with Clarendon. It is known by various terms: athleticism, the games cult or the games ethic.[8] It was a remarkable phenomenon which assisted substantially in the transformation of an expanding private secondary school system on the back of increasing national prosperity. It remains insufficiently appreciated as a brilliant system of social engineering bringing educational order out of disorder, establishing successful patterns of institutional cohesion and conformity, offering an effective training for imperial careers and serendipitously creating leisure activities which have contributed hugely to the leisure revolution of the twentieth century.

The Games Ethic, of course, began in the mid-nineteenth century in English public schools with pressing problems of discipline and survival. Here the concern is with the diffusion of the Cult into the schools of the Scottish middle classes where, as some have put it, it played a fundamental (and disgraceful) part in the 'Anglicizing' of their male offspring. However, this 'Anglicization' in fact, on closer scrutiny, certainly welcomed and supported by the Scottish (and Northern Irish and Welsh) middle classes, was as much an assimilation into a *British* middle-class cultural identity: a fusion of a set of manners, mores, beliefs and attitudes which allowed Scots access to higher levels of imperial careers by making the 'British' boys of Scottish middle class parents virtually indistinguishable in values, dress and behaviour, if not accent, from the larger community of middle and upper middle class boys in English public schools. Central to this process of cultural cloning was the late nineteenth century games field and its associated educational, social and moral connotations. Was Braveheart betrayed?

John Snell (1629–97), an Ayrshire landowner, left the revenues of his estate on his death to finance the Snell Exhibitions to Balliol College, Oxford, for scholars born and educated in Scotland. In the second half of the nineteenth century this gave rise to educational consequences for Scotland far removed, it can be confidently asserted, from those Snell had had in mind in the second half of the seventeenth century. Two Scottish educationalists, of the time, who were in the vanguard of a revolution in educational principles and practices, were both recipients of the Exhibitions in their youth: Hely Hutchinson Almond (1832–1903) and John Guthrie Kerr (1853–1937).

Hely Hutchinson Almond and 'Lorettonianism'

Hely Hutchinson Almond was a zealot, crusader and revolutionary – in educational terms. He was admired; he was emulated; he inspired. His influence reached out beyond Scotland – to English public schools and ancient universities, to distant colonial territories and institutions. Within Scotland he played a fundamental role in reforming educational precept and practice, in re-shaping, through neophytes, private and state schools and in challenging the prejudices of the middle classes in matters of health, hygiene, exercise and education.[9]

Almond had a most profound contempt for the inhibited, hidebound conservatism of the Scottish middle classes. He castigated them unceasingly for their views on schooling, clothing, exercise and diet. Above all, he frowned severely on their attitudes to exercise; in their view it was 'a childish pastime for men, and even for boys – a frivolous and useless occupation.'[10] He strenuously rebutted this atavistic view and wished to bring up Scottish middle class youth 'in the habit of fighting convention' as far as they dared and could!'[11]

In 1862 he purchased a small private school in Musselburgh called Loretto. He made it famous throughout the British Empire.[12] At Loretto he established his gospel of good living which he called 'Lorettonianism'. It was a way of life embracing 'an elaborate and systematic programme of health education covering food, clothes, physical exercise, sleep, fresh air and cold baths'.[13] In practical terms this resulted in a daily timetable as follows: '6 hours study, 10 hours sleep, 1½ hours at meals, 1 hour free after meals, 1 hour drawing or singing, ½ hour prayers or assembly, ½ hour in the gymnasium, 2½ hours at games, 1 hour leisure!'[14] It was arguably the most complete, rigorous and sustained programme for the education of the body

– if not the mind – in British education at the time. Almond was absorbed in the creation of a system of education that embraced 'the most important of all sciences – the science of health.'[15] It was based on involvement, observation and reflection. It had four sources of inspiration: Balliol College, Oxford, Herbert Spencer, John Ruskin and Archibald MacLaren.[16]

In late adolescence, in the late 1840s, Almond read Classics at Glasgow University. He found that experience boring. After several years of a diet of morning classical studies he left Glasgow for Oxford, in his own words 'pale-faced, having had nothing to do with my afternoons but roam aimlessly about streets and roads … '.[17] In 1850 he went to Balliol as the recipient of a Snell Exhibition. He found this experience exciting. His biographer, R.J. Mackenzie, wrote of it: 'It is not too much to say that it opened his mind to the existence of a new set of virtues. His love of the open air, his passion for health, his appreciation of manly endeavour … were to him the gifts of the river'.[18] More than this, he found the experience inspirational. In later life, he asserted: 'I have no hesitation in saying, that but for the boats, etc., at Oxford, I could have had no hold as a schoolmaster, and but insufficient vigour for the work or life'.[19]

He decided to become a radical educationalist. His chosen task was to return to Scotland and win over the sons of the middle classes to his personal ideals of masculine health and hardiness. It should be recognized, however, that Almond was as conventional as he was unconventional: he was an enthusiastic advocate of the period ideological shibboleths of the English upper middle-class educational system. More on this later.

'Lorettonianism', therefore, was an odd amalgam of radicalism and conservatism. It was also a curious combination of individualism and conformity. Loretto had no house system, the supreme instrument of late nineteenth century public school 'social engineering' that was crucial in bringing order out of anarchy in the schools – too much shared power with other masters for Almond's liking. Neither did Almond allow the ornate symbols of athletic success that decked the athletes ('bloods') of other public schools – too much pupil power for Almond's liking. He was the 'plain Methodist'; others were 'High Anglicans'.[20] Nevertheless, within a framework of idiosyncratic individualism Loretto had its own corporate symbols of being all designed in Almond's own image: the open neck shirt, the knee-length flannel trousers, the capless head, the strong boots.[21] These were 'Almond's symbols of institutional conformity of Lorettonianism or Rationality'.[22]

Almond's 'manifesto' was a curious mixture of realism and romanticism, which appeared over and over again throughout his life in journals, magazines, and newspapers including *Health, Journal of Education, New Review, Nineteenth Century, Scotsman, Spectator, Tatler* and *The Times*. He preached a Spencerian gospel at the same time as he endorsed a Jeffriesian idyll of moral, muscled, informed men. His icon was an odd version of the noble, black savage – only in Almond's version, he was white and living in Scotland not Africa. To the ambitions of Spencer and the dreams of Jeffries, Almond added the aesthetic beliefs of John Ruskin, especially his assertion that 'a chalk stream does more for education than a hundred national schools',[23] and the pragmatic exercises of Archibald MacLaren, particularly those set out in his *A System of Physical Education, Theoretical and Practical.*[24]

Almond was an ideological synthesist. He was a Scottish educational missionary to the Scots – and he meshed the ideas of his four ideological missionaries to the British (and other) middle classes into the doctrine of 'Rationality', as he liked to call 'Lorettonianism',[25] that was uniquely his own. At the same time he was a whole-hearted subscriber to the prevailing and essentially English moralistic and muscular credo of the Games Ethic:

> The sincere belief of many, however romantic, misplaced or myopic, [was] that exercise was a highly effective means of inculcating valuable instrumental and impressive educational goals: physical and moral courage, loyalty and co-operation, the capacity to act fairly and take defeat well, the ability to both command and obey. These were the famous ingredients of character training which the public schools considered their pride and their prerogative.[26]

The ethic, up to a point, was undoubtedly 'a neologism born of moral passion'.[27] By 1880 it dominated the British public school system. Almond was an early convert. He once wrote:

> Games in which success depends on the united efforts of many, and which also foster courage and endurance, are the very life blood of the public school system. And all the more self-indulgent games or pursuits contain within themselves an element of danger to school patriotism and might, if they permanently injured the patriotic games, cause public schools to fail in their main object, which we take to be the production of a grand breed of men for the service of the British nation.[28]

Thus the conventional as well as the unconventional characterised Loretto. This conventionalism, incidentally, embraced a deeply entrenched anti-intellectualism. Almond emphatically preferred 'vigorous manhood, full of courage' to 'the languid, lisping babbler about art ... '.[29] He was at one with many English colleagues and certainly most pupils.

Two other mainstream convictions ensured that Almond was British by ideological choice and not 'English' by pedagogical persuasion. Almond was a fiercely aggressive muscular Christian of the Kingsleyan variety: 'he preached the period virtues of developing the broad chest, the tireless stride and the strong body for Christ'.[30] With militant zeal (in more than a theological sense) he deprecated the 'ailing emancipated body' of ascetic Christianity and applauded 'the powerful frame' – far more pleasing to God – of the muscular Christian. He advocated a vigorous and virile spirituality. 'Why, oh why', he once pleaded, 'cannot there be a holy alliance between the athlete and the Christian?'[31] And, with more than religious intentions, he pressed his boys to consecrate their robust bodies as living sacrifices to God Almighty:

> ... cannot the glowing examples of the long line of Christian heroes, – from him whose peerless manhood received its crown, when he was led forth in crippled and worn-out old age to die outside the walls of Rome, down to the last company of young recruits, whose self-denying devotion to missionary work has given new dignity to athletic prowess – nerve you to consecrate your bodies to God's service; to regard your limbs, your brains, your lungs, all your vital functions and powers, as loans from Him, which you are bound to turn to the very best account, so that you may repay Him His own with much usury?[32]

This consecration had a strongly terrestrial motivation – the Imperial Mandate. Musselburgh Neo-Spartanism was a preparation for colonial Christian proselytism: 'Almond had an unsullied vision of his manly Lorettonians as salvationists carrying Christ's banner to heathen places ... with a confidence bred of muscular and moral superiority'.[33]

Almond was a passionate imperialist. Every year he delivered the same sermon on the same day – the 19 June. It was known in the School as the 'Waterloo Sermon' but its formal title was 'The Divine Governance of Nations'. It has much in common with the chauvinistic outpouring of imperialistic fervour of a fellow Scot, J.A. Cramb, in his *Reflections on the Origins and Destiny of Imperial Britain*.[34] In a phrase, it was replete with jingoism, bigotry and racism. And totally in keeping with the militarist tone of the public schools of the time,[35] it preached martial (and missionary) self-sacrifice to its schoolboys – who should model themselves, Almond asserted, on imperial martyrs and heroes. Their spilt blood was the lifeblood of a powerful nation.

Rather than lose their national identity Almond's pupils paraded it with some success at the English ancient universities. In late Victorian and Edwardian 'Oxbridge', at least on the playing fields, it sometimes seemed less that England had 'colonized' Scotland and more the other way about, largely as a consequence of Almond's successful inculcation of 'Lorettonianism' in his school at Musselburgh. In 1900, for example, the *Public School Magazine* contained a sketch entitled 'The Triumph of

Loretto'. It depicted a unique occasion: two Lorettonians, the respective captains of the Cambridge and Oxford XV's of the year, soberly shaking hands before the annual match and declaring, 'I think we've met before!' This meeting was the high point of a success on Oxford and Cambridge playing fields in the last quarter of the nineteenth century which was quite astounding. Loretto, this small, unpretentious and rather odd school, had five rugby blues and one cricket blue at Oxford in 1880. The next year, eight out of the nine Lorettonians at Oxford played rugby for the University. In addition, one was captain of the cricket eleven and another president of the boat club. Three years later Loretto had eleven full blues at Oxford and seven played in the University match. Finally, between 1884 and 1891 four Lorettonians held the captaincy of the Oxford XV.[36]

Occupationally 'Lorettonianism', of course, was a shrewd and pragmatic approach to imperial employment. The Caledonian chorus in the late nineteenth-century sang with enthusiasm 'Let's say welcome to Britain'. From British membership Scots gained fame and fortune and a clear sense of proud imperial identity, and a passport to all these things for the middle classes was private education. Scottish prosperity and pride came in part in the wake of the successful emulation of English public school mores.

In 1905 the *Harmsworth Encyclopaedia* provided a list of the most famous British public schools.[37] Loretto was among them. It had been highly influential in the previous twenty-five years. In Scotland, Fettes, and in England, Sedburgh, owed much to Almond's innovations. Loretto's stock stood high not only in Britain but the Empire. One of the most distinguished schools in New Zealand, Wangannui, was an exact copy of Almond's Loretto. Furthermore, the exclusive Scottish public schools of Blairlodge, Glenalmond and Merchiston borrowed heavily from Loretto, inspired either directly by Almond's actions and ideas or indirectly by the appointment of Old Lorettonians committed to them. However, even more critical to the adoption of the Games Ethic in Scottish education was the influence of Almond on Edinburgh Academy through the Old Lorettonian R.J. Mackenzie, Rector from 1889 to 1902. Edinburgh Academy's Almondian innovations became in time part and parcel of the curriculum of the famous Scottish middle class day schools, and then eventually the state secondary schools. Through a steady process of diffusion the permanent dissemination of Almond's ideas on a wide front was achieved (see Table 1). Ideological diffusion, however, was a rather complex matter!

> Headmasters subscribed to the games ethic for three important reasons. It assisted in the process of social distancing, by creating for the school the essential features of identity and status. In terms of social

engineering, it brought about the much sought after 'esprit de corps'; it was also widely believed that it provided a sound method for character building. And finally, it came in time to be part of a gentleman's education which helped in turn to produce an imperial elite.[38]

It was not a linear progression, as has been suggested, from Scottish private boarding school to private day school to state day school.[39] Masters from the public schools of Scotland in some instances moved directly to state schools.[40]

TABLE 1

DIFFUSION OF THE GAMES ETHIC IN SCOTLAND: SOME EARLY SOURCES

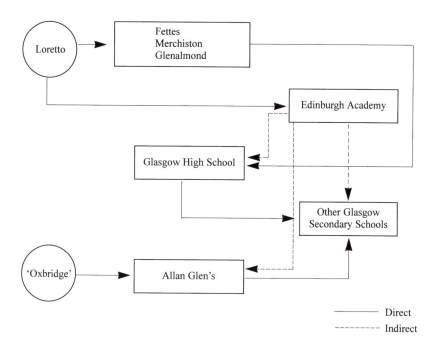

Furthermore, the Universities of Oxford and Cambridge played a larger role in ideological dissemination than simply inspiring Almond and Kerr (see Table 2). A process of 'circular causality' characterized the public school system in Britain at least up to the Second World War: 'Bloods' (athletic heroes) played games at school, played games at 'Oxbridge' and returned to school to play and coach. The stranglehold 'Oxbridge' had on public school posts ensured substantial conservatism.[41] The 'varsity'

TABLE 2[42]

VARSITY BACKGROUNDS OF STAFF OF FETTES, MERCHISTON AND
GLENALMOND SCHOOLS

GLENALMOND		MERCHISTON		FETTES	
Oxford	23	Oxford	16	Oxford	18
Cambridge	27	Cambridge	11	Cambridge	18
Trinity, Dublin	1	London	1	Edinburgh	1
London	2	Durham	1	no details	2
Edinburgh	1	Aberdeen	1		
no details	5	Edinburgh	1		
		Glasgow	2		
		St. Andrew's	2		
		Trinity, Dublin	1		
		no details	3		
TOTAL	59	TOTAL	42	TOTAL	39

backgrounds of staff of Fettes, Merchiston and Glenalmond are interesting in this latter context.

Merchiston staff proved to be keen Scottish 'explorers'. They spread throughout the highlands, lowlands and central region and occupied some 29 teaching posts in these areas. Two of them, H. Ellicot and F.S. Goodwin, whom we shall meet later, played a central role in the evolution of the games ethic and games provision at Glasgow High School 'as well as aiding and abetting John Guthrie Kerr ... in his programme of proselytism through the Glasgow area'.[43]

It is time now to turn to an inspirationalist in the state system who, like Almond, owed his initial Pauline conversion to the values emanating from the English public school system and carried forward to 'Oxbridge' and Balliol, and who, like Almond, made a similar strenuous effort to ensure that these values were adopted and adapted in Scotland into a British system of middle class education. The setting for this effort could not, in many ways have been more unhelpful, but commitment, energy and determination found a way.

John Guthrie Kerr

John Guthrie Kerr became headmaster of Allan Glen's School in Glasgow in 1890; Hely Hutchinson Almond became headmaster of Loretto in Musselburgh in 1862. In the years between 1862 and 1890 the Games Ethic had slowly spread throughout the middle-class schools of Scotland. Consequently Kerr inherited a school in an urban system in the West of

Scotland that was ripe for change. He owed much, indirectly, to Almond and his influence, but he owed more, directly, to the Snell Exhibitions and the consequent access they afforded to Oxford University.

Kerr was an exceptional undergraduate at Glasgow University (1871–74) with the result that in 1874 he won a Snell Exhibition to Balliol College. He was there for two years. Its influence on him was similar to its influence on Almond. His eyes were opened to a broad vision of education: as he saw it – a Renaissance in ideals and action. In 1876 he returned to Scotland. He was first a teacher at Kilmarnock Academy and then a lecturer at the Church of Scotland Glasgow Teacher Training Centre.

Loretto and Allan Glen's were like chalk and cheese. In 1853 a Glasgow businessman, Allan Glen, established a school to provide a practical education for boys planning to enter trade or business. Subsequently, in response to developments in Scottish education in the following decades, the school became a state school.[44] Most importantly, however, as a result of support from the Science and Art Department at South Kensington and a private Act of Parliament in 1878, it evolved as 'a secondary (day) school, in which the utmost is made of science as a general instrument of education'.[45]

Before the arrival of Kerr it was firmly in the tradition of Scottish state secondary schools. The Games Ethic of the Scottish private middle class schools had not yet percolated downwards to it, despite the fact that, increasingly, throughout all Scottish secondary schools, as Robert Anderson has remarked, 'The character was now to be cultivated as well as the intellect, personal influence of the teacher over pupil replaced formal relationships, and schools began to take an official interest in ... sport.'[46]

Unquestionably Kerr brought southern university influences and experiences back to his northern school. In his 1894 inaugural address as President of the Educational Institute of Scotland he spoke enthusiastically of the need for a broad conception of the purpose of school studies and greeted with equal enthusiasm the changes for the better, as he saw them, now characterising Scottish education. This was not surprising. He had taken the lead in bringing about these changes:

> His innovatory policy of *mens sana in corpore sano* was cultivated systematically ... it was part of wider 'civilising' processes which involved a school song, concerts, magazine and more symbolic gestures, such as the creation of new school colours of light and dark blue combining quite deliberately the colours of two great English seats of learning to which pupils would now go in increasing numbers.[47]

All these calculated innovations comprised an attempt at a British model of education that allowed his Scots access to employment in Britain's empire. It was not Anglicization in action. This is a far too simplistic interpretation of what transpired at Allan Glen's. Its strength – science education – was assiduously promoted: 'Kerr himself was proud of the special, utilitarian emphasis of his Scottish science school. He had no foolish aspirations to model Allan Glen's *wholly* [emphasis added] on the games-playing, classics-orientated schools of the English upper classes.'[48]

The nature of Allan Glen's was once well described by a school governor, Professor George Ramsay:

> It is not so much a Technical School as a Science School. It does not profess to teach the technical details of any special calling or profession – these can only be learnt in actual life inside the profession itself – what it professes to do is to use Science as an instrument for training and developing the mind combining with science just as much literary teaching and no more, as it is necessary for every educated man to possess for this purpose. Science constitutes the main work, the foundation work of the school.[49]

This emphasis was in marked contrast to England and Wales. Sir Robert Morant, the highly influential Secretary of State for Education from 1903 to 1911 was committed to the tradition of 'muscular Christianity' (more accurately of course, 'muscular Darwinism')[50] and 'used all his enormous influence to place in the key positions at the Board (of Education) men educated at the public schools and the older universities',[51] with the result that by means of the Regulations for Secondary Schools of 1904, the scientific emphasis of the higher grade schools gave way to the liberal education of the Grammar Schools, themselves based on the English public school, Morant's chosen model for state education, which reflected his admiration for life in the public school system – 'the very citadel of secondary education.'[52]

Occupational possibilities, as Kerr fully recognized, were enhanced not diminished by retention of a utilitarian education based on the industrial experiences and entrepreneurial skills of the 'second city of the empire'. As John MacKenzie has remarked: 'despite the suggestion that superiority in education was a myth created by later nationalists ... , it is generally agreed that there was a different attitude towards education in Scotland, including ... above all, valuable specialisation'.[53] In a sense this emphasis on science and technology was, to an extent, a late nineteenth and early twentieth-century small-scale equivalent of the Scottish Enlightenment. To quote Colley on the eighteenth-century with reference to the later context of the nineteenth and twentieth centuries, ' ... as both sides of the border came to recognise there were senses in which Scotland was not England's peer but its superior'.[54]

While English schoolboys were over represented in careers in imperial administration, Scottish schoolboys were over represented in imperial technical and scientific careers: 'there can be little doubt that throughout the Empire, Scots characteristically dominated public works, and medical, botanical, forestry and engineering services'.[55] At Allan Glen's, on speech days, at assembly, in the magazine, there was frequent mention of scientific or industrial successes. In 'the second city of the Empire' imperial careers fittingly were followed with pride but adjutants in Indian regiments and district administrators in Africa were in short supply. Instead the boys heard of the sterling efforts of former pupils in the Indian Public Works Board and the Colonial Medical Service.[56]

Long after Kerr had given up his headship, he strongly asserted his belief in the essential role of science in Allan Glen's: 'I stand by the Ramsay motto 'Cum Scientiae Humanitas' with scientiae as the inceptive agent'.[57] What Kerr sought to achieve, and arguably succeeded in achieving, was not the Anglo-Saxon colonisation of Scottish education but an educational act of union between Scotland and England, perhaps symbolised best by the introduction of a school song (along southern public school lines) to foster *esprit de corps* which incorporated and added a cacophonous line making mention of indigenous tradition: 'we chip, file and turn very hard'! No colonization here. No echo here of those wonderfully banal lines, typical of the English public school, caught so amusingly yet so trenchantly in *The Lanchester Tradition* celebrating the founder of that mythical establishment:

> John Buss, John of us
> Played good cricket and made no fuss'![58]

In fact, Kerr made more of an effort than most of the English public schools (day or boarding) at the time to bridge C.P. Snow's two cultures. And this was a very Scottish effort; a product of the intelligent recognition of the mutually reinforcing occupational value of 'indigenous' and 'foreign' cultures.

In effect, Allan Glen's achieved something of a harmonious balance between vocationalism and liberalism and could well have served a useful model for the English public schools in an increasingly technological age, and thus perhaps saved them from the later savage criticisms of irrelevance, atavism and inertia.[59] The school sensibly, in the context of the times, embraced the English public school games ethic, but at the same time retained a Scottish 'public' school science ethic.[60] It had the best of both worlds – a state of affairs certainly appreciated by the middle classes of Glasgow suburbia who increasingly supported the school in larger and larger numbers. The achievement of this balance was noted in 1913 with pride in the annual Speech Day address of Dr Henry Dyer, Vice Chairman of the Glasgow School Board. Allan Glen's, he observed, was now almost 'as distinguished for its athletic as its science training'.[61] At the same Speech Day the Reverend John G. Duncan, Vice Convenor of the High Schools Committee of the Glasgow Board of Education and the Reverend J. Fraser Graham, Convenor of the Committee on the High Schools of the School Board of Glasgow, also praised the school for holding the balance between science and sport.

Kerr resigned from his post of headmaster of Allan Glen's in 1917. Greatly moved by the tragedies of the Western Front he devoted himself to the nursing of its victims. However, in a real sense, he never left the school. His influence remained powerful. In the years after the Great War the consolidation of a system of 'British' education continued. The 'Kerrian balance' was carefully maintained and academic and athletic performance assiduously and successfully cultivated. And with the Games Ethic firmly established throughout the Scottish system of education – private and public – Allan Glen's steadily accumulated the blazers, badges, colours, sportswear and 'the athletic facilities, trophies, teams and records inseparable from a top drawer school of the period'.[62] It also pursued a period social 'Darwinian' enthusiasm for competition and victory – and went from strength to strength, regionally and nationally.

This 'Darwinism' was promulgated by Kerr himself well into the twentieth century. When, in October 1931, the Old Boy's Club presented the school with the Kerr Memorial Plaque, Kerr himself was present at the unveiling ceremony, and delivered a speech entitled 'No obstacle – no progress; no fight, no joy of conflict.' In it, at one point, he declared, 'It is in personal effort and a sense of contest, in the things of the mind and the muscles, that youth will best attain to intellectual manhood, moral courage and physical fitness and so promote efficiency for service to the world.'[63] It was a Scottish rhetoric of 'British balance'. It was also a celebration of educational synthesis realized in his lifetime and in his school. It was also a paean to achieved imperial access. It was Scotland and England united to Scotland's advantage:

> Kerr's ambition for his pupils certainly included the intended erosion of traditional Scottish educational attitudes and it was, in part, a deliberate deracination process. He wanted to produce not simply recruits for Clydeside industry but Scots who would feel comfortable among English educated competitors and colleagues in the professions. To this extent his policy had, as a primary objective, the Anglicisation and de-parochialism of his pupils. Adoption of the

fashion of the playing fields was one significant means of achieving this.'[64]

This observation is certainly correct but Kerr's model involved more than adoption. It also involved adaptation. It was the work of both an idealist *and* a pragmatist. Kerr was committed to 'the laying of broad and sure foundations for liberal culture [and] the building up of energy and character'.[65] To this end, he borrowed English fashion, but he was also a Scottish conservative and created a 'British' model of education embracing the best, as he saw it, of Scottish and English practice in the interests of his pupils.

Concluding Remarks

Today the 'victim' theory is popular in the media but, as one historian has written with reference to the Empire, Britain, and more specifically Scotland:

> The concept of the eternal victim fits ill with the recent reaction against viewing the indigenous peoples of the Empire, or for that matter the subordinate classes of Britain, as essentially passive. The notion that such people are always the objects of dominant behaviour, the absorbers of a superior culture doomed to twitch to the electrodes of imperial energy, has been rejected. The idea that they meekly respond to the images imposed upon them by copying the stereotype itself is to stretch the concept of self-oppression beyond credulity.[66]

Such constructions, he continued, may comfort the dominant power or class but they hugely underestimate the considerable capacity of inferior cultures and classes 'to maintain a hidden integrity'.[67] There was nothing covert in the integrity of Almond and Kerr.

Almond and Kerr were both radicals and reformers. Both worked with elements of Scottish educational tradition, and rejected others. Both, in their different ways, created an education that was a *combination* of Scottish and English elements. Both ensured that Scottish youth benefited from these disparate combinations. Both ensured, with others, that Scotland figured confidently, and to some effect, in the British Empire. Neither ever lost his sense of national identity or pride.

Other Scottish schools and schoolmasters were attracted by 'the seductive ideology'[68] for some or all of the reasons that inspired Almond and Kerr: improved social status, pupil access to attractive careers and a British imperial identity. Interesting samples from Glasgow are readily to hand and furnish further evidence of Scottish middle class attempts to develop a 'British' identity through schooling in the Late Victorian and Edwardian periods. One outstanding exemplar is Glasgow Academy, a proprietary day school founded in 1846.[69] In its early years it placed an unequivocal emphasis on high academic standards. Its former pupils did the school proud: in the 1870s, for example, the school received frequent mention in Glasgow University's Honours Lists. 'Survival could be interpreted in simple terms', it has been shrewdly noted, 'the school had to attract large numbers of boys from middle class families and to gain a reputation for high academic standards. Parents would look for academic honours and in the Academy they got them'.[70] By 1888 the school had the reputation of being one of the two best in Scotland. However by the 1890s it looked beyond Glasgow University for career credentials. Increasingly the Rector drew the attention of parents to Oxford University and then the Indian Civil Service. A later Rector added Woolwich, Sandhurst and the Royal Engineering College to the list. A wider set of credentials than the mere academic now appeared necessary to stamp metaphorically a useful British caste mark on Glaswegian foreheads. Unsurprisingly, cricket – the pre-eminent symbol of imperial consolidation and civilisation[71] – now received increasing attention.

The school's poor performance in earlier years was now causing disquiet. In 1891 remedial action was taken. Lional Lyde, former English public schoolboy and Oxford graduate, was appointed from a leading Scottish public school, Merchiston Castle, in large part, it would appear, due to his ability at and interest in the activities on the games field. He was sent proudly from Merchiston Castle to Glasgow Academy with this crucial testimonial from Merchiston's headmaster: 'His attainments, enthusiasm, sympathy with the young and keen interest in games which as former captain in an English Public School, he understands thoroughly, have made him a distinct force in our life here'.[72] In the educational climate of the times no praise could be more fulsome or more valuable. In the words of Christopher Loughlan, it was 'a most telling appointment'.[73]

There was, however, much more to come at the turn of the century as Glasgow Academy made strenuous efforts to acquire the essential credentials of a modern middle class school indistinguishable from any other in the British Isles. Cultural 'cloning' was essential for imperial careers. Games were now played in school time; a Games Committee of Masters was appointed to oversee major and minor games; Saturday morning became 'sacrosanct for the playing of (games)'.[74] A headmaster of impeccable contemporary credentials was now appointed – Edwin Temple, schoolboy at Glenalmond and Fettes (two famous Scottish public, boarding schools), graduate of Cambridge, master at Glenalmond. He added the final polish to the patina of a public school image: a school magazine, a cadet corps and extensive playing fields. However, according to Loughlan, Scottish pragmatism ensured that the worst athletic excesses 'witnessed ... in English public schools in the period 1860–1900 were rarely observed'.[75] A British not an English identity was the objective.

This socialisation bore fruit. In the *Chronicle* in 1908 we read: 'One of the nice things about footer in India is that the teams are composed of players from a great number of schools. In our team, Rugby, Haileybury, Marlborough, Sandhurst, Bedford, Kelvinside Academy, Edinburgh Academy and Watson's are among the schools represented ... in addition Winchester, Sedburgh, Cheltenham, Loretto and Fettes.'[76]

Loughlan, with exact appreciation, sums up the significance of this inclusion. 'This was like a 'Who's Who' of the rugby playing fraternity in one part of the imperial community of India ... the school had made it!'[77] In the Centenary publication an assessment of the (British) significance of the 'new education' was offered: 'it has provided our city, our country, India and the Empire with men ... to raise this country both morally and materially to the great position it occupies in the world today'.[78]

Elsewhere in the city strenuous moral and material efforts were being made to provide for imperial careers. Glasgow High School was one of the designated Higher Class schools created by the 1872 Education (Scotland) Act. It was the responsibility of the Glasgow School Board set up in the wake of the Act. Throughout the 1870s and 1880s token gestures only were made towards the new athletic ethos. Facilities were poor, some distance from the school and shared with another local secondary school. In 1901 H.J. Spencer arrived as Rector. He was an educationalist 'vitally concerned with the development of sporting activities'.[79] An old boy of Nottingham High School, and a graduate of St. John's College, Cambridge, with teaching experience at Edinburgh Academy, he strongly endorsed major games. It is wholly reasonable to suggest in the light of the evidence already presented above, that his appointment was far from accidental. It was certainly fortuitous. Now followed rapidly the creation of the essential moralistic apparatus of a sound school of the period. It included a school 'war' song for the playing field and a cadet corps. In 1903 Spencer moved on to greater things – the Headmastership of University College, London – but 'the pattern ... had been set',[80] and when Oxbridge educated Shirley Goodwin became headmaster in 1909 his ambitions were unexceptional. Under his aegis the onward march of period educational priorities was relentless: colours, challenge cups, form matches, further elevation of major games, pursuit of adequate equipment and facilities. The latter priority was an especially serious one:

At present the existence of a School Library, the Magazine, the

Literary and Musical Societies, the splendid Officers' Training Corps, proves how fully alive the school authorities are to the importance of corporate effort by the boys. But the games – the finest agency of all – find their value discounted. Glasgow High School is perhaps the only school in its class in Scotland which is not adequately provided for in this manner ... Glasgow Academy and Watson's College are among the great day schools in Scotland whose pupils are comparable in number with those attending the High School, and they both possess excellently equipped playing fields.[81]

Emulation for survival was a fundamental requirement. The relationship between emulation and survival in the *post* school years was well brought out by a letter from a former pupil, James F. Dyer, to his old school on his experiences in India. According to Dyer, the 'High' man's success depends less on academic achievement and more on straight shooting, hard riding and a passable game of tennis, hockey, cricket and football.[82] In short, he had to be a clubbable man with clubbable connections and capacities – smoothly in the public school mould: 'One cannot help working harmoniously', wrote Dyer, 'with a man with whom one has perhaps golfed in the morning, played tennis in the afternoon and had a quiet rubber in the evening.'[83] The evidence is clear. The late nineteenth-century headmasters of the leading Glasgow middle class day schools were, for the most part, carefully chosen for their public school and Oxbridge experiences, values and attitudes. They, in turn, often appointed staff in their own image. And this was true of the whole of Scotland. The English and Scottish public (boarding) schools provided models to imitate. Cultural cloning was the ambition – in pursuit of imperial middle class careers. The middle class schools of Glasgow were certainly no longer simply Scottish but they were clearly not English. They were British institutions training Scots for the British Empire. As such they furnish fascinating illustrations of ethnic adaptation in the interests of survival, security and prosperity. And sport was central to this adaptation and to the cloning process that followed in its wake.

The Games Ethic transformed the Scottish educational culture of the late nineteenth and early twentieth centuries. Its significance for Scottish class structure, career access, recreational culture, and eventually renascent nationalism has never been fully understood, appreciated or investigated. Academic myopia has seen the study of sport as an element of culture for far too long as 'a frivolous and useless occupation'.[84] All that is now changing as it should. The study of sport in Scottish society is steadily becoming a subject of some interest and some importance. In the Caledonian Groves of Academe, as in similar Groves elsewhere, *inter alia* its functions – as moral metaphor, cultural bond, political symbol, religious manifestation and emancipatory inspiration – are now at last being investigated.

NOTES

1. Sir Alastair Dunnett, 'Let's say Goodbye to Britain', *The Independent*, 12 Sept. 1996, p.16.
2. *The Independent*, 16 Sept. 1996, p.17.
3. Linda Colley, *Britons: Forging the Nation 1707–1837* (New Haven, CT, 1992), p.119.
4. Ibid., p.120.
5. Ibid., p.125.
6. John M. MacKenzie, 'Essay and Reflection: On Scotland and the Empire', *The International History Review*, Vol.XV, No.4 (Nov. 1993), p.721.
7. See, for example, John Chandos, *Boys Together* (London, 1984), *passim.*
8. See J.A. Mangan, *Athleticism in the Victorian and Edwardian Public School: The Emergence and Consolidation of an Educational Ideology* (Cambridge, 1981), prologue.
9. Ibid., *passim.*
10. See Christopher Loughlan, 'The Games Ethic, Seductive Ideology and the Second City', M.Ed. thesis, University of Glasgow, 1988.
11. J.A. Mangan, 'Almond of Loretto: Scottish Educational Visionary and Reformer', *Scottish Education Review*, Vol.11, No.2 (Nov. 1979), pp.97–106.
12. R.J. MacKenzie, *Almond of Loretto* (Edinburgh, 1905), p.264.
13. Quoted in MacKenzie, *Almond of Loretto*, p.327.
14. Mangan, *Athleticism*, p.58.
15. Mangan, 'Almond of Loretto', p.100.
16. Report of the Royal Commission on Physical Training (Scotland), 1903, Vol.11, 414, Q9774.
17. Mangan, 'Almond of Loretto', p.101.
18. See Mangan, *Athleticism*, pp.48–58.
19. MacKenzie, *Almond of Loretto*, p.13.
20. Ibid., p.16.
21. Mangan, *Athleticism*, p.163.
22. Ibid.
23. Ibid.
24. Quoted in John Evans, *John Ruskin* (London, 1952), p.314.
25. See Mangan, 'Almond of Loretto', p.99. For a Discussion of 'Lorettonianism', see Mangan, *Athleticism*, pp.54–5.
26. Mangan, *Athleticism*, p.9.
27. The term is to be found in R.A. Nisbet, *The Sociological Imagination* (New York, 1970), p.23.
28. *Lorettonian*, Vol.IV, No.15 (June 1882), p.57.
29. Mangan, 'Almond of Loretto', p.102.
30. Mangan, *Athleticism*, p.53.
31. Quoted in J.A. Mangan, 'Hely Hutchinson Almond: Iconoclast, Anglophile and Imperialist', *Scottish Journal of Physical Education*, Vol.12, No.3 (Aug. 1984), p.40.
32. Ibid.
33. Ibid.
34. See J.A. Mangan, 'Duty unto Death: English Masculinity and Militarism in the Age of the New Imperialism', in J.A. Mangan (ed.), *Tribal Identities: Nationalism, Europe, Sport* (London, 1996), pp.20–21.
35. Ibid., *passim*, and also J. A. Mangan, '"Muscular Militaristic and Manly": the British Middle Class Hero as Moral Messenger', in Richard Holt and J.A. Mangan (eds.), *European Heroes: Myth, Identity, Sport* (London, 1996), pp.28–47.
36. MacKenzie, *Almond of Loretto*, pp.122–3.
37. Mangan, *Athleticism*, p.5.

ANAL CLONING FOR COLONIAL CAREERS

38. Loughlan, 'The Games Ethic … ', summary.
39. J.A. Mangan, 'Imitating their Betters and Disassociating from their Inferiors: Grammar Schools and the Games Ethic in the Late Nineteenth and Early Twentieth-Centuries', in Nicholas Parry and David McNair (eds.), *The Fitness of the Nation: Proceedings of the 1982 Annual Conference of the History of Education Society of Great Britain* (London, 1983), p.10.
40. Ibid., p.11.
41. Ibid., p.10.
42. Ibid., p.11.
43. Ibid.
44. J.A. Mangan, 'Catalyst of Change: John Guthrie Kerr and the Adaptation of an Indigenous Scottish Tradition', in J.A. Mangan (ed.), *Pleasure, Profit and Proselytism: British Culture and Sport at Home and Abroad, 1700–1914* (London, 1988), pp.87–8.
45. Ibid., p.88.
46. Robert Anderson, 'Secondary Schools and Scottish Society in the Nineteenth Century', unpublished paper delivered to the Scottish History of Education Society, Autumn 1985, p.8.
47. Mangan, 'John Guthrie Kerr', p.90.
48. Ibid., p.91.
49. *Allan Glen's Monthly*, Vol.XX (Jan. 1911), p.2.
50. See J.A. Mangan, 'Social Darwinism and Upper-Class Education in Late Victorian and Edwardian England', in J.A. Mangan and James Walvin (eds.), *Manliness and Morality: Middle Class Masculinity in Britain and America, 1800–1940* (Manchester, 1987), pp.135–59.
51. Quoted in Mangan, 'Imitating their Betters', p.24.
52. Ibid.
53. MacKenzie, 'Scotland and Empire', p.732.
54. Colley, *Britons: Forging the Nation*, p.119.
55. MacKenzie, 'Scotland and Empire', p.732.
56. Mangan, 'John Guthrie Kerr … ', pp.95–6.
57. Ibid.
58. G.F. Bradby, *The Lanchester Tradition* (London, 1914; 1954 edn consulted), p.41.
59. See Mangan, *Athleticism*, Epilogue, *passim.*
60. Mangan, 'John Guthrie Kerr … ', p.96.
61. Ibid.
62. Ibid., p.101.
63. Ibid.
64. Ibid., p.102.
65. *Allan Glen's Magazine*, Vol.XXIII (Feb. 1914), p.1.
66. MacKenzie, 'Scotland and Empire', p.732.
67. Ibid.
68. This attractive expression is used by Christopher Loughlan in his thesis, 'The Games Ethic', mentioned earlier.
69. See Loughlan, 'The Games Ethic … ', *passim.*
70. Ibid., p.30.
71. See J.A. Mangan, 'Prologue: Britain's Chief Spiritual Export: Imperial Sport as Moral Metaphor, Political Symbol and Cultural Bond', in J.A. Mangan, *The Cultural Bond: Sport, Empire, Society* (London, 1992), pp.1–10.
72. Quoted in Loughlan, 'The Games Ethic … ', p.31.
73. Ibid.
74. Ibid., p.32.
75. Ibid., p.33.
76. Ibid., p.36.
77. Ibid.
78. Ibid., p.37.
79. Ibid., p.46.
80. Ibid., p.48.

81. Ibid., p.50.
82. Ibid., pp.52–53.
83. Ibid., p.53.
84. Mangan, *The Cultural Bond*, pp.8–9.

Select Bibliography

Acton, T. and G. Mundy (eds.), *Romani Culture and Gypsy Identity* (Hertford, 1997).

Adair, D., 'Respectable, Sober and Industrious? Attitudes to Alcohol in Early Colonial Adelaide', *Labour History*, No.70 (1986), pp.16–26.

Adair, D., 'Declarations of Difference: Attempts to Exclude Non-Whites from late Colonial Australia', *Flinders Journal of History and Politics*, No.16 (1993), pp.131–55.

Adair, D. and W. Vamplew, *Sport in Australian History* (Oxford, 1997).

Allison, L., *The Changing Politics of Sport* (Manchester, 1993).

Anderson, B., *Imagined Communities: Reflections on the Origin and Spread of Nationalism* (London, 1983).

Andrews, D.L., 'Deconstructing Michael Jordan: Reconstructing Post-Industrial America', *Sociology of Sport Journal*, Vol.13 (1996), pp.315–18.

Andrews, D.L., 'The Fact(s) of Michael Jordan's Blackness: Excavating a Floating Racial Signifier', *Sociology of Sport*, Vol.13 (1996), pp.125–58.

Appadurai, A., 'Disjuncture and Difference in the Global Cultural Economy',*Theory, Culture and Society*, No.7 (1990), pp.207–36.

Bairner, A., 'Sportive Nationalism and Nationalist Politics: A Comparative Analysis of Scotland, the Republic of Ireland, and Sweden', *Journal of Sport & Social Issues*, Vol.20, No.3 (1996),pp.314–35.

Bale, J., 'Sport and National Identity: A Geographical View', *British Journal of Sports History*, Vol.3, No.1 (1986), pp.18–41.

Bercovich, S., *The Rites of Assent: Transformations in the Symbolic Construction of America* (New York, 1993).

Berlant, L., 'America, "Fat", the Fetus', *Boundary 2,* Vol.21, No.3 (1994), pp.145–94.

Billig, M., *Banal Nationalism* (London, 1995).

Blain, N., Boyle, R. and H. O'Donnell, *Sport and National Identity in the European Media* (Leicester, 1993).

Bloom, W., *Personal Identity, National Identity and International Relations* (Cambridge, 1990).

Bogen, E., *Immigration in New York* (New York, 1987).

Bordo, S., *Twilight Zones: The Hidden Life of Cultural Images from Plato to O.J.* (Berkeley, CA, 1997).

Borrie, W.D., *The European Peopling of Australia: A demographic history 1788–1988* (Canberra, 1994).

Bourdieu, P., 'Sport and Social Class', *Social Science Information*, Vol.17, No.6 (1978), pp.819–40.

Bowker, M., *On Guard for Thee: An Independent Review of the Free Trade Argument* (Hull, 1988).

Boyce, D.G., *Nationalism in Ireland* (London, 1995).

Boyd, T., 'The Day the Niggaz Took Over: Basketball, Commodity Culture, and Black Masculinity', in A. Baker and T. Boyd (eds.), *Out of Bounds: Sports, Media, and the Politics of Identity* (Bloomington, IN, 1997), pp.123–42.

Bradley, H., 'Dempsey to Open Basketball Duel by Tossing Sphere', in Joe Lapchick Scrapbooks (1927).

Bradley, J., 'Inventing Australians and Constructing Englishness: Cricket and the Creation of a National Consciousness, 1860–1914', *Sporting Traditions*, Vol.11, No.2 (1995), pp.46–50.

Bradley, J., *Ethnic and Religious Identity in Scotland* (Aldershot, 1995).
Brand, J., *The National Movement in Scotland* (London 1978).
Breuilly, J., *Nationalism and the State* (Manchester, 1993).
Broome, R., 'Professional Boxers in Eastern Australia, 1930–1979', *Aboriginal History*, Vol.4, No.1 (1980), pp.87–100.
Broome, R., *Aboriginal Australians: Black Response to White Dominance, 1788–1980* (Sydney, 1982).
Brown, M.B., 'Basketball, Rodney King, Simi Valley', in M. Hill (ed.), *Whiteness: A Critical Reader* (New York, 1997), pp.102–16.
Brown, S.J., 'Outside the Covenant: The Scottish Presbyterian Churches and Irish Immigration, 1922–38', *The Innes Review*, Vol.XLII, No.1 (1991), pp.19–45.
Búrca, M. de, *The GAA: A History of the Gaelic Athletic Association* (Dublin, 1980).
Butler, J., *Bodies that Matter: On the Discursive Limits of "Sex"'* (New York, 1993).
Campbell, T. and P. Woods, *The Glory and the Dream: The History of Celtic FC, 1887–1986* (Edinburgh, 1986).
Cashman, Richard, *Paradise of Sport: The Rise of Organised Sport in Australia* (Melbourne, 1995).
Cashmore, Ernest, *Black Sportsmen* (London, 1982).
Chandos, J., *Boys Together* (London, 1984).
Christie, J.R., *Ben Johnson: The Fastest Man on Earth* (Toronto, 1988).
Clarke, J., *New Times and Old Enemies: Essays on Cultural Studies and America* (London, 1991).
Clarke, S.A., 'Fear of a Black Planet: Race, Identity Politics, and Common Sense', *Socialist Review*, Vol.21, No.2 (1991), pp.37–59.
Cole, C. and D.L. Andrews, 'Look – Its NBA Showtime!: Visions of Race in the Popular Imaginary' in N.K. Denzin (ed.), *Cultural Studies: A Research Volume* (Greenwich, 1996).
Cole, C., 'American Jordan: P.L.A.Y., Consensus and Punishment', *Sociology of Sport Journal*, Vol.13, No.4 (1996), pp.366–97.
Colley, L., *Britons: Forging the Nation 1707–1837* (New Haven, CT, 1992).
Collins, Jock, *Migrant Hands in Distant Lands: Australia's Post-War Migration* (Second Edition, Leichardt, NSW, 1991).
Connolly, W.E., *The Ethos of Pluralization* (Minneapolis, 1995).
Cooney, J., *Scotland and the Papacy* (Edinburgh, 1982).
Cornell, S. and D. Hartman, *Ethnicity and Race: Making Identities in a Changing World* (London, 1998).
Corris, P., *Lords of the Ring: A History of Prize-Fighting in Australia* (North Ryde, NSW, 1980).
Crenshaw, K.W., 'Color-Blind Dreams and Racial Nightmares: Reconfiguring Racism in the Post-Civil Rights Era', in T. Morrison and C.B. Lacour (eds.), *Birth of a Nation'hood: Gaze, Script and Spectacle in the OJ Simpson Case* (New York, 1997), pp.97–168.
Crick, B., (ed.), *National Identities: The Constitution of the United Kingdom* (Oxford, 1991).
Cronin, M., 'Defenders of the Nation? The Gaelic Athletic Association and Irish Nationalist Identity', *Irish Political Studies*, Vol.11 (1996), pp.1–19.
Cumann, Lúthcleas Gael, *A Century of Service 1884–1984* (Dublin, 1984).
Curtice, J. and D. Seawright, 'The Decline of the Scottish Conservative and Unionist Party, 1950–1992: Religion, Ideology or Economics?' *Contemporary Record (The Journal of Contemporary British History)*, Vol.9, No.2 (1995), pp.319–42.

Curtis, L., *Ireland: The Propaganda War* (London 1984).

Daly, J.A., *Elysian Fields: Sport, Class and Community in Colonial South Australia* (Adelaide, 1982).

Daly, J.A., *The Adelaide Hunt: A History of the Adelaide Hunt Club, 1840-1986* (Adelaide, 1986).

Daniels, S., *Fields of Vision: Landscape, Imagery and National Identity in England and the U.S.* (Cambridge, 1993).

Davies, R., 'Singing Away Canada's Soul: Culture, Identity and the Free Trade Agreement', *Harper's*, Vol.278 (1989), pp.43–7.

Department of National Heritage, *Sport: Raising the Game* (London, 1995).

Derrida, J., *Positions* (Chicago, IL, 1981).

Devine, T.M. (ed.), *Irish Immigrants and Scottish Society in the Nineteenth and Twentieth Centuries: Proceedings of the Scottish Historical Studies Seminar, University of Strathclyde, 1989/90* (Edinburgh, 1990)

Diamond, S., *Roads to Dominion: Right-Wing Movements and Political Power in the United States* (New York, 1995).

Docherty, G. and P. Thompson, *100 Years of Hibs 1875/1975* (Edinburgh, 1975).

Dunning, E.G., 'Sport in the Process of European Integration', unpublished paper presented at the Macht und Ohnmacht im neun Europa Conference, Vienna, 1992.

Dyson, M.E., *Between God and Gangsta Rap: Bearing Witness to Black Culture* (New York, 1996).

Elias, N., *What is Sociology?* (London, 1978).

Elias, N., *The Germans* (Cambridge, 1996).

Elias, N. and J.L. Scotson, *The Established and the Outsiders: A Sociological Enquiry into Community Problems* (London, 1994).

Eliott, R.S.P. and J. Hickie, *Ulster: A Case Study in Conflict Theory* (London, 1971).

Encel, Sol (ed.), *The Ethnic Dimension: Papers on Ethnicity and Pluralism by Jean Martin* (Sydney, 1981).

Equinas, R., *Michael and Me: Our Gambling Addiction, My Cry for Help* (San Diego, CA, 1993).

Evans, J., *John Ruskin* (London, 1952).

Finn, G.T.P., 'Racism, Religion and Social Prejudice. Irish Catholic Clubs, Soccer and Scottish Society – Part I', *International Journal of the History of Sport*, Vol.8, No.1 (1991), pp.72–95.

Finn, G.T.P., 'Racism, Religion and Social Prejudice. Irish Catholic Clubs, Soccer and Scottish Society – Part II', *International Journal of the History of Sport*, Vol.8, No.3 (1991), pp.370–97.

Frankenburg, R., 'Whiteness and Americaness: Examining Constructions of Race, Culture and Nation in White Women's Life Narratives', in S. Gregory and R. Sanjek (eds.), *Race* (New Brunswick, 1994), pp.62-77.

Fryer, Peter, *Staying Power: The History of Black People in Britain* (London, 1984).

Gallagher, T., *Glasgow: The Uneasy Peace* (Manchester, 1987).

Gallico, P., *Farewell to Sport* (New York, 1938).

Gate, Robert, *Gone North: Welshmen in Rugby League*, Vol.1 (Ripponden, 1986).

Gate, Robert., *Rugby League: An Illustrated History* (London, 1989).

Gay, P. du (ed.), *Production of Culture/Cultures of Production* (London, 1997).

Gellner, E., *Nations and Nationalism* (Oxford, 1983).

George, N., *Elevating the Game: Black Men and Basketball* (New York, 1992).

Gilroy, P., *The Black Atlantic: Modernity and Double Consciousness* (London, 1993).

Giroux, H.A., *Disturbing Pleasures: Learning Popular Culture* (New York, 1994).

Gooding-Williams, R. (ed.), *Reading Rodney King: Reading Urban Uprising* (New York, 1993).

Gray, H., 'Television, Black Americans and the American Dream', *Critical Studies in Mass Communication*, Vol.6 (1989), p.376.

Gray, H., *Watching Race: Television and and Struggle for "Blackness"* (Minneapolis, MN, 1995).

Greene, B., *Hang Time: Days and Dreams with Michael Jordan* (New York, 1992).

Greene, B., *Rebound: The Odyssey of Michael Jordan* (New York, 1995).

Grossberg, L., *We Gotta Get Out of This Place: Popular Conservatism and Postmodern Culture* (London, 1992).

Guibernau, M., *Nationalisms: The Nation State and Nationalism in the Twentieth Century* (Cambridge, 1996).

Guillory, J., *Cultural Capital* (Chicago, IL, 1993).

Haines, R., 'Shovelling Out Paupers?: Parish-Assisted Emigration from England to Australia, 1834–1847', in E. Richards (ed.), *Visible Immigrants 2: Poor Australian Immigrants in the Nineteenth Century* (Canberra, 1991), pp.33–68.

Haines, R., 'The Idle and the Drunken Won't Do There: Poverty, the New Poor Law and Nineteenth Century Government Assisted Emigration to Australia from the United Kingdom', *Australian Historical Studies*, Vol.28, No.108 (1997), pp.1–21.

Hall, S., 'The Rediscovery of "Ideology": Return of the Repressed in Media Studies', in M. Gurevitch *et al.* (eds.), *Culture, Society and the Media* (London, 1990), pp.56–90.

Hall, S., 'What is This "Black" in Black Popular Culture?', in D. Morley and K.H. Chen (eds.), *Stuart Hall: Critical Dialogues in Cultural Studies* (London, 1996), pp.465–75.

Hall, S. and P. du Gay (eds.), *Questions of Cultural Identity* (London, 1996).

Hall, S., Held, D. and A. McGrew (eds.), *Modernity and its Futures* (Cambridge, 1992).

Hall, S., Critcher, C., Jefferson, T., Clarke, J. and B. Roberts, *Policing the Crisis: Mugging, the State, and the Law and Order* (London, 1979).

Hallinan, C.J., 'Aborigines and Positional Segregation in Australian Rugby League', *International Review for the Sociology of Sport*, Vol.2, No.2 (1991).

Handley, J.E., *The Irish in Scotland* (Glasgow, 1974).

Harker, R., 'Bourdieu–Education and Reproduction', in *An Introduction to the Work of Pierre Bourdieu* (London, 1990), pp.87–110.

Harmstorf, I. and M. Cigler, *The Germans in Australia* (Melbourne, 1985).

Harmstorf, I. and P. Schwerdtfeger (eds.), *The German Experience of Australia, 1833–1938* (Adelaide, 1988).

Harris, B., *The Proud Champions: Australia's Aboriginal Sporting Heroes* (Crows Nest, NSW, 1989).

Hastings, A., *The Construction of Nationhood. Ethnicity, Religion and Nationalism* (Cambridge, 1997).

Hay, Roy, '"Making Aussies" or "What Soccer is all about": Soccer and European Migrants to Australia, 1945–93', Bradman, Balmain, Barellan and Bocce, Australian Culture and Sport Conference, Australian Sports Commission/ Australian Defence Forces Academy conference at the Australian Institute of Sport, Canberra, 8–9 October 1993.

Hay, Roy, 'British Football, Wogball or the World Game? Towards a social history of Victorian Soccer', in John O'Hara (ed.), *Ethncity and Soccer in Australia, Studies in Sports History Number 10* (Campbelltown, 1994), pp.44–79.

Hayes, L., Hogan, V. and D. Walsh, *Heroes of Irish Sporting Life* (Dun Laoghaire, 1995).

Healy, J., 'Nat Holman Player and Coach', Copy in Holman file, Naismith Memorial Basketball Hall of Fame (no date).

Hickie, T., *They Ran with the Ball: How Rugby Football Began in Australia* (Melbourne, 1993).

Hill, David, *Out Of His Skin: The John Barnes Phenomenon* (London, 1989).

Hirst, J.B., *Convict Society and Its Enemies* (Sydney, 1983).

Hobsbawm, E.J., 'Introduction: Inventing Traditions' and 'Mass Producing Traditions: Europe, 1870–1914', in E.J. Hobsbawm and T.O. Ranger (eds.), *The Invention of Tradition* (Cambridge, 1983).

Hobsbawm, E.J., *Nations and Nationalism since 1780: Programme, Myth and Reality* (Cambridge, 1996).

Hogan, M., *The Sectarian Strand: Religion in Australian History* (Ringwood, 1987).

Hollander, Z., *The NBA Official Encyclopaedia of Pro Basketball* (New York, 1979).

Holmes, J.W., *Life with Uncle* (Tornot, 1981)

Holt, R., *Sport and the British: A Modern History* (Oxford, 1989).

Horton, P., 'Rugby Union Football and its Role in the Socio-Cultural Development of Queensland, 1882–91', *International Journal for the History of Sport,* Vol.9, No.1 (1992), pp.119–31.

Houlihan, B., *Sport, Policy and Politics: A Comparative Analysis* (London, 1997).

Howell, R.A. and M.L. Howell, *The Genesis of Sport in Queensland* (St. Lucia, 1992).

Hughson, John, 'Football, Folk Dancing and Fascism: Diversity and Difference in Multicultural Australia', *Australian and New Zealand Journal of Sociology,* Vol.33 (1997), pp.167–86.

Humphries, T., *Green Fields: Gaelic Sport in Ireland* (London, 1996).

Hutchinson, J. and A.D. Smith (eds.), *Ethnicity* (Oxford, 1996).

Huttenback, R.A., 'No Strangers Within the Gates: Attitudes and Policies Towards the Non-White Residents of the British Empire of Settlement', *Journal of Imperial and Commonwealth History,* No.1 (1972/3), pp.279–92.

Inglis, K.S., *The Australian Colonists: An Exploration of Social History, 1788–1870* (Melbourne, 1974).

Jackson, S.J. and D.L. Andrews, 'Excavating the (Trans)national Basketball Association: Locating the Global/Local Nexus of America's World and the World's America', *Australian Journal for American Studies,* Vol.15, No.1 (1996), pp.57–64.

Jackson, S.J., 'Disjunctural Ethnoscapes: Ben Johnson and the Canadian Crisis of Racial and National Identity', Paper presented at the Crossroads International Cultural Studies Conference, Tampere, Finland, 1–4 July 1996.

Jackson, S.L., 'Gretzky, Crisis and Canadian Identity in 1988: Rearticulating the Americanization of Culture Debate', *Sociology of Sport Journal,* Vol.11 (1994), pp.428–46.

James, C.L.R., *Beyond a Boundary* (London, 1963).

Jarvie, G. and G. Walker (eds.), *Scottish Sport in the Making of the Nation: Ninety Minute Patriots?* (London, 1994).

Jeffords, S., *Hard Bodies: Hollywood Masculinity in the Regan Era* (New Brunswick, 1993).

Jenkins, B and S.A. Sofos (eds.), *Nation and Identity in Contemporary Europe* (London, 1996).

Johnson, L. and D. Roediger, '"Hertz, Don't Do It?" Becoming Colourless and Staying

Black in the Crossover of O.J.Simpson', in T. Morrison and C. B. Lacour (eds.), *Birth of Nation'hood: Gaze, Script and Spectacle in the O.J. Simpson Case* (New York, 1997), pp.17–23.

Jones, J.M., 'Whites are from Mars, O.J. is from Planet Hollywood: Blacks don't support O.J. and Whites just don't get it', in M. Fine, L. Weis, L.C. Powell and I.M. Wong (eds.), *Off White Readings on Society, Race, and Culture* (New York, 1997), pp.251–8.

Jupp, James (ed.), *Ethnic Politics in Australia* (Sydney, 1984).

Jupp, James (ed.), *The Australian People* (Sydney, 1988).

Keirnan, C., 'Home Rule for Ireland and the Formation of the Australian Labour Party, 1883 to 1891', *Australian Journal of Politics and History,* Vol.38, No.1 (1992), pp.1–11.

Kellas, J.G., *The Politics of Nationalism and Ethnicity* (London, 1991).

Kendrick, S., 'Scotland, Social Change and Politics', in D. McCrone, D. Kendrick and P. Straw (eds.), *The Making of Scotland: Nation, Culture and Social Change* (Edinburgh, 1989).

King, S., 'The Politics of the Body and the Body Politic: Magic Johnson and the Ideology of Aids', *Sociology of Sport Journal,* Vol.10, No.3 (1993), pp.270–85.

Klein, A., 'Borderline Treason: Nationalisms and Baseball on the Texas–Mexican Border', *Journal of Sport & Social Issues,* Vol.20, No.3 (1996), pp.296–313.

Kuper, S., *Football Against the Enemy* (London, 1994).

Langman, L., 'From Pathos to Panic: American Character Meets the Future', in P.Wexler (ed.), *Critical Theory Now* (London, 1991), pp.165–241.

Lapchick, Richard, *Scrapbooks,* Boston, MA.

Lapierre, L., *If you this country: Facts and Feelings on Free Trade* (Toronto, 1987).

Leonard, 'Lank', 'Celtics Win and Take Eastern Division Title', *Philadelphia Inquirer,* 15 March 1928, p.22.

Leonard, 'Lank', 'Joe Lapchick and Davey Banks are "Mutt and Jeff" of Professional Basketball', in Joe Lapchick Scrapbooks, 1927. Richard Lapchik, Boston, MA.

Levine, P., *Ellis Island to Ebbets Field* (Chicago, 1992).

Lipsitz, G., 'The Greatest Story Ever Sold: Marketing and the O.J. Simpson Trial', in T. Morrison and C.B. Lacour (eds.), *Birth of a Nation'hood: Gaze, Script, and Spectacle in the O.J. Simpson Case* (New York, 1997), pp.3–29.

Lisee, J.F., *In the Eye of the Eagle* (Toronto, 1990).

Long, J., Tongue, N., Spracklen, K. and B. Carrington, *What's The Difference? A Study of the Nature and Extent of Racism in Rugby League* (Leeds, 1995).

Lucas, D., *The Welsh, Irish, Scots and English* (Canberra, 1987).

Lule, J., 'The Rape of Mike Tyson: Race, the Press and Types', *Critical Studies in Mass Communication,* Vol.12 (1995), pp.176–195.

MacClancy, J. (ed.), *Sport, Identity and Ethnicity* (Oxford, 1996).

MacClancy, J., 'Sport, Identity and Ethnicity' and 'Nationalism at Play: The Basques of Vizcaya and Athletic Bilbao', in J. MacClancy (ed.), *Sport, Identity and Ethnicity* (Oxford, 1996), pp.181–200.

MacDonagh, O., Mandle, W.F. and P. Travers (eds.), *Irish Culture and Nationalism, 1750–1950* (Canberra, 1983).

MacDonagh, O., *The Sharing of the Green: A Modern Irish History for Australians* (St. Leonards, NSW, 1996).

Macintosh, D., Bedecki, T. and C.E.S. Franks, *Sport and Politics in Canada* (Kingston, 1987).

MacKay, J.R., *The Hibees: The Story of Hibernian Football Club* (Edinburgh, 1986).

MacKenzie, J.M., 'Essay and Reflection: On Scotland and the Empire', *International History Review*, Vol.XV, No.4 (1993).

MacKenzie, R.J., *Almond of Loretto* (Edinburgh, 1905).

McAuley, E., 'Rich has Edge on Collegian for Pivot Job', Joe Lapchick Scrapbook, 1992.

McCaffrey, L., *Textures of Irish America* (Syracuse, New York, 1992).

McConnochie, K., Hollinsworth, D. and J. Pettmann (eds.), *Race and Racism in Australia* (Wentworth Falls, NSW, 1982).

McDermott, P., *Gaels in the Sun* (Drogheda, 1970).

McDonald, M.G., 'Michael Jordan's Family Values: Marketing, Meaning and Post-Regan America', *Sociology of Sport Journal*, Vol.13, No.4 (1996), pp.344–65.

McFarland, E., *Protestants First: Orangeism in 19th Century Scotland* (Edinburgh, 1990).

McGrory, J., *A Lifetime in Paradise* (Glasgow, 1975).

McKay, J., '"Just Do It": Corporate Slogans and the Political Economy of "Enlightened Racism"', *Discourse: Studies in the Cultural Politics of Education*, Vol.16, No.2 (1995), pp.191–201.

McLaren, B., *Talking of Rugby* (London, 1992).

McQueen, H., *A New Britannia: An Argument Concerning the Social Origins of Australian Radicalism and Nationalism* (Melbourne 1976).

Maguire, J., 'Globalization, Sport Development, and the Media/Sport Production Complex', *Sport Science Review*, Vol.2, No.1 (1993), pp.29–47.

Maguire, J., 'Globalization, Sport and National Identities: "The Empire Strikes Back"?', *Loisir et Société*, Vol.16, No.2 (1993), pp.293–322.

Maguire, J., 'Sport, National Identities and Globalization', in J. Bale (ed.), *Community, Landscape and Identity: Horizons in a Geography of Sports* (Keele, 1994).

Maguire, J., 'Sport, Identity Politics, and Globalization: Diminishing Contrasts and Increasing Varieties', *Sociology of Sport Journal*, Vol.11, No.4 (1994), pp.398–427.

Maguire, J. and J.C. Tuck, 'Pride and Patriotism: Rugby Union and National Identity in a United Sporting Kingdom?', unpublished paper presented at the International Sociology of Sport Association Conference 'Sport: Social Problems and Social Movements', Rome, 1995.

Maguire, J., 'Blade Runners: Canadian Migrants, Ice Hockey, and the Global Sports Process', *Journal of Sport & Social Issues*, Vol.20, No.3 (1996), pp.335–60.

Maharaj, G., 'Talking Trash: Late Capitalism, Black (Re)productivity, and Professional Basketball', *Social Text*, Vol.50 (1997), pp.97–110.

Mandle, W.F., *The Gaelic Athletic Association and Irish Nationalist Politics, 1884–1924* (London, 1987).

Mangan, J.A., 'Almond of Loretto: Scottish Educational Visionary and Reformer', *Scottish Education Review*, Vol.11, No.2 (Nov. 1979), pp.97–106.

Mangan, J.A., *Athleticism in the Victorian and Edwardian Public School: The Emergence and Consolidation of an Educational Ideology* (Cambridge, 1981).

Mangan, J.A., 'Hely Hutchinson Almond: Iconoclast, Anglophile and Imperialist', *Scottish Journal of Physical Education*, Vol.12, No.3 (Aug. 1984), pp.38–42.

Mangan, J.A., 'Muscular Militaristic and Manly: The British Middle Class Hero as Moral Messenger', in R. Holt and J.A. Mangan (eds.), *European Heroes: Myth, Identity, Sport* (London, 1986), pp.28–47.

Mangan, J.A., *The Games Ethic and Imperialism* (Harmondsworth, 1986 and London, 1998).

Mangan, J.A. (ed.), *Pleasure, Profit and Proselytism: British Culture and Sport at Home and Abroad* (London, 1988).

Mangan, J.A., *The Cultural Bond: Sport, Empire, Society* (London, 1992).

Mangan, J.A. (ed.), *Tribal Identities. Nationalism, Europe, Sport* (London, 1996).

Markey, R., 'Populist Politics: Racism and Labour in NSW, 1880–1900', in A. Curthoys and A. Markus (eds.), *Who are Our Enemies? Racism and the Australian Working Class* (Sydney, 1978).

Markus, A., *Fear and Hatred: Purifying Australia and California, 1850–1901* (Sydney, 1979).

Marqusee, M., ' Sport and Stereotype: From Role Model to Muhammad Ali', *Race & Class*, Vol.36, No.4 (1995), pp.1–29.

Martin, J.L., *The Migrant Presence* (Sydney, 1978).

Mason, T., *Association Football and English Society, 1863–1915* (London, 1980).

Medhurst, K., 'The Basques and the Catalans', *The Minority Rights Group Report*, No.9 (London, 1987).

Melling, Phil, 'Definitions for the Definers, not the Defined', *The Sports Historian*, No.16 (May 1996), pp.16–32.

Mennell, S., 'The Formation of We-Images: A Process Theory', in C. Calhoun (ed.), *Social Theory and the Politics of Identity* (Oxford, 1994).

Mercer, K., *Welcome to the Jungle: New Positions in Black Cultural Studies* (New York, 1994).

Merchant, L. (ed.), *Neighbours Taken for Granted* (New York, 1966).

Miles, R., *Racism* (London, 1989).

Miller, K., 'Class Culture and Immigrant Group Identity in the United States: The Case of Irish-American Ethnicity', in V. Yans-McLaughlin (ed.), *Immigration Reconsidered* (New York, 1990), pp.122–53.

Moffett, S.E., *The Americanization of Canada* (Toronto, 1972).

Moore, Andrew, *The Mighty Bears! A Social History of North Sydney* (Sydney, 1996).

Moorehouse, B., 'Repressed Nationalism and Professional Football: Scotland versus England', in J.A. Mangan and R. Small (eds.), *Sport, Culture and Society* (London, 1986).

Moorehouse, B., 'Scotland versus England; Football and Popular Culture', *International Journal of Sport*, No.4 (1987), pp.189–202.

Morrison, T. and C.B. Lacour (eds.), *Birth of a Nation'hood: Gaze, Script, and Spectacle in the O.J. Simpson Case* (New York, 1997).

Mosely, Philip, *Ethnic Involvement in Australian Soccer, 1950–1990* (Canberra, 1995).

Moseley, P.A., Cashman, R., O'Hara, J. and H. Weatherburn, *Sporting Immigrants* (Crows Nest NSW, 1997).

Mozley, A., 'Evolution and the Climate of Opinion in Australia, 1840–76', *Victorian Studies*, No.10 (June 1967), pp.411–30.

Muirhead, I.A., Rev., 'Catholic Emancipation in Scotland: The Debate and the Aftermath', *Innes Review*, Vol.24, No.2 (1973), pp.103–20.

Murphy, Brian, *The Other Australia: Experiences of Migration* (Melbourne, 1993).

Murray, B., *The Old Firm: Sectarianism, Sport and Society in Scotland* (Edinburgh, 1984).

Nairn, T., *The Break-Up Of Britain: Crisis and Neo-Nationalism* (London, 1977).

Naughton, J., *Taking to the Air: The Rise of Michael Jordan* (New York, 1992).

Nauright, J. and T.J.L. Chandler, *Making Men: Rugby and Masculine Identity* (London, 1996).

O'Farrell, P., *The Irish in Australia* (Sydney, 1987).

O'Farrell, P., 'St. Patrick's Day in Australia', *Journal of the Royal Australian Historical Society,* Vol.81, No.1 (1995), pp.1–16.

O'Connor, R., *German Americans* (Boston, MA, 1968).

O'Hara, John, (ed.), *Ethnicity and Soccer in Australia, ASSH Studies in Sports History*, No.10 (Campelltown, 1994).

Oommen, T.K., *Citizenship, Nationality and Ethnicity* (Cambridge, 1997).

Paric, L. *et al.*, 'Croats in the Australian Community', Report for Australian Federal Bureau of Immigration, Population and Multicultural Research, 1996.

Partington, G., *The Australian Nation: Its Irish and British Roots* (Kew, Vic., 1994).

Pavkovic, Aleksandar, Koscharsky, Halyna and Adam Czarnota (eds.), *Nationalism and Postcommunism: A Collection of Essays* (Aldershot, c.1995).

Polley, M., *Moving the Goalposts: A History of Sport and Society since 1945* (London, 1998).

Postal, B., Silver, J., and R. Silver (eds.), *Encyclopaedia of Jews in Sports* (New York, 1965).

Price, C., *The Great White Walls are Built: Restrictive Immigration to North America and Australia, 1836–1888* (Canberra, 1974).

Ramdin, Ron, *The Making of the Black Working Class in Britain* (Aldershot, 1987).

Rathet, Mike and Don R. Smith, 'We're Here to Play Football', in Richard Whittingham (ed.) *The Fireside Book of Pro Football* (New York, 1989).

Reeves, J.L. and R. Campbell, *Cracked Coverage: Television News, the Anti-Cocaine Crusade and the Regan Legacy* (Durham, 1984).

Reid, R., 'Tracking the Immigrants: Assisted Movement to Nineteenth-Century New South Wales', in *Visible Immigrants 1: Neglected Sources for the History of Australian Immigration* (Canberra, 1989), pp.23–46.

Reinerman, C. and H.G. Levine, 'The Crack Attack: Politics and Media in America's Latest Drug Scare', in J. Best (ed.), *Images of Issues: Typifying Contemporary Social Problem* (New York, 1989).

Richards, E. (ed.), *The Flinders History of South Australia: Social History* (Adelaide, 1986).

Robertson, R., *Globalization: Social Theory and Global Culture* (London, 1992).

Rokkan, S. and D. Urwin, *Economy, Territory and Identity: Politics of Western European Peripheries* (London, 1983).

Rosenwaike, I., *Population History of New York City* (Syracuse, NY, 1972).

Rowe, D., 'Accommodating Bodies: Celebrity, Sexuality, and "Tragic Magic"', *Journal of Sport and Social Issues*, Vol.18, No.1 (1994),pp.6–26.

Ryan, Greg, *Forerunners of the All Blacks* (Canterbury, NZ, 1993).

Sandell, J., 'Out of the Ghetto and Into the Marketplace: Hoop Dreams and the Commodification of Marginality', *Socialist Review,* Vol.25, No.2 (1995), pp.57–82.

Schmelz, R., 'Ancient Australian Leisure', *Sport and Leisure*, No.5 (1984), p.5.

Scott, M., *From Nation to Colony* (Lindsay, Ont., 1988).

Shaw, D., 'The Politics of Futbol', *History Today*, Vol.35 (Aug. 1985), pp.38–42.

Silverman, B., *The Jewish Athletes Hall of Fame* (New York, 1989).

Sloop, J.M., 'Mike Tyson and the Perils of Discursive Constraints: Boxing, Race, and the Assumption of Guilt', in A. Baker and T. Boyd (eds.), *Out of Bounds: Sports, Media, and the Politics of Identity* (Bloomington, IN, 1997).

Smith, A.D., *National Identity* (Harmondsworth, 1991).

Smith, A.D., *Nations and Nationalism in a Global Era* (Cambridge, 1995).

Smith, D. and G. Williams, *Fields of Praise: The Official History of the Welsh Rugby Union 1881–1981* (Cardiff, 1980).

Smith, David, 'People's Theatre: A Century of Welsh Rugby', *History Today*, Vol.31, (March 1981), pp.30–35.

Smith, G., *Canada and the Canadian Question* (Toronto, 1971).

Smith, S., *Second Coming: The Strange Odyssey of Michael Jordan from Courtside to Home Plate and Back Again* (New York, 1995).

Smout, T.C., 'Perspectives on the Scottish Identity', *Scottish Affairs*, Vol.6 (1993), pp.101–13.

Sugden, J. and A. Bairner, A., *Sport, Sectarianism and Society in a Divided Ireland* (Leicester, 1993).

Sullivan, E., 'Ed Sullivan's Sports Whirl', *New York World*. Joe Lapchick Scrapbooks, 1926.

Tatz, Colin, *Obstacle Race: Aborigines in Sport* (Sydney, 1995).

Thomas, C., *The History of the British Lions* (Edinburgh, 1996).

Thompson, Cec, *Born on the Wrong Side* (London, 1995).

Thorpe, W., 'Archibald Meston and Aboriginal Legislation in Colonial Queensland', *Historical Studies,* Vol.21, No.82 (1984), pp.48–56.

Tkalcevic, Mato, *Croats in Australia: An Information and Resource Guide* (Burwood, 1988).

Unikoski, Rachel, *Communal Endeavours: Migrant Organisations in Melbourne* (Canberra, 1978).

Vamplew, Wray, *The Turf: A Social and Economic History of Horse Racing* (London, 1986).

Vamplew, Wray and Brian Stoddart (eds.), *Sport in Australia: A Social History* (Melbourne, 1994).

Wacquant, L.J.D., 'The New Urban Color Line: The State and the Fate of the Ghetto in Postfordist America', in C. Calhoun (ed.), *Social Theory and the Politics of Identity* (Oxford, 1994).

Walker, G. and T. Gallagher, *Sermons and Battle Hymns: Protestant Popular Culture in Modern Scotland* (Edinburgh, 1990).

Waterhouse, R., 'Popular Culture and Pastimes' in N. Meaney (ed.), *Under New Heavens: Cultural Transmission and the Making of Australia* (Melbourne, 1989), pp.237–86.

Watson, M., *Rags to Riches. The Official History of Dundee United* (Dundee, 1985).

West, C., *Race Matters* (Boston, MA, 1994).

Whitelock, D., *Adelaide: A Sense of Difference* (Adelaide, 1985).

Wilson, B. and Sparks, R., 'It's Gotta be the Shoes: Youth, Race and Sneaker Commercials', *Sociology of Sport Journal*, Vol.13, No.4 (1996), pp.398–427.

Wilson, B., '"Good Blacks" and "Bad Blacks": Media Constructions of African-American Athletes in Canadian Basketball', *International Review for the Sociology of Sport*, Vol.32, No.2 (1997), pp.177–89.

Wilson, B., *Celtic: A Century with Honour* (London, 1988).

Wittke, C., *The Irish in America* (New York, 1956; revised 1970).

Woolcock, H.R., *Rights of Passage: Emigration to Australia in the Nineteenth Century* (New York, 1978).

Notes on Contributors

Daryl Adair is a Lecturer in Sports Humanities, Centre for Sports Studies, University of Canberra, Australia. He is the author, with Wray Vamplew, of *Sport in Australian History* (Oxford, 1997).

David L. Andrews is an Assistant Professor in the Department of Human Movement Sciences and Education, the University of Memphis. His research and teaching interests include the critical analysis of contemporary sport, and the cultural politics of advertising.

Joseph M. Bradley holds a Ph.D. and is author of *Ethnic and Religious Identity in Modern Scotland* (Avebury, 1995), and *Sport, Culture, Politics and Scottish Society: Irish Immigrants and the Gaelic Athletic Association* (John Donald, 1998). His research interests include the sociology of sport, Scottish and Irish politics, culture, identity and the Irish diaspora.

Cheryl Cole is an Assistant Professor in the Department of Kinesiology, Women's Studies and the Unit for Criticism and Interpretive Theory at the University of Illinois, Urbana-Champaign. She is currently completing a book which examines the relations among the construction of embodied deviance, sport and national identity in post-war America.

Tony Collins has contributed to, among others, *The International Journal of the History of Sport*, the *New Dictionary of National Biography* and the *Encyclopaedia of World Sport*. His thesis on the causes and consequences of the 1895 rugby schism – Rugby's Great Split: Class, Culture and the Origins of Rugby League Football – is published by Frank Cass.

Mike Cronin is Senior Research Fellow at De Montfort University, Leicester. He is the author of *The Blueshirts and Irish Politics* (Dublin, 1997) and the editor of *The Failure of British Fascism* (London, 1996). He is currently working on *Sport and Nationalism in Ireland: Gaelic Games, Soccer and Irish National Identity* (Dublin, forthcoming 1998) and has published widely on the links between sport and national identity in Ireland.

Roy Hay is a Senior Lecturer in Economic and Social History at Deakin University, Geelong, Victoria, Australia. His publications include *The Origins of the Liberal Welfare Reforms, 1906–1914* (London, 2nd edn, 1983), *The Development of the British Welfare State, 1880–1975* (London, 1978), and a series of articles on sport, ethnicity and migration.

Steven J. Jackson is a Senior Lecturer in the School of Physical Education, the University of Otago, where he teaches courses in the Sociology of Sport, and Sport, Media and Culture. His research interests include sport and national identity, sport and the media, the globalization of culture and sports violence.

Joseph Maguire did his Ph.D. in sociology at Leicester University and is currently a Reader in the Sociology of Sport at Loughborough University. He has lectured widely in universities in North America and Europe, and is currently the president of the International Sociology of Sport Association. He is co-author of *Sport and Leisure in Social Thought* (Champaign, IL, 1993), and *The Global Sports Arena* (London, 1994). His research interests include globalization, national identity, migration and violence in sport.

J.A. Mangan is Professor of Cultural History and the Director of the International Research Centre for Sport, Socialisation and Society, Strathclyde University. He is the author and editor of numerous books and articles on sport, culture and society and has lectured on these topics in Africa, the Americas, Asia, Australasia and Europe. He was the Inaugural Chairman of the British Society for Sports History and is a fellow of the Royal Historical Society and the Royal Anthropological Institute. He is the founder and executive academic editor of the Cass journals *The International Journal of the History of Sport*, *The European Annual Review of the History of Sport*, and *Culture, Sport, Society*, and the series 'Sport in the Global Society'.

David Mayall is Senior Lecturer in History at Sheffield Hallam University with teaching and research interests in the history of immigration and ethnic identity. He has had published various articles on the history of Gypsies and is the author of *Gypsy Travellers in Nineteenth Century Society* (Cambridge, 1988) and *English Gypsies and State Policies* (Hatfield, 1996). He is also a co-editor (with Professors John Burnett and David Vincent) of the three-volume *The Autobiography of the Working Class: An Annotated, Critical Bibliography* (Hemel Hempstead, 1984–89). He is currently writing a book on the historical construction of Gypsy identity from the sixteenth to the twentieth centuries.

Murry R. Nelson is Professor of Education and American Studies at the Pennsylvania State University. He teaches courses in both social studies curriculum and American Studies and conducts research in both areas, particularly in the history of curriculum and of early professional basketball. The third edition of his *Children and Social Studies* (Harcourt, Brace) was published in 1998 and his *The Originals – The New York Celtics Invent Modern Basketball* (Bowling Green Press/Popular Press) will be published in late 1998.

Jason Tuck is a lecturer in Sports Studies at King Alfred's University College, Winchester. He is in the process of completing his doctorate from Loughborough University on the topic of rugby union and national identity. Jason is a graduate of Roehampton Institute and completed an MA in the Sociology of Sport at Leicester University. Findings from his research have been presented at a variety of international conferences, including the annual symposium of the International Sociology of Sport Association.

Index